IMAGES
of America

SAN AUGUSTINE COUNTY

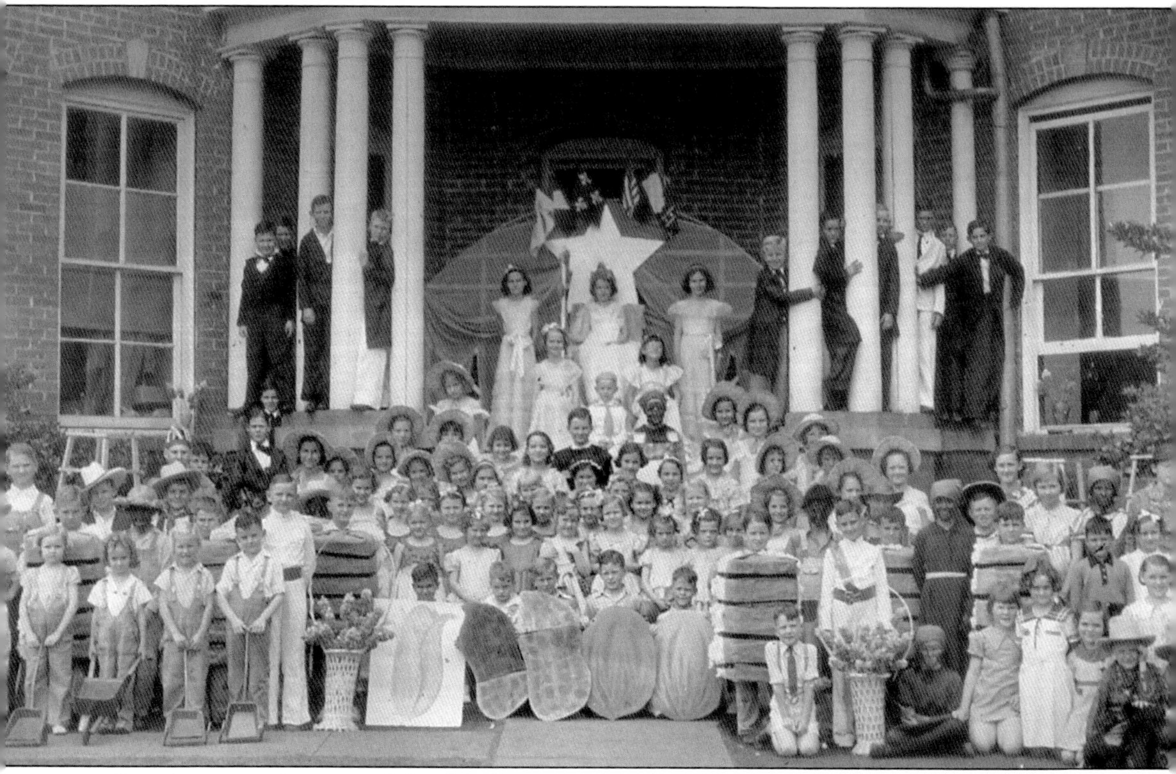

San Augustine Grammar School pupils are pictured on the steps of their 1907 elementary school during the Texas Centennial year, celebrating 100 years of Texas Independence from 1836 to 1936. In the May 1936 issue of *Hi-Life* (newspaper of San Augustine High School), the event was reported as follows: " 'Bluebonnet Land,' a pageant portraying the leading historical events of the Lone Star State, was presented by the grammar school pupils, Friday night, April 10, 1936, at the high school auditorium. Among the events portrayed were: the signing of the Texas Declaration of Independence, the mission builders, and a sketch history of Austin's colony. Various products and resources, such as fruits, vegetables, sulfur, oil, cotton, grain, and wild flowers, were portrayed in an effective manner. The cowboys and balloon dancers added color to the event. Twenty-one pupils dressed as Texas Bluebonnets, with 'Texas' on her throne, formed the background for the stage. Many happy memories were recalled by the older members of the audience when the old time square dance was presented by the pupils in dress typical of the 'square dance days.' " Artist/historian Richard Murphy (left) and Joe Holcombe are the two young cowboys on the first row, extreme right. (Courtesy of Dr. Curtis and Mary Jean Haley.)

ON THE COVER: Around 1918, a group of young men formed the San Augustine Band. They were self-appointed musicians who played for various functions in San Augustine County and for dances held upstairs in the 1884 Hollis Hall. The friendships forged among this unusual assortment of men became cherished memories that lasted throughout their lifetimes. Pictured here are, from left to right, (first row) Babe Sossaman, Cade Downs, Robert Hall, a Mr. Ballinger, N. J. McKnight, and Loven Hall; (second row) Bill McKnight, a Mr. James, Briney Sossaman, W. E. Hicks, and Matt Johnson. The Sossamans came from a family of silversmiths. The McKnights owned the bottling company, making Coca-Cola and an orange drink. W. E. Hicks became a dentist, and Cade Downs was president of First National Bank for several decades. Matt Johnson owned a successful grocery business. Little is known about the others. (Courtesy of Richard Murphy.)

IMAGES
of America

SAN AUGUSTINE COUNTY

John and Betty Oglesbee

ARCADIA
PUBLISHING

ISBN 978-0-7385-7937-5

Published by Arcadia Publishing
Charleston SC, Chicago IL, Portsmouth NH, San Francisco CA

Printed in the United States of America

Library of Congress Control Number: 2010928319

For all general information contact Arcadia Publishing at:
Telephone 843-853-2070
Fax 843-853-0044
E-mail sales@arcadiapublishing.com
For customer service and orders:
Toll-Free 1-888-313-2665

Visit us on the Internet at www.arcadiapublishing.com

To the people of present-day San Augustine County who never forget to preserve and protect our history and heritage for future generations

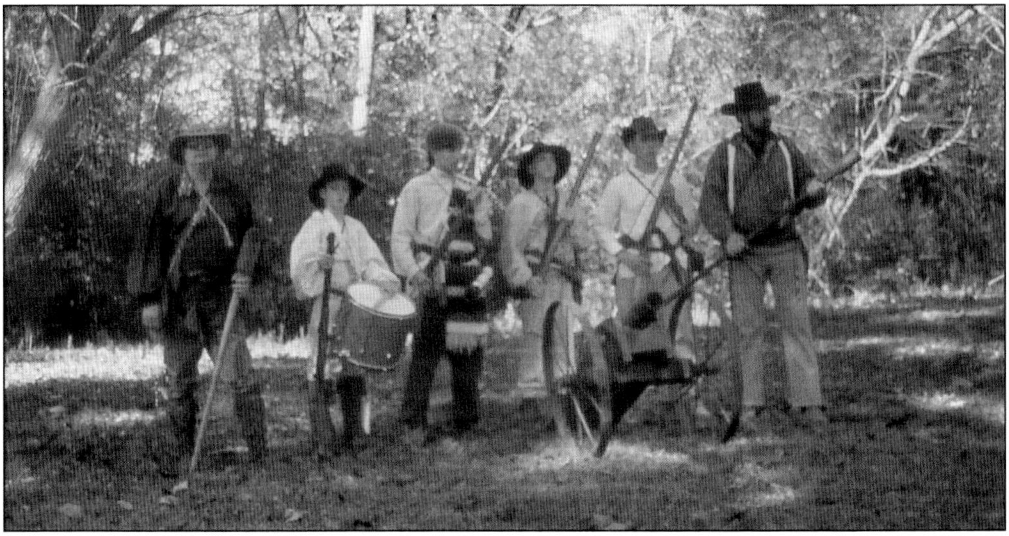

The Ayish Bayou Militia, under the leadership of Knights of San Jacinto LaVon Tindall and Billy Johnson, has performed at numerous area events over the past 10 years with a small cannon and black-powder muskets. The group of high school–age boys was formed under the auspices of the Alexander Horton Chapter, Sons of the Republic of Texas, San Augustine County, Texas. (Photograph by the author.)

Contents

Acknowledgments

When embarking upon a project requiring the collection of more than 200 vintage images from friends, acquaintances, organizations, and other sources, a certain measure of trust and cooperation is involved. We are deeply appreciative to all who have generously shared their treasured photographic memorabilia with us.

A great deal of credit is due our friend Richard Murphy, who opened his vast repository of images to us for use in this book. Murphy, a writer, artist, and historian in his own right, also provided original sketches for several early-day scenes in the book for which no photographs are available.

Without the efforts and cooperation of Stephen Hays, publisher/editor of the 94-year-old *San Augustine Tribune,* many images would not have been available to us. His able assistant, Crystal Horne Sowell, was especially helpful in locating specific images from the newspaper's archives.

Many friends spent time sorting through old family albums and candid photographs reflecting the life and times of early San Augustine, while others helped to identify people in images from past generations. Our sincere thanks go to Nelsyn and Julia Wade, James Williams, Martha Butts, R. D. Griffin, Dr. Curtis and Mary Jean Haley, Alfred Broden, Charles and Sharon Bradberry, Judge Charles Mitchell, Jerry Payne, Stephanie Kardell, Sandra Calpakis, Dorothy Mae Tannery Wilkerson, Tony Ball, Verline Stewart, McXie Whitton Martin, Val and Lucy Sharp, Mayme McClure, Joe Bryan and Nancy Bickley, Doniece Smith, Sharon Pollard, Shane Mathews, Gwendolyn Hall Odom, Marshall McMillan, Leeon Ware, Marion and Patti Neill, A. E. (Jake) Whitton, Holly Fussell Flynt, Mary Jane Stripling, Evelyn Watts, Carol Wayne Vaughn, SAISD superintendent Walter Key, Velma Teagle, Agnes Sparks, Linda Goller, Ann Nichols, Inez Sparks, Bette Hodges of Neillrae Music, Christ Episcopal Church, Redland Lodge No. 3, Mission Dolores Museum, San Augustine Public Library, and the offices of Orgain, Bell, and Tucker. Thanks to all!

Mention must also be made of the vintage images available from the U.S. Library of Congress, some of which were taken by U.S. government photographers Russell Lee in 1939 and John Vachon in 1943. Few counties in America are so fortunate as to have been a part of those remarkable times during the presidency of Franklin D. Roosevelt.

Special recognition is due Wendi McElhaney Thornburgh, owner of Picture Perfect Photography in San Augustine, who scanned the images used inside the book. Her positive attitude and professional expertise made the project fun and rewarding for all of us.

Finally, we are most appreciative of the supportive role played by Luke Cunningham, Winnie Rodgers, and Ryan Easterling, our Arcadia Publishing editors, who were always available to encourage and assist as this project moved along toward completion.

INTRODUCTION

Ninety percent of the men who engaged in the strife for Texas Independence had walked the streets of San Augustine.

–Louis Nardini, in *No Man's Land*

These men, often with their friends and families, entered Texas by way of El Camino Real de los Tejas, designated a National Historic Trail in 2004. The ancient trace had been blazed in 1691 by Domingo Teran de los Rios, newly appointed governor in the Spanish province of Texas. Variously identified as the Old Spanish Trail, San Antonio Road, and King's Highway, the timeworn roadbed stretched from the interior of Mexico, crossed the Rio Grande, and then meandered in an easterly direction across Texas into Louisiana. Teran was accompanied by Fr. Damien Massanet, whose idea of establishing seven permanent Catholic missions along the way appealed to Spanish authorities. Their claim to Texas could be defended against French encroachment, and at the same time, the Catholic faith could be introduced to the Caddo Indian tribes of eastern Texas. In accordance with this plan, Mission Nuestra Senora de los Dolores de los Ais was established in 1717 on the Ayish Bayou. The documented site covers a large area near the present-day city of San Augustine.

Near Mission Dolores was the large ranch, Tequitana, part of four leagues granted to Antonio Leal by the king of Spain in 1800. A few years later, Edmund Quirk purchased the Leal grant.

Many immigrants entering Texas from Louisiana in the early 1800s came by way of James Gaines ferry on the Sabine River, traveling west to the Ayish Bayou District and the village soon to be named San Augustine, the first settlement of consequence along El Camino Real. "The Redlands" was often the name used for the area, for its iron-rich crimson soil.

By the early 1820s, Elisha Roberts, Nathan Davis, John Bodine, John and Matthew Cartwright, Philip Sublett, John Chumley, and Alexander Horton, among other immigrants, had settled in the San Augustine area. Alexander Horton described the locale in his memoirs:

> When I first came to San Augustine in 1824, I found this to be the most beautiful country I had ever seen. The woods were clear of any undergrowth, covered over with large red oaks, hickory, blackjacks, walnuts, and post oaks. The hills and valleys were covered with a rich covering of grass from twelve to twenty-five inches high, and the creeks and bottomlands had a rich growth of cane. It was a most lovely and desirable country . . . a land suitable for the right kind of man.

Horton later remarked that the wild game was so plentiful he could sit on his front porch and shoot turkey, bear, and deer.

Dr. George Louis Crocket (1861–1936) in *Two Centuries in East Texas: A History of San Augustine County and Surrounding Territory From 1685* described the founding of San Augustine as follows:

In 1832 at a mass meeting of the people a committee of fifteen men was appointed to select the spot on which the town should be located." Riding on horseback over various locations in the region, they chose the east bank of the Ayish Bayou for the town site, an area encompassing 645 acres in the Edmund Quirk grant. Purchase price was $200. Crocket continued: "It is interesting to note that this spot was thus, for the third time, selected as the most suitable location for a permanent settlement: first by the Ais Indians who placed their village here, next by the Spaniards who located their mission here, and last by this committee of American settlers."

Surveyor Thomas McFarland was selected to survey the town site and sell the lots. It is believed that San Augustine was the first town in Texas laid out on the purely American plan—356 lots on 48 city blocks with two lots in the center for a courthouse square and all streets 40 feet wide.

From these humble beginnings sprang the earliest and oldest American town of Texas, often called the "Eastern Gateway to Texas," a place of culture, religion, education, and immense political and economic influence. William Seale in *San Augustine in the Texas Republic* wrote: "Architecturally the San Augustinians built an environment eminently superior to any town in Texas—with the exception of Galveston—prior even to the Civil War." Seale continued: "Lawyers were everyplace—Thomas J. Rusk, J. Pinkney Henderson, Henry W. Sublett, Napoleon B. Thompson, William B. Ochiltree, Benjamin Rush Wallace—and so on. Businessmen who had no knowledge of the law kept close to their attorneys."

Louis Nardini in *No Man's Land* stated: "San Augustine became a most important port of entry, second only to Galveston. It may very well be called the Cradle of Texas Independence, for it is said that any man entering San Augustine, be he French, Spanish, or American, became a Texan."

Sam Houston was first nominated commander in chief of the Texan forces at San Augustine by his friend Philip Sublett. The state's first governor, James Pinckney Henderson, lived here, as did Oran Milo Roberts, a later governor. A list of early Texas families associated with San Augustine County must include the familiar names of Cullen, Sharp, Cartwright, Sublett, Rusk, LeGrand, Garrett, Blount, Horton, Greer, Ingram, Parker, Teel, Thomas, and Roberts.

In the *Southwestern Historical Quarterly, Volume 3, Number 1,* published in July 1899, former San Augustine resident Emma B. Shindler spoke of many of the men listed above with these words:

> Is this not a galaxy of names worthy to adorn the history of the proudest town in Texas? . . . Ah! Those old days when San Augustine was adorned with the presence of men and women whose names live in history! . . . Know that all the men I have mentioned, with but two or three exceptions, had wives, women worthy of their positions and the times. And Sam Houston . . . who led our fathers to victory . . . took his loving wife to the old, old, town of which I write to show her to his friends . . . Sam Houston always found a welcome with the Red Landers . . . San Augustine, in the years that have come and gone, has passed through many and great changes, but the footprints are there . . . The fine forests that surround her, the oil and ore that lie in her bosom, the fertility of her soil, will yet bring her to the front.

Churches were established throughout San Augustine County, with several denominations being first in Texas. Education was a top priority. San Augustine was often called "The Athens of Texas" for her centers of learning: San Augustine University, Wesleyan College, and later the University of Eastern Texas. By 1850, Redland Lodge and Rising Star Chapter founded the Masonic Institute, with two separate schools, the Masonic Male Institute and the Masonic Female Institute. The Masonic schools operated successfully until the Civil War.

This pictorial history of San Augustine County and its environs is an effort to depict the emergence of this historic settlement, the lives of its people in the generations that followed, and the far-reaching significance it bears to all facets of the formative years of Texas.

A bright future is ahead for 21st century San Augustine County with recent discoveries in oil and gas and continuing successes in her poultry and timber industries.

One

First American Settlement of Texas

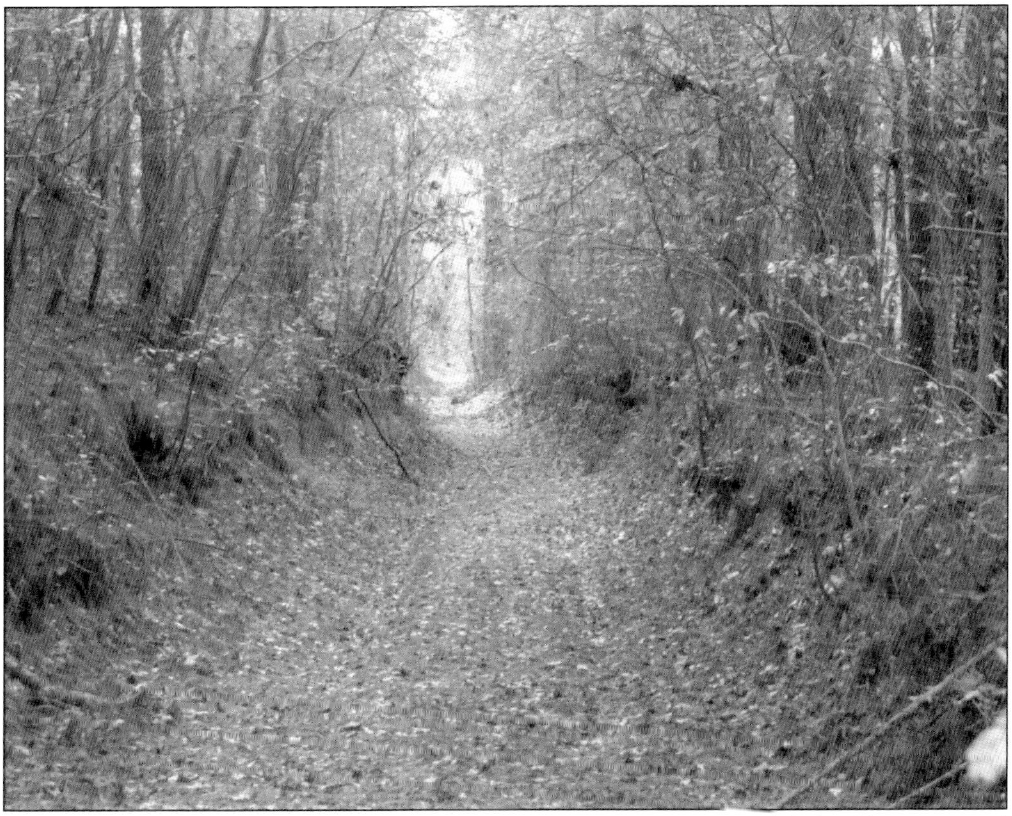

This well-worn trail is a section of the original route of El Camino Real de los Tejas National Historic Trail, about 10 miles east of San Augustine near Texas Highway 21. According to Hodding Carter in *Doomed Road of Empire*, "There is no trail of the Spaniard in the Americas that had more significance in the shaping of North American history than the King's Highway. Ultimately it became the main route of the masses of colonists as they came to claim this unknown frontier." (Photograph by the author.)

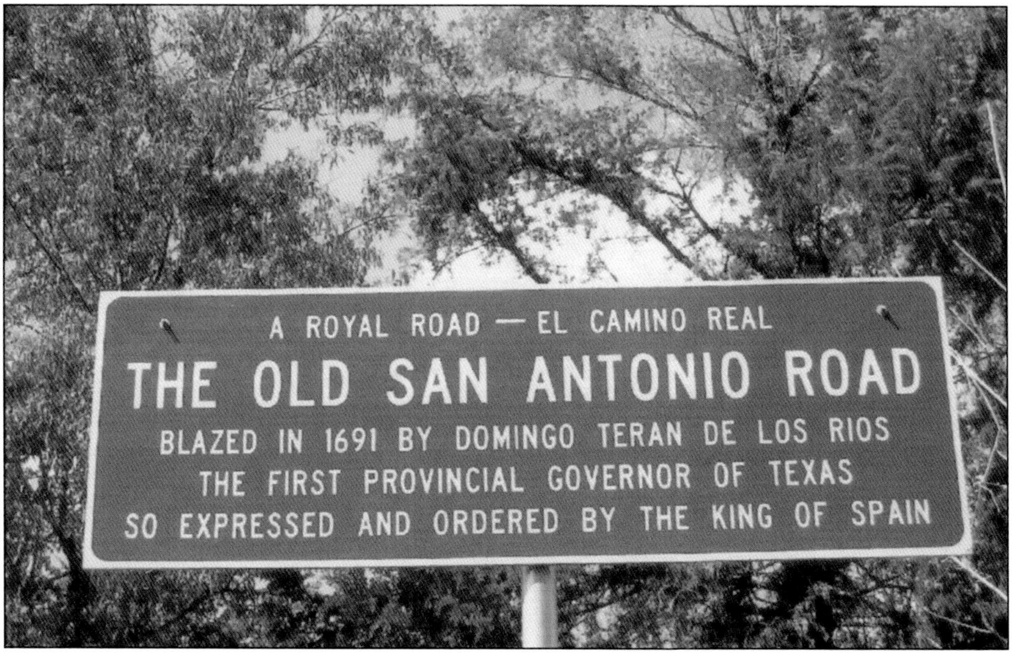

These explanatory highway signs appear at intervals along Texas Highway 21. El Camino Real de los Tejas became a National Historic Trail in October 2004 after many years of committed effort on the part of historians, lawmakers, and private citizens. After passage, trail sponsor Sen. Kay Bailey Hutchison wrote: "This corridor is not just a highway, it is the foundation of an inspirational past and, with this designation, will become an even more important academic and economic aspect of Texas." A logo and signage depicting the significance of the ancient trace has been developed by the National Parks System and El Camino Real de los Tejas National Historic Trail Association. (Photograph by the author.)

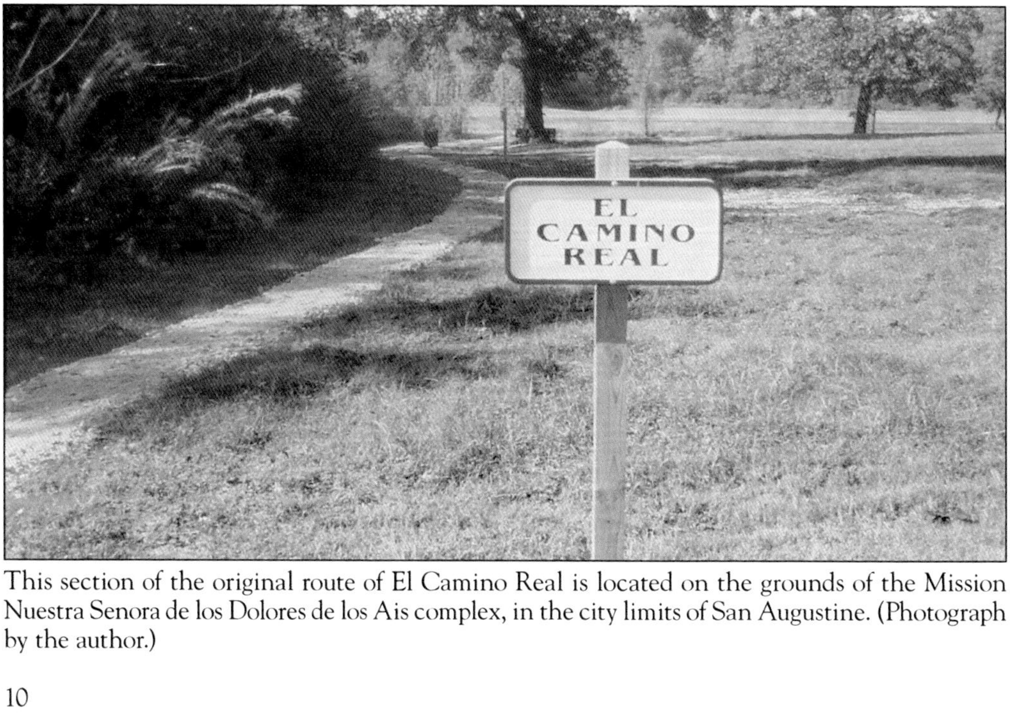

This section of the original route of El Camino Real is located on the grounds of the Mission Nuestra Senora de los Dolores de los Ais complex, in the city limits of San Augustine. (Photograph by the author.)

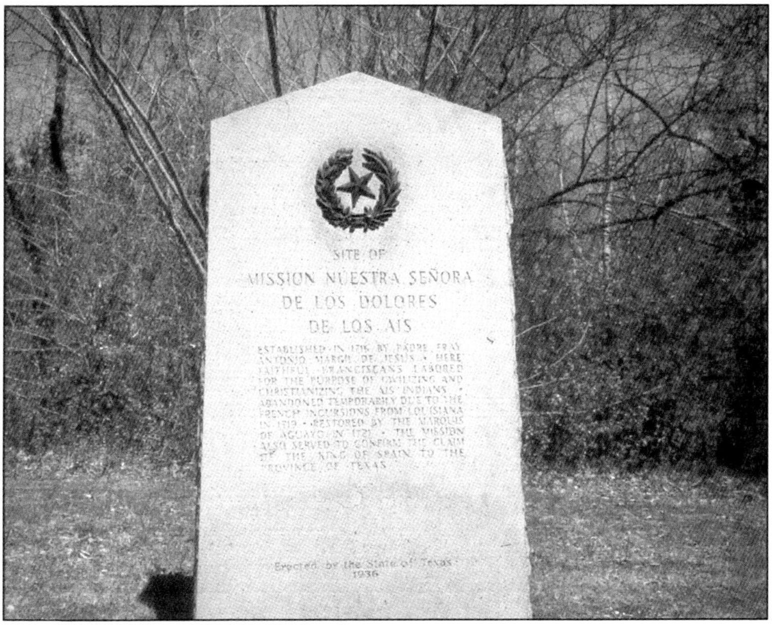

The exact location of Mission Dolores has been fully documented since the early 1800s. This informational marker was erected during the Texas Centennial in 1936. (Photograph by the author.)

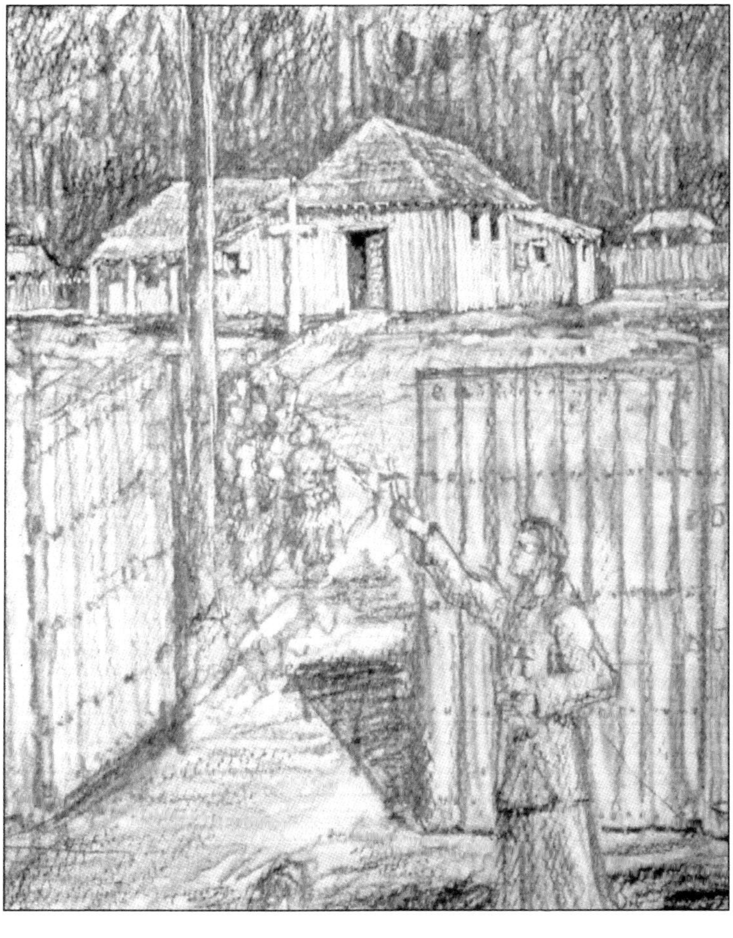

San Augustine native son Raiford L. Stripling, widely acknowledged as "The Restoration Architect of Texas," sketched his concept of the Mission Dolores compound in the 1960s. Spanish records indicate that there were seven buildings, including a chapel, quarters for the priests, and dwellings for the soldiers who provided military protection for the mission. (Courtesy of Mission Dolores Museum; photograph by the author.)

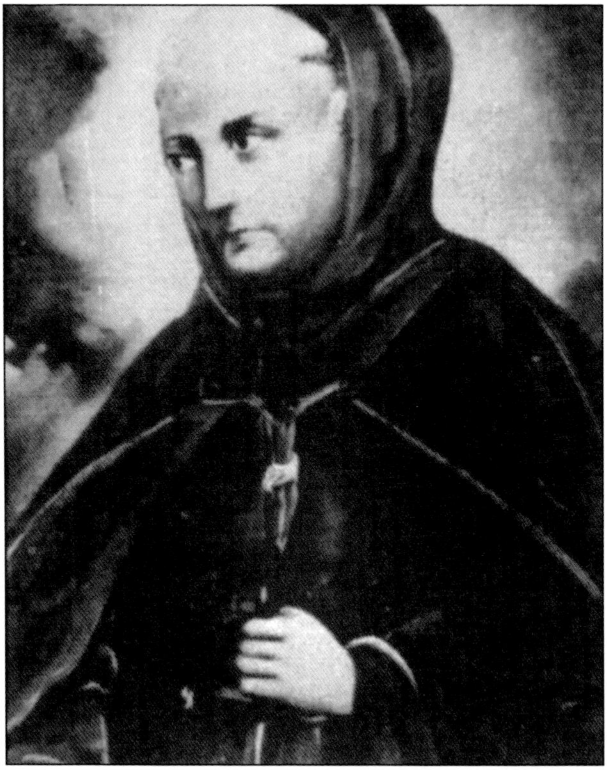

Fr. Margil de Jesus called Mission Dolores his "Precious Pearl." All friars of this Zacatecan mission served under his leadership. The soles of Father Margil's feet were reportedly "as hard as mules' hooves" from walking barefoot between the East Texas missions. He loved to stand atop "Mission Hill" overlooking the pristine valley through which meandered the ever-flowing Ayish Bayou, the source of water for inhabitants and crops. (Author's collection.)

Architect Raiford Stripling lends a hand to archaeologist Kathleen Gilmore from the University of North Texas during a Mission Dolores dig in 1972. (Courtesy of Mission Dolores Museum director Al Broden.)

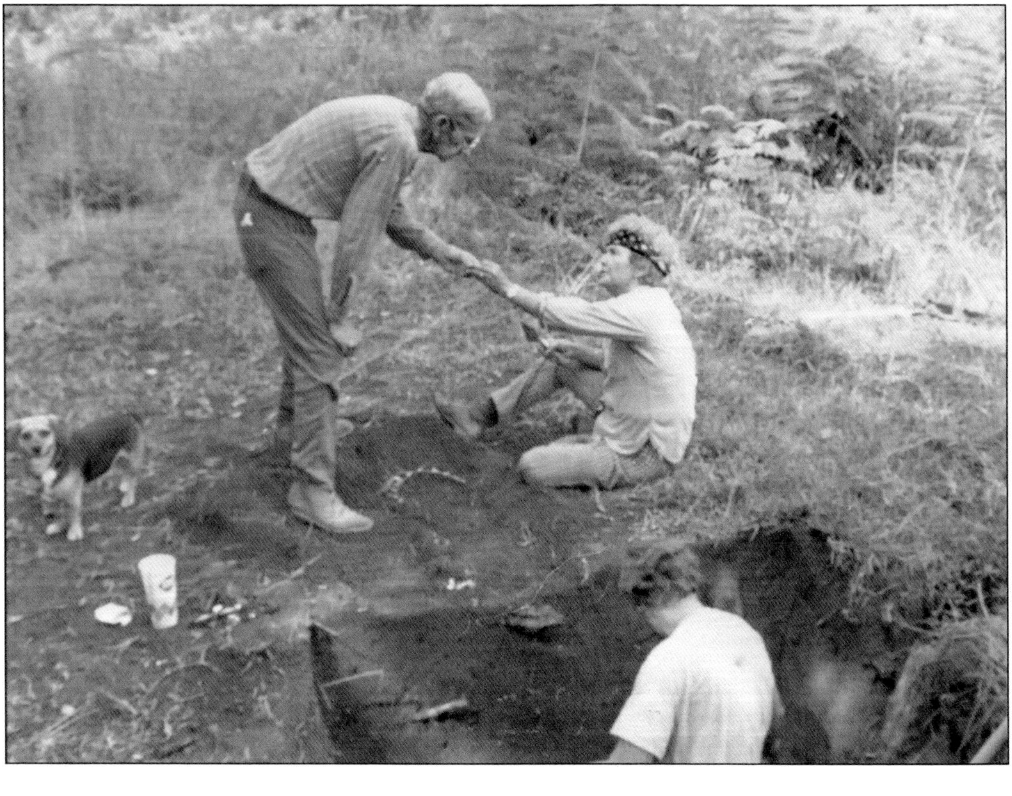

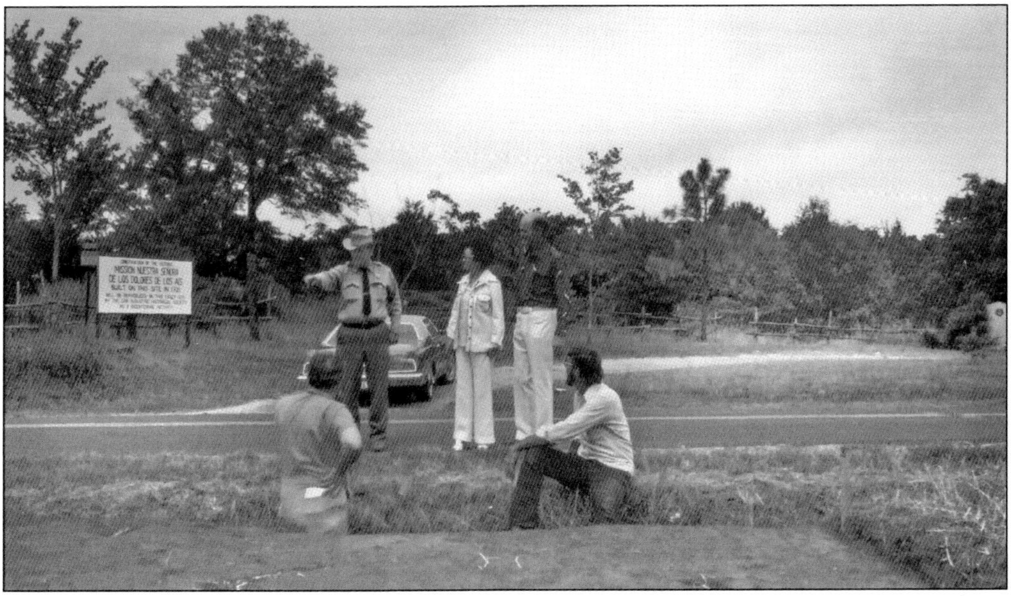

Archaeologist Dr. Jim Corbin, Stephen F. Austin State University, was at the Mission Dolores site in 1977 during an investigative dig. He returned on two later occasions, in 1979 and 1984, for additional archaeological work. Pictured are, standing from left to right, San Augustine County sheriff Nathan Tindall, city councilwoman Frances Maxwell, and David Maxwell. Dr. Corbin (right) is seated in the trench. (Courtesy of *San Augustine Tribune.*)

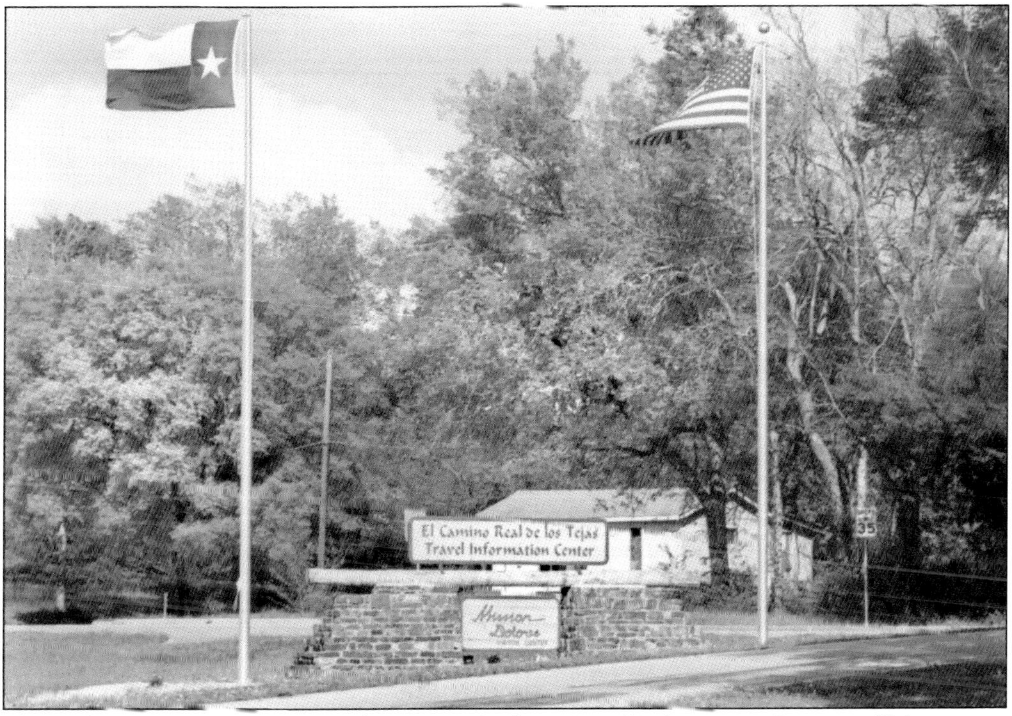

This is the impressive entrance to the Mission Dolores Travel Information Center and Museum on Highway 147 South, three blocks from the San Augustine County courthouse square. (Photograph by the author.)

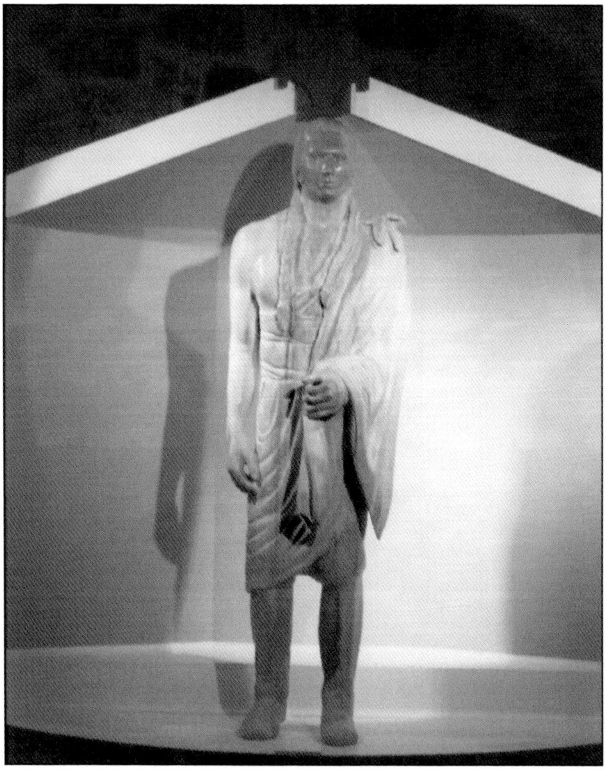

This woodcarver's depiction of an Ais Indian is 5 feet tall. The original statue occupies a prominent place in the Mission Nuestra Senora de los Dolores de los Ais Museum, located within the documented mission area. The Ais were not prone to congregate inside the mission grounds, nor accept the Catholic faith. However, the men seemed amenable to assist the priests with crop cultivation, and the women worked inside the mission compound helping with household chores. Dr. George Crocket wrote, "There is no report of a single example of a healthy, stalwart Christian Indian. Results of the friars' work seem to have been of a social and medical nature rather than spiritual character." (Photograph by the author.)

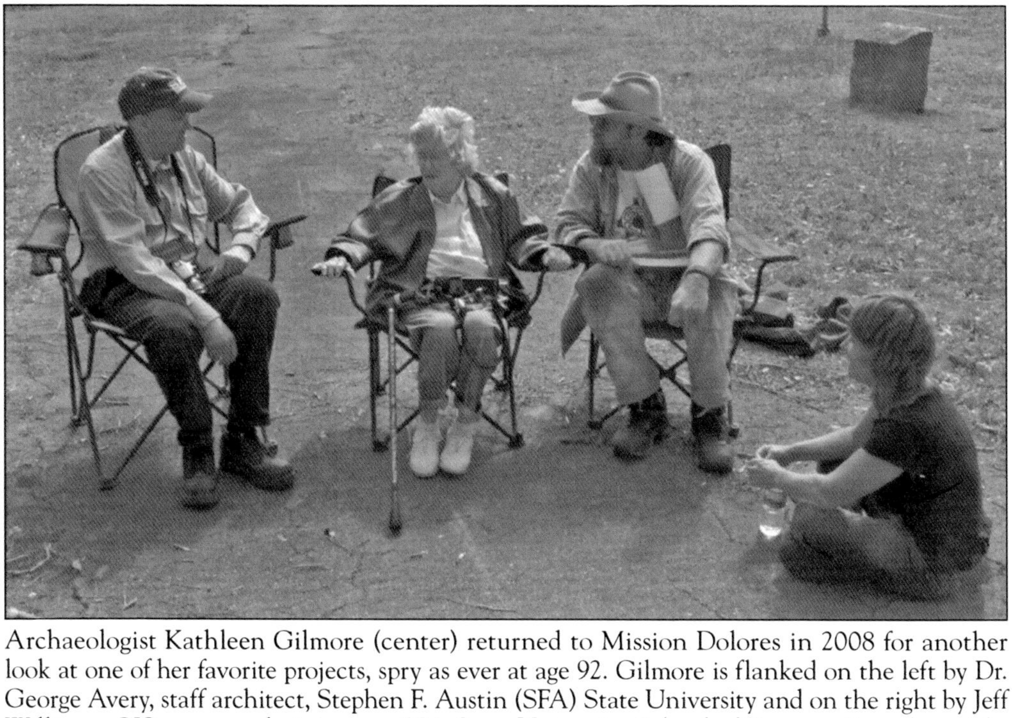

Archaeologist Kathleen Gilmore (center) returned to Mission Dolores in 2008 for another look at one of her favorite projects, spry as ever at age 92. Gilmore is flanked on the left by Dr. George Avery, staff architect, Stephen F. Austin (SFA) State University and on the right by Jeff Williams, GIS systems administrator, SFA State University School of Forestry. Seated on right is area archaeologist Connie Hodges. (Photograph by Al Broden.)

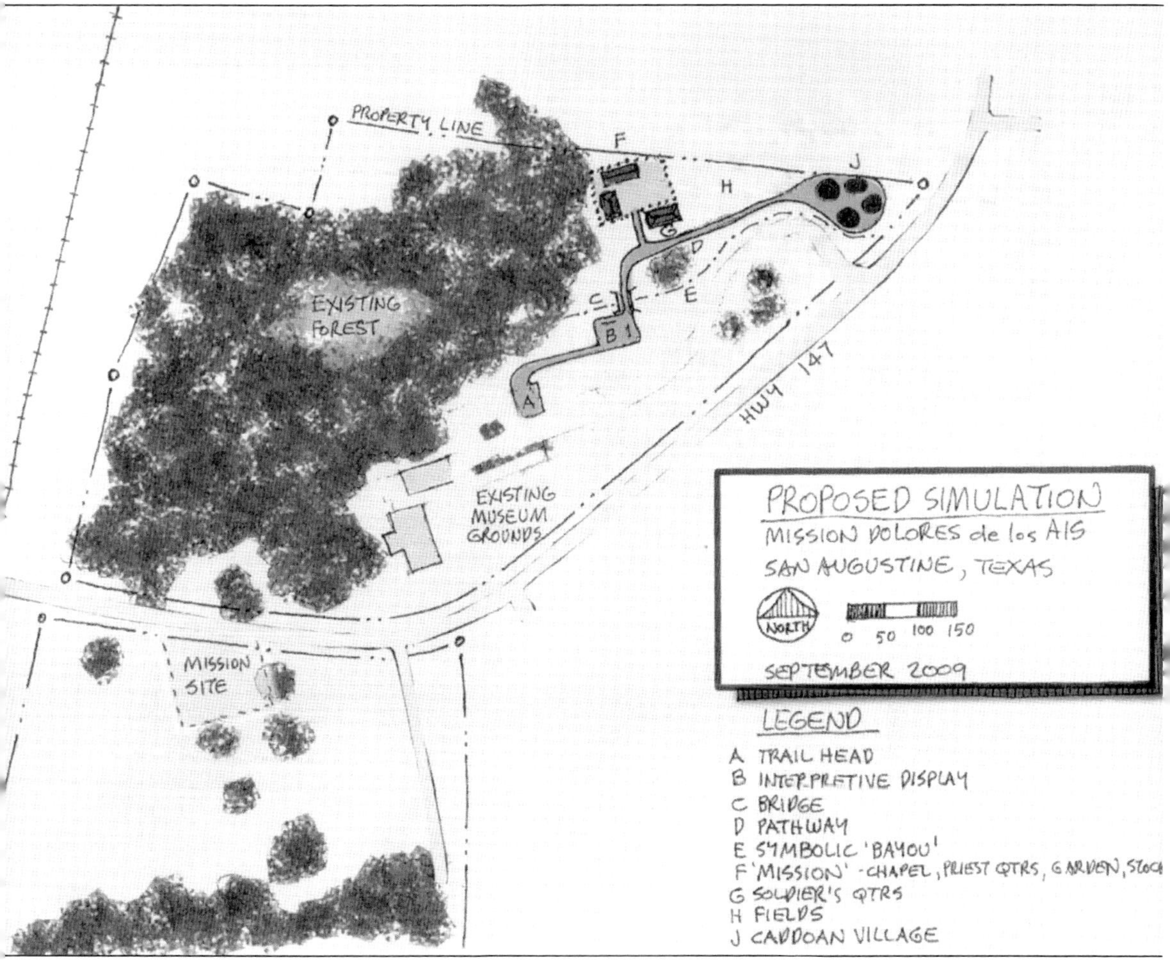

This proposed simulation of Mission Dolores was conceived by Mark Wolf of San Antonio, an architect specializing in Spanish Colonial structures. Dr. Jim Bruseth, director of the archaeology division, Texas Historical Commission, and Dr. George Avery of Stephen F. Austin State University are working with the San Augustine County Historical Society in implementing this significant historical and educational project. The simulation, located to the extreme right of the Mission Dolores Travel Information Center and Museum complex, will feature a trail head, an interpretative display, and a bridge, pathway, and symbolic "Ayish Bayou." The mission compound will include a chapel, priests' quarters, and soldiers' dwellings plus gardens, fields, and stockade. Nearby will be the rounded thatched huts of a Caddoan village. All seven structures will be constructed as authentically as possible in the Spanish Colonial architecture style, with a view of representing the overall appearance of a piney woods mission. (Simulation sketch courtesy of San Augustine County Historical Society.)

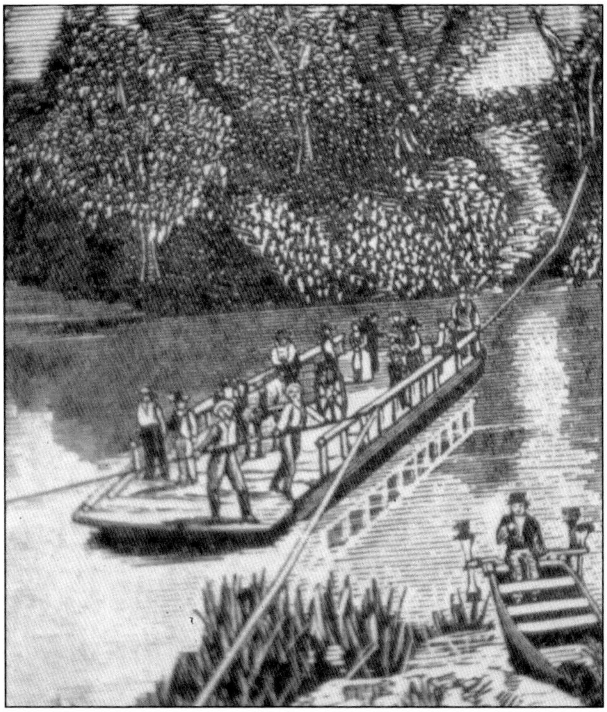

Several ferries operated on the Sabine River as early as 1794. Author Edna White in *East Texas Riverboat Era* wrote: "The main stream of immigrants, both overland and those coming via the Red River by steamboat, merged at Natchitoches, Louisiana, the last outpost of Anglo-American civilization on the wilderness trek, then followed the King's Highway to Gaines Ferry, where they crossed the Sabine River." James Gaines had purchased the ferry in 1819. He operated the Gaines Ferrying House on the Texas side of the Sabine River, where Stephen F. Austin and his guide Erasmo Seguin stayed during Austin's first visit to Texas in 1821. (Author's collection.)

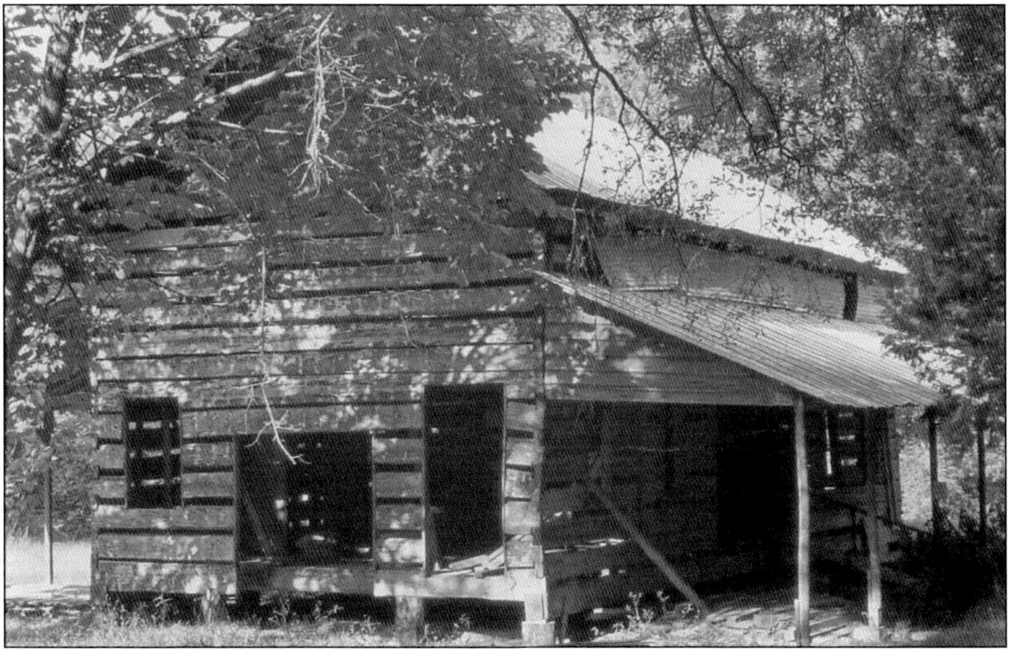

The 1818 Gaines-Oliphint House, also built by James Gaines, is cited as the oldest log house in Texas. It was moved from the west bank of the Sabine River during the building of Toledo Bend Reservoir and is currently being restored in the Pendleton Harbor subdivision through the efforts of the James Frederick Gomer Chapter, Daughters of the Republic of Texas, Hemphill, Texas. Unfortunately, the Gaines Ferrying House did not survive the move. (Photograph by the author.)

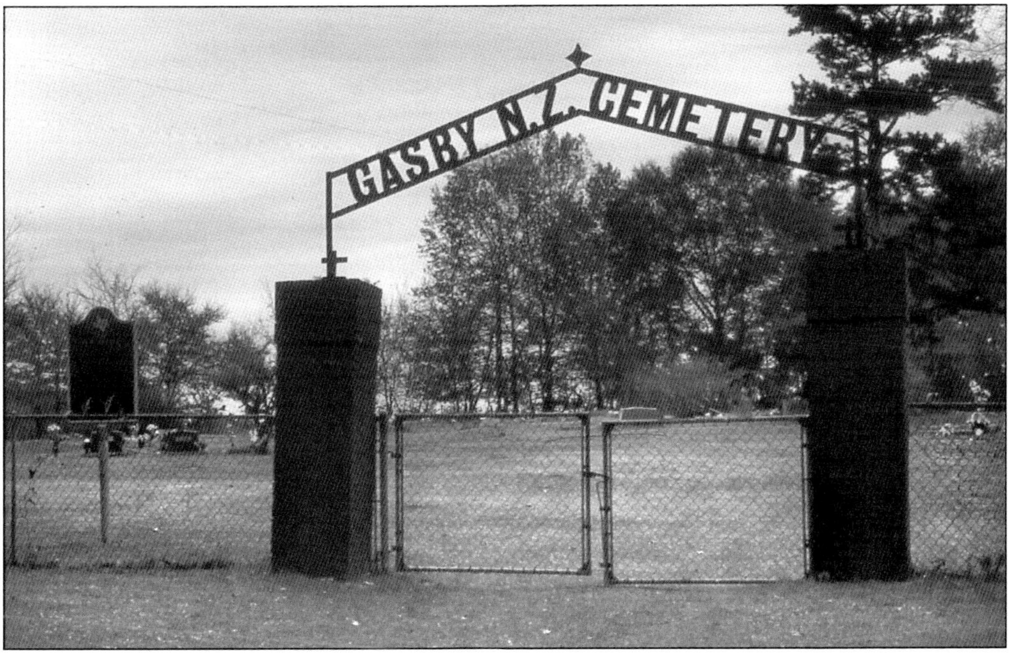

The historic Gasby New Zion Cemetery, named in honor of freedman William Gasby, is located on an original section of El Camino Real. Gasby was a successful entrepreneur who owned a cotton gin and blacksmith shop. Skilled in surveying, he was instrumental in laying out the village of Geneva, Texas, on El Camino Real. (Photograph by the author.)

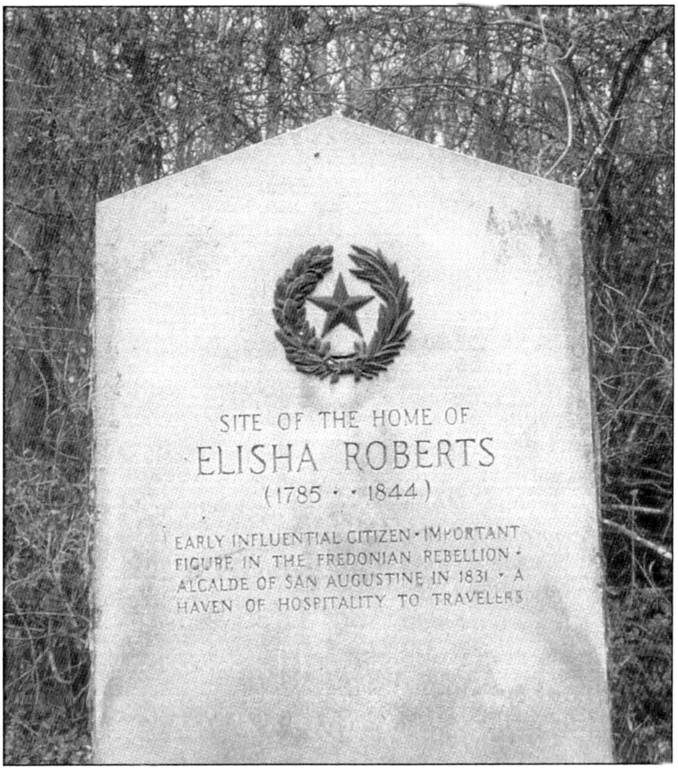

Elisha Roberts was one of the early influential settlers of the Ayish Bayou District, arriving in 1824. Elected alcalde in 1831, he "held court" on the front porch of his home and tavern, where friends and neighbors sought the counsel and advice of this remarkable man. Roberts was one of the 15 men who chose the town site of San Augustine in 1832. This marker was erected during the Texas Centennial in 1936. (Photograph by the author.)

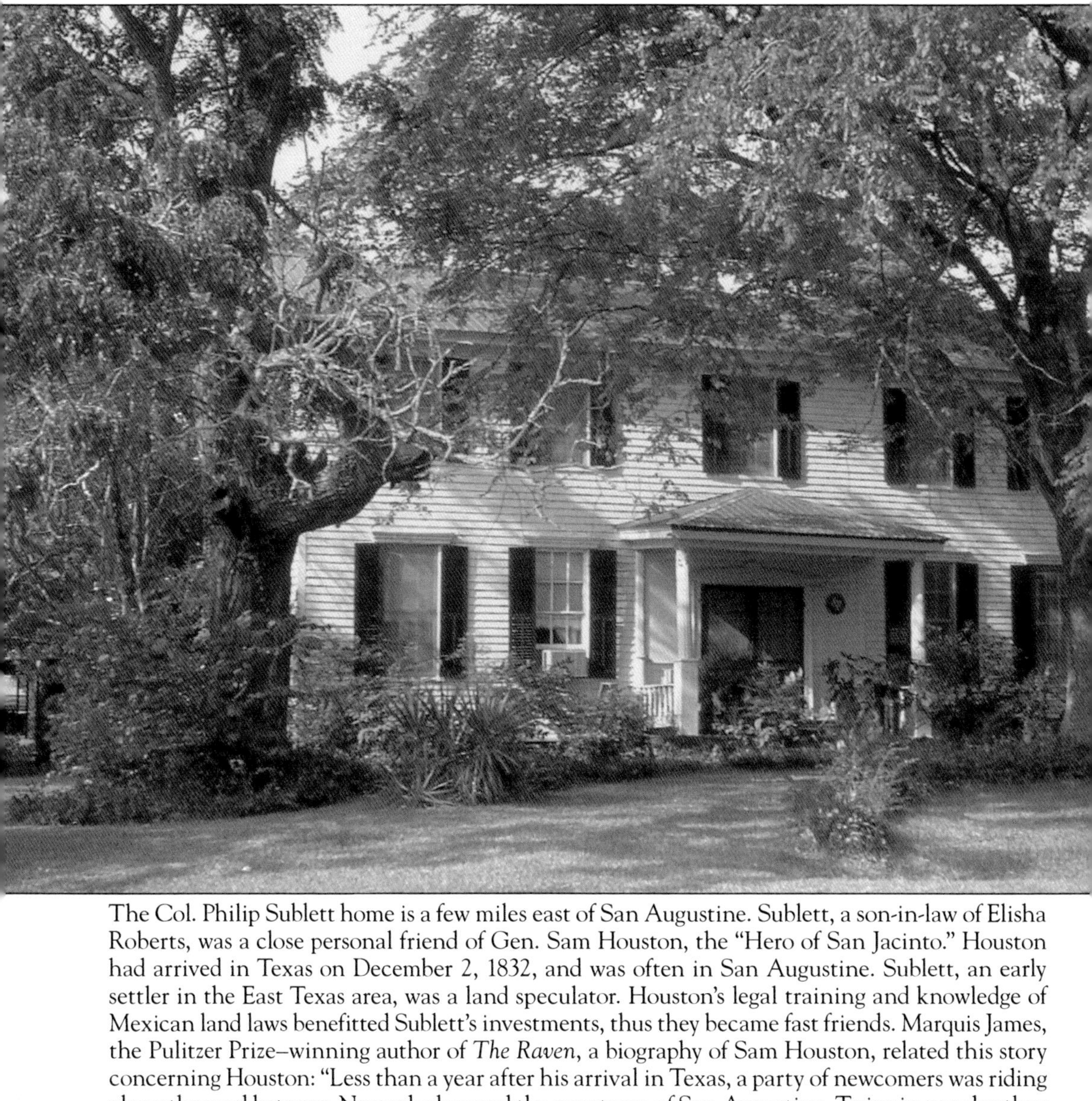

The Col. Philip Sublett home is a few miles east of San Augustine. Sublett, a son-in-law of Elisha Roberts, was a close personal friend of Gen. Sam Houston, the "Hero of San Jacinto." Houston had arrived in Texas on December 2, 1832, and was often in San Augustine. Sublett, an early settler in the East Texas area, was a land speculator. Houston's legal training and knowledge of Mexican land laws benefitted Sublett's investments, thus they became fast friends. Marquis James, the Pulitzer Prize–winning author of *The Raven*, a biography of Sam Houston, related this story concerning Houston: "Less than a year after his arrival in Texas, a party of newcomers was riding along the road between Nacogdoches and the new town of San Augustine. Twice in one day they passed a splendidly mounted horseman whose polite bows attracted favorable comment, especially from the ladies. That evening the party inquired who the civil stranger might be. 'That,' they were told, 'is Governor Houston, and he says there is going to be war in Texas before long and he means to figure in it.' " After the battle for Texas Independence was won on April 21, 1836, Houston spent several months in the Sublett home recuperating from a serious ankle wound. The home pictured was constructed in 1874 and was built to the exact specifications of the original 1830 Sublett home that had burned. Sublett was the first to nominate Sam Houston as commander of the Texan forces before the war, a nomination later ratified in Nacogdoches. After independence, Colonel Sublett encouraged Houston, along with many other San Augustinians, to enter the race for president of the new Republic of Texas. Houston agreed, with the comment, "The crisis demands it." He was elected by a large majority in September 1836. (Photograph by the author.)

Alexander Horton came to the Ayish Bayou District in 1824 as a lad of 14. His detailed diary and memoirs chronicle the life and times of the early settlers to the eastern section of Texas, with a special focus on events occurring in the San Augustine County area. Horton was Gen. Sam Houston's first aide-de-camp in the struggle for Texas Independence. In the years following, Horton continued to serve Texas as lieutenant colonel of the Mounted Gunmen of Texas protecting the frontier in 1837 and as captain in the Mounted Volunteers in campaigns against Mexico and Native American unrest in 1838. He was land commissioner for San Augustine County in 1837 and served a term in the Texas legislature in 1874. (Sketch by Richard Murphy, descendant of Colonel Horton.)

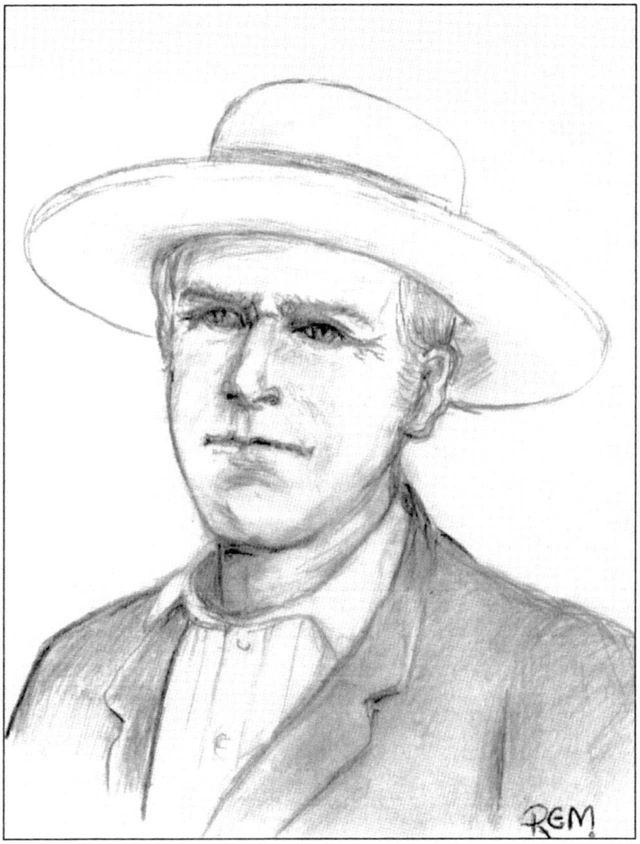

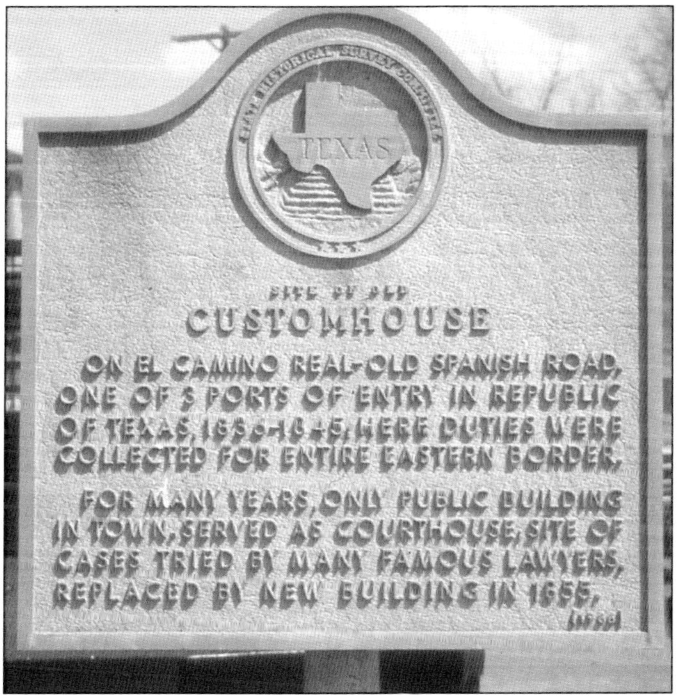

Customs Service of the Republic of Texas existed from June 1837 to February 1846. After Texas was annexed to the United States, the collection of customs was abolished. Historian Dr. George L. Crocket wrote, "For many years the customhouse was the only municipal building in town. Duties were collected on goods coming from the United States. San Augustine was third in importance of the ports of entry under the Republic of Texas, only Galveston and Matagorda ranking above it. One end of the rectangular building was used as a courthouse." (Photograph by the author.)

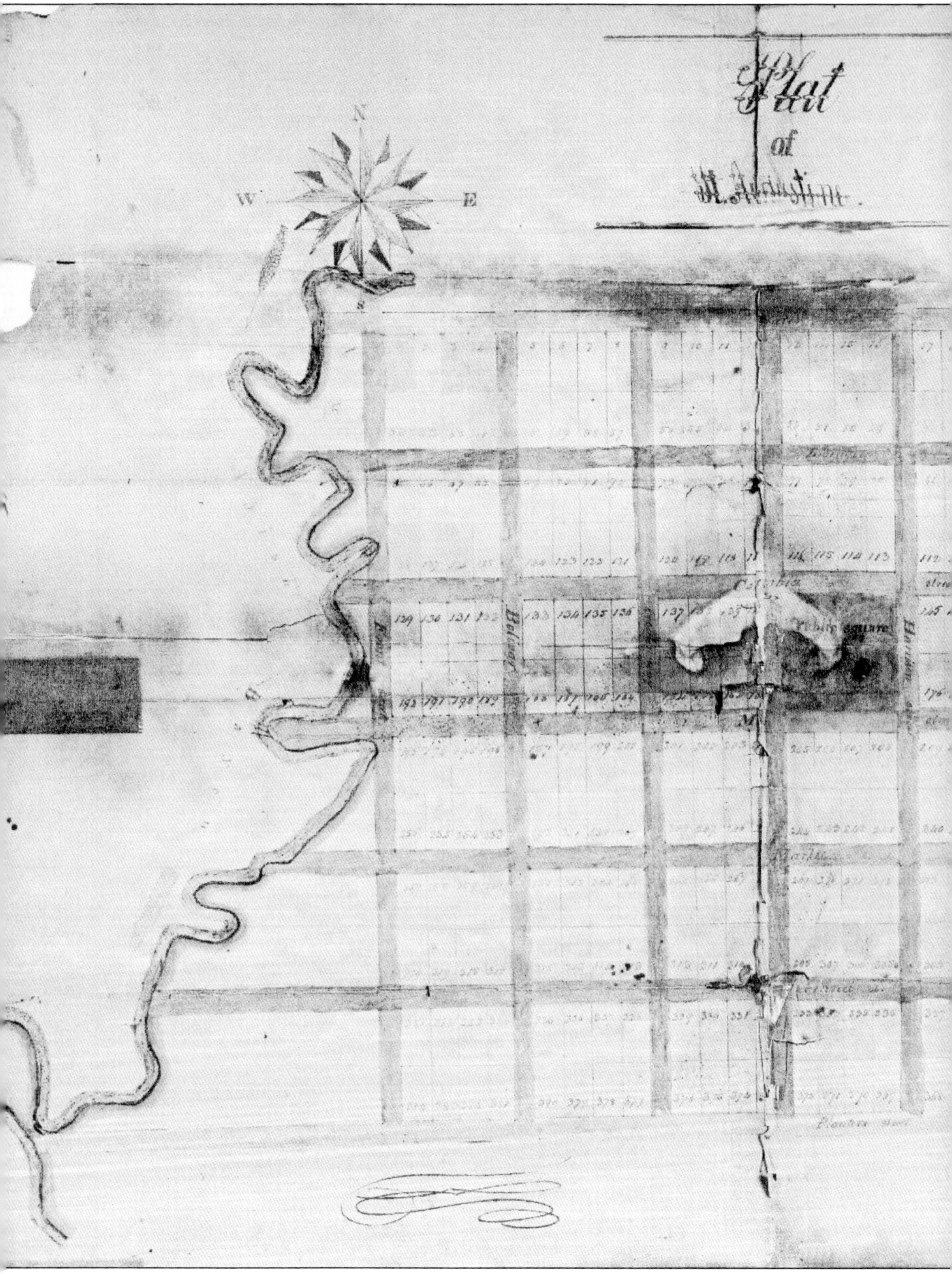
Plat
of
N
W
E
S

During San Augustine's formative years, and with the arrival of more settlers, it became apparent that a permanent town site needed to be selected. Dr. George L. Crocket, the San Augustine County historian extraordinaire, relates the story: "Thus, in 1832 at a mass meeting of the people, a committee of fifteen men was selected to choose a location. The committee consisted of William McFarland, Shedrack Thomas, Henry W. Augustine, David Huffman, Wyatt Hanks, James Hanks, John G. Love, William Garrett, Alexander Horton, David Renfroe, Achilles E.C. Johnson, Elisha Roberts, David O. Warren, Matthew Cartwright, and Philip A. Sublett. The chosen location included 640 acres on the east side of the Ayish Bayou, containing the old Mission Dolores site, and bounded on the west by the Bayou and on the south by the King's Highway (El Camino Real), for a sum of $200. The original plat of San Augustine was drawn by surveyor Thomas McFarland in 1833, the first town in Texas to be laid out on the American plan: i.e., 48 blocks divided into 356 lots, each 80 feet wide and 160 feet deep, separated by streets 40 feet wide, with two lots near the center for a public square. The names McFarland gave the streets have survived the test of time (Main, Columbia, Ayish, Market, Harrison, Liberty, Livingston, Milam, and others) with one exception. Montezuma, the street where the Custom House was located, was later changed to Montgomery." With magnification, the street names can be read. (Plat courtesy of Stephanie Kardell and Sandra Calpakis.)

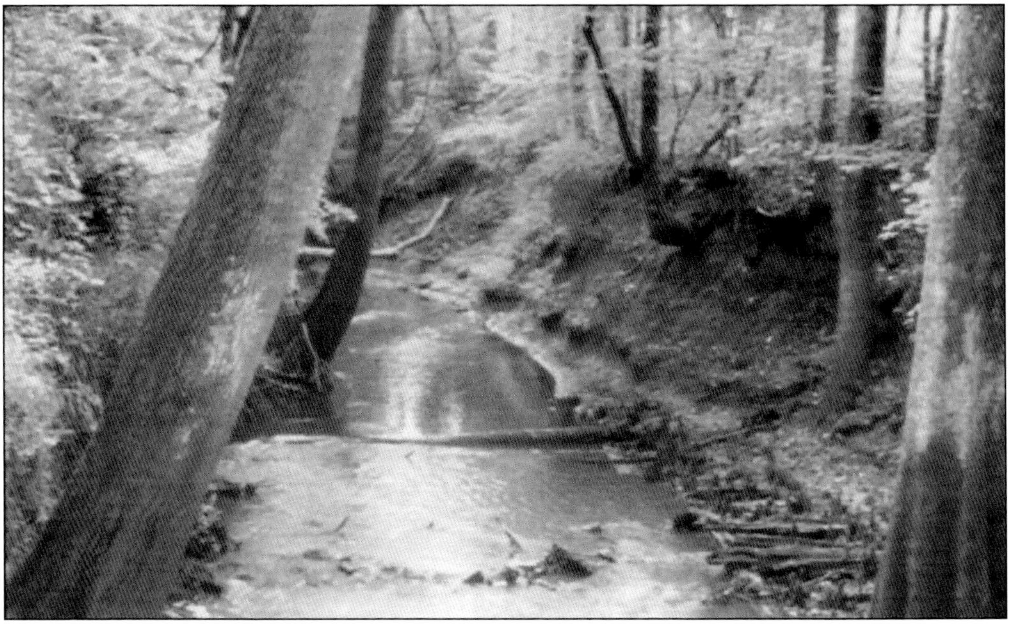

The Ayish Bayou became the lifeblood of the early settlers to the San Augustine area, furnishing a rich fertile bottom for their crops and power for their gristmills and multiple sawmills. This stream runs the entire length of San Augustine County amid towering pines and sturdy hardwoods. Its headwaters bubble up from a spring on the north end of the original Edmund Quirk land grant, about 5 miles from the city of San Augustine. (Photograph by the author.)

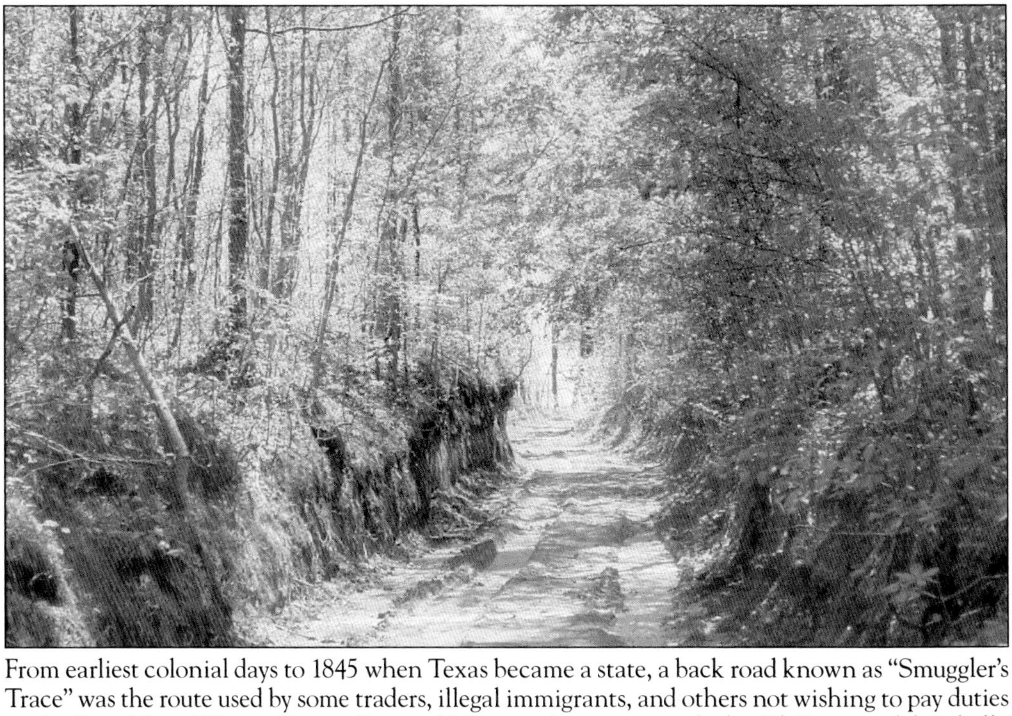

From earliest colonial days to 1845 when Texas became a state, a back road known as "Smuggler's Trace" was the route used by some traders, illegal immigrants, and others not wishing to pay duties to the Republic of Texas. Originally an old Native American trail, this El Camino del Caballo (horse and mule road, or contraband trace) still exists. (Photograph by the author.)

Matthew Cartwright was one of the early successful entrepreneurs in San Augustine County, a substantial citizen who was fair in his dealings. Cartwright's business ventures included land investments, two retail stores in the downtown area, and an active cotton farming operation. (Courtesy of Stephanie Kardell and Sandra Calpakis.)

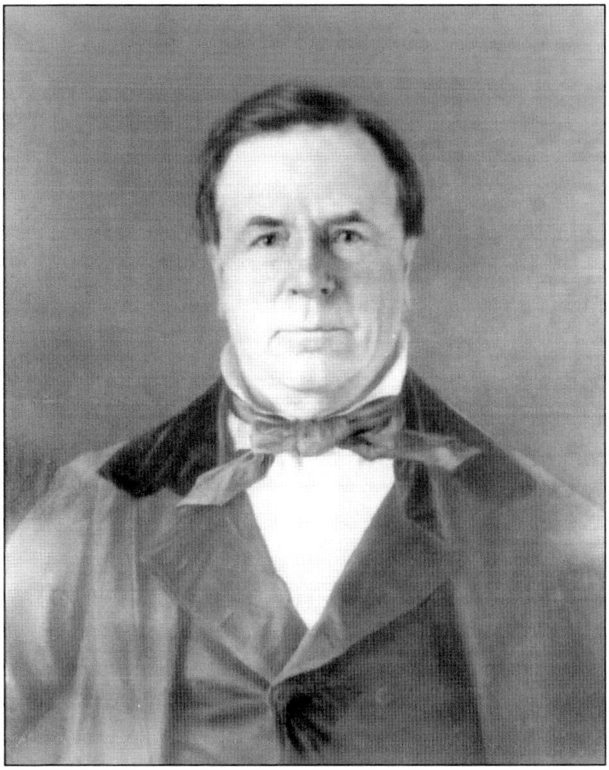

An oxen-drawn wagon is pictured along the unpaved El Camino Real, now Main Street in San Augustine. Notice the woman in the wagon holding a baby. In the background is the Greek Revival–style office of Matthew Cartwright. (Courtesy of Stephanie Kardell and Sandra Calpakis.)

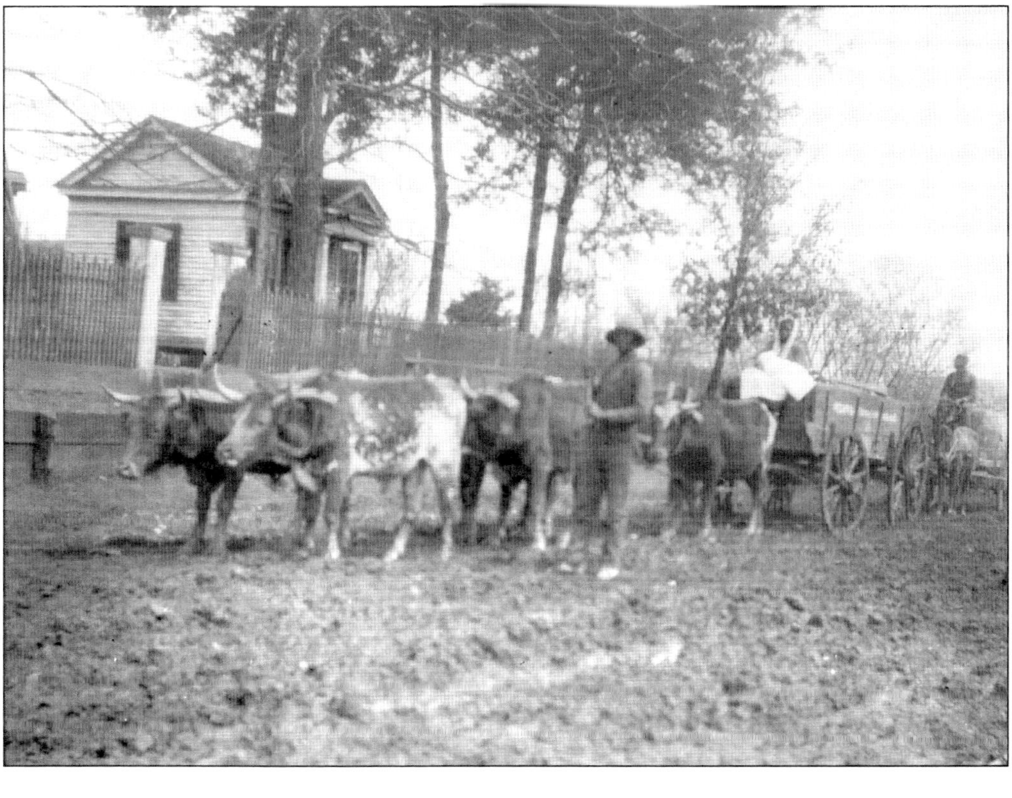

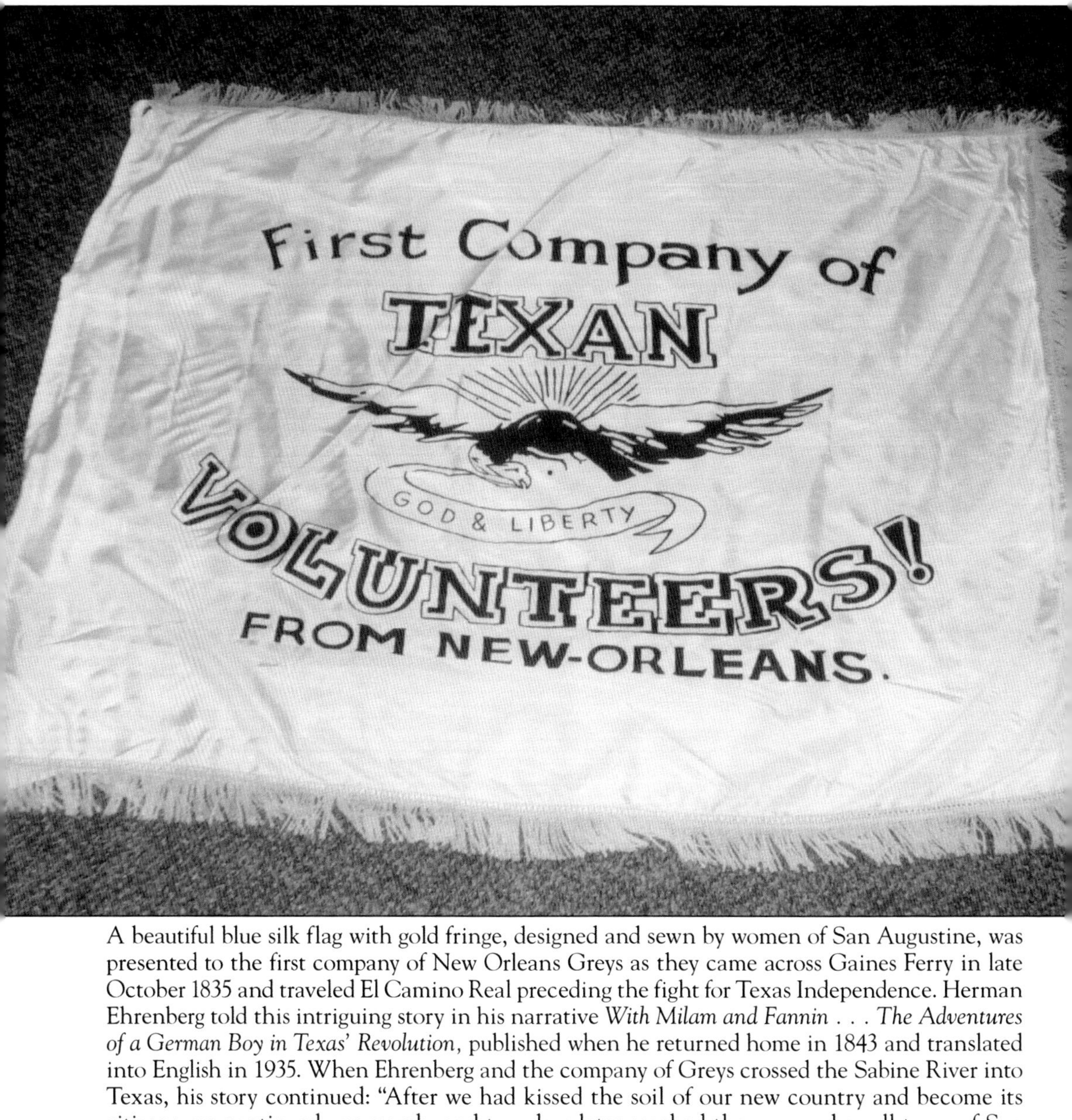

A beautiful blue silk flag with gold fringe, designed and sewn by women of San Augustine, was presented to the first company of New Orleans Greys as they came across Gaines Ferry in late October 1835 and traveled El Camino Real preceding the fight for Texas Independence. Herman Ehrenberg told this intriguing story in his narrative *With Milam and Fannin . . . The Adventures of a German Boy in Texas' Revolution*, published when he returned home in 1843 and translated into English in 1935. When Ehrenberg and the company of Greys crossed the Sabine River into Texas, his story continued: "After we had kissed the soil of our new country and become its citizens, we continued our march, and two days later reached the new and small town of San Augustine . . . Nothing could surpass the generous and cordial reception which the settlers gave us. But what pleased our company beyond everything else was the sight of large beefsteaks and roasts, prepared especially for us, lying before huge fireplaces . . . the meat was put into hot china dishes and laid on the tables by the hospitable colonists . . . As we sat down to eat, the simple, laconic 'Help yourselves' of our hosts was the only ceremony used . . . It must have been eleven o'clock when our party broke up and retired for the night. Our beds consisted of heaps of bear and buffalo skins, upon which we slept soundly until sunrise." This replica of the historic flag was made by Children of the American Revolution and presented to the Mission Dolores Museum. (Courtesy of Mission Dolores Museum; photograph by the author.)

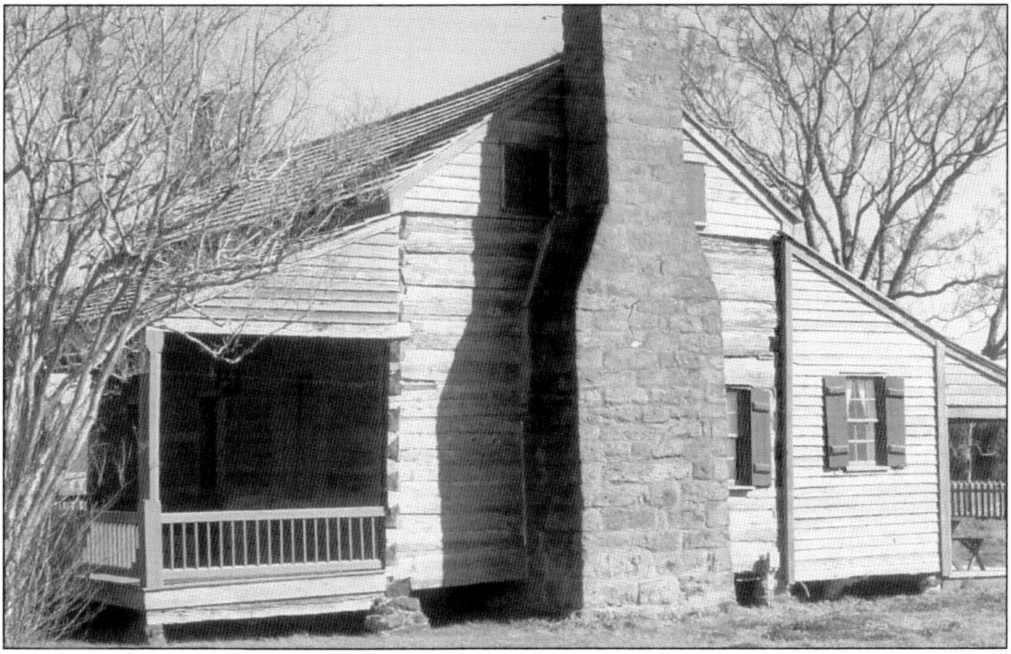

The Milton Garrett home was built in 1826 and faces El Camino Real a few miles west of San Augustine. Battle scars from yesteryear and bullet holes from Native American skirmishes were intentionally left in the doors and walls by architect Raiford Stripling during the home's restoration. The chimney is of rock quarried from behind the house. (Photograph by the author.)

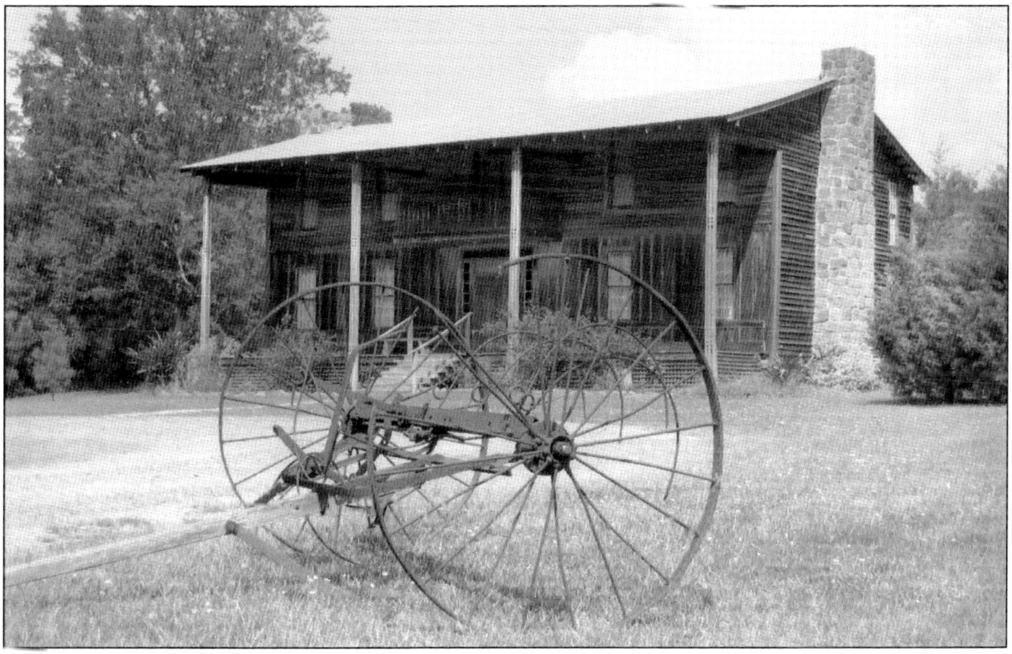

The Flournoy-Granberry House, better known as the Halfway House, was built in 1841. Thirteen miles west of San Augustine, it was a welcome stopping place for travelers headed to Nacogdoches along El Camino Real. Owner Samuel Flournoy was postmaster there in 1843 during Republic of Texas days. (Photograph by the author.)

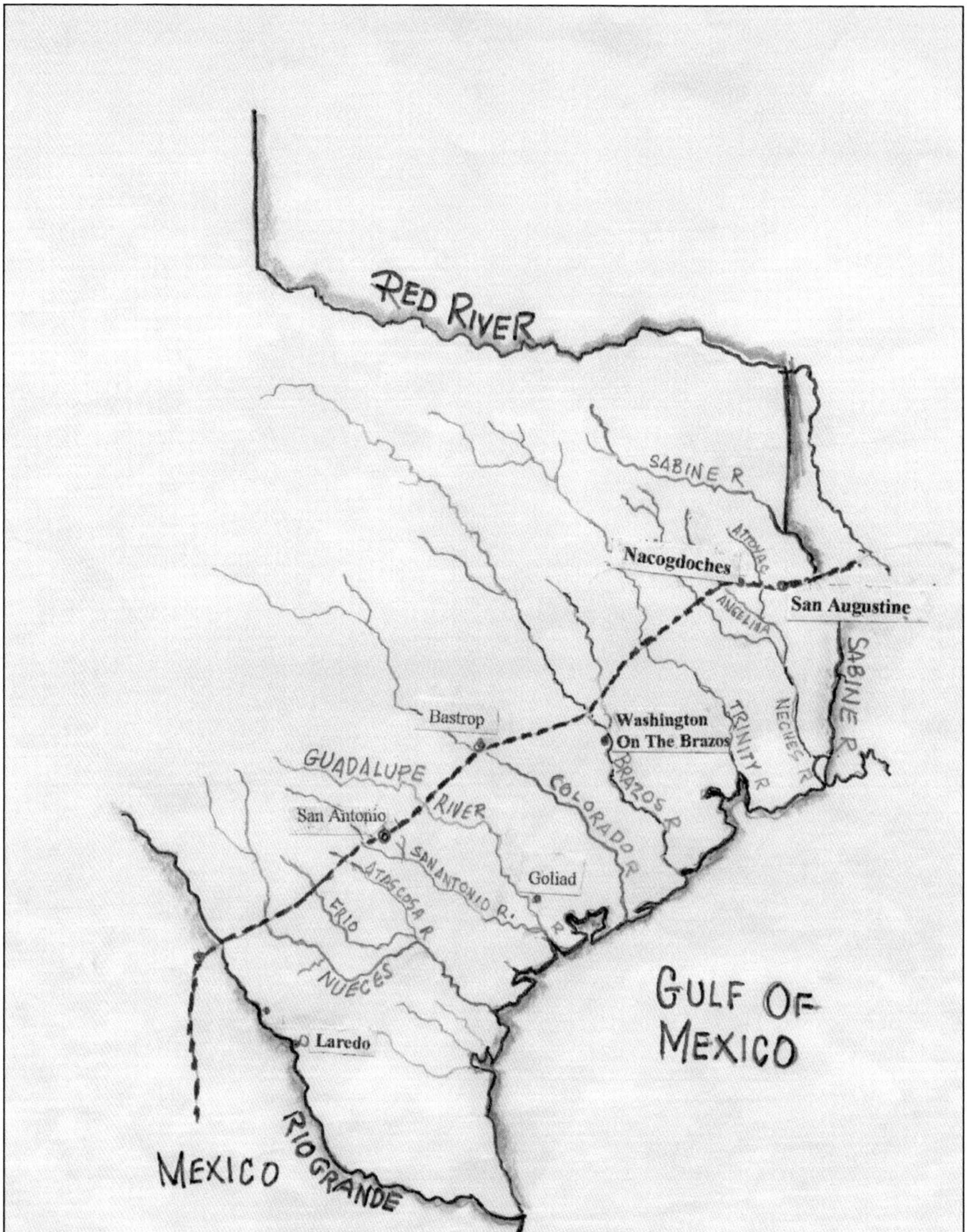

Independence Bound: This drawing shows the route taken in 1836 by David Crockett and many others who fought for Texas Independence at the Alamo in San Antonio, Texas. Today the Alamo is the most revered historic site (and the most visited) in the state of Texas. The Daughters of the Republic of Texas are custodians of the Alamo. Admission is free. (Sketch by Richard Murphy.)

Two

THE WAY WE WERE

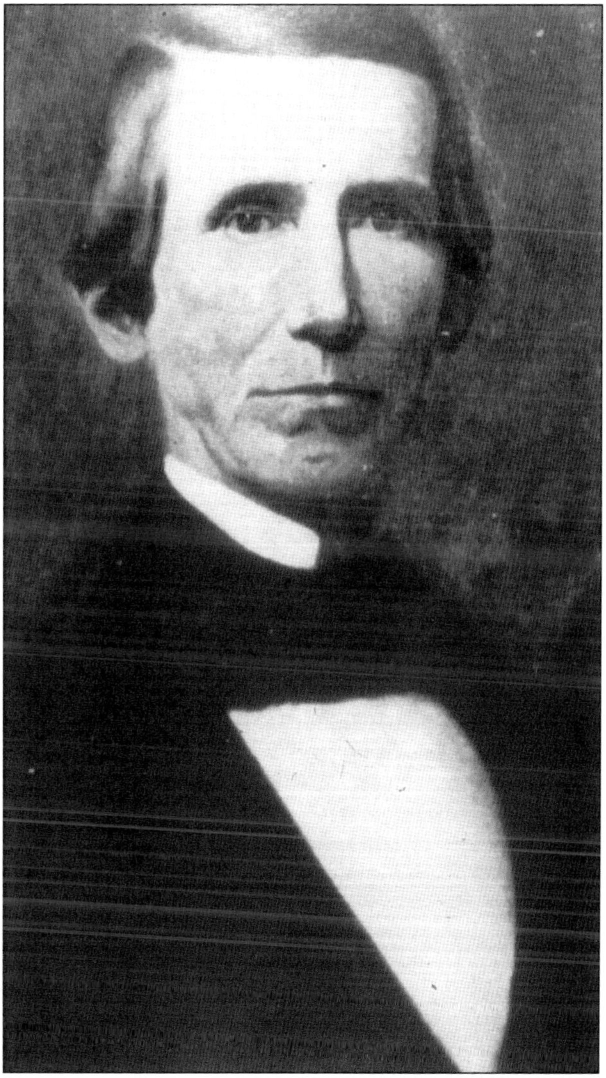

According to Dr. George L. Crocket in *Two Centuries in East Texas*, James Pinckney Henderson came to Texas "in her hour of greatest need in the spring of 1836." In 1837, Pres. Sam Houston chose him as attorney general for the Republic of Texas. Later, after the death of Stephen F. Austin, he assumed the office of secretary of state. He met his future wife, Frances Cox, while in Paris as the Texas envoy to England and France. After their marriage they settled in San Augustine, where Henderson entered law practice with Thomas J. Rusk and Kenneth L. Anderson. In 1845, when Texas became a state, he was elected her first governor. According to Mary D. Farrell, biographer of Frances Cox Henderson, "Frances studied law and became proficient enough in the subject to carry on the law practice when James had to be away on state business. When Henderson moved to Austin for his two-year term, his wife remained in San Augustine. One of her major contributions was to establish Episcopal churches in San Augustine, Rusk, Palestine, and Nacogdoches." (Author's collection.)

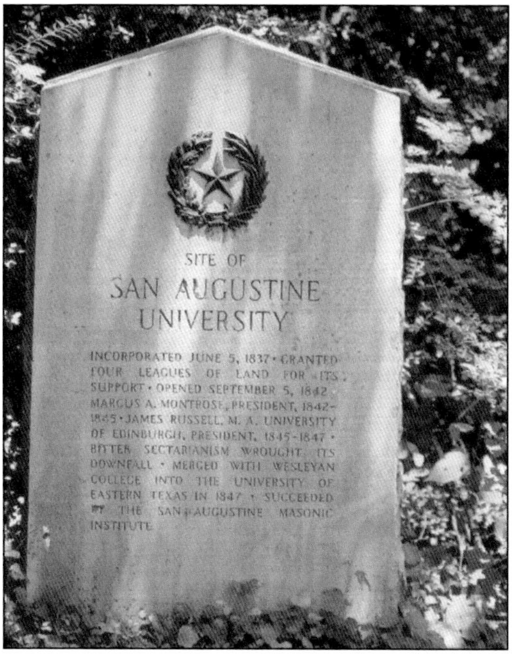

Many settlers who came to San Augustine County were people of superior education and ambitious goals. During the Texas Centennial in 1936, markers were placed at the locations of the state's first schools. San Augustine University was founded in 1837 (pictured at left), and Wesleyan College was founded in 1844. Neither lasted but a few years. In 1848, Oran M. Roberts combined the two schools into the nondenominational University of Eastern Texas. For a detailed pictorial history of the San Augustine County schools, the authors recommend *Schools of San Augustine County* by Harry P. and Kelly Noble, published in 2007. (Photograph by the author.)

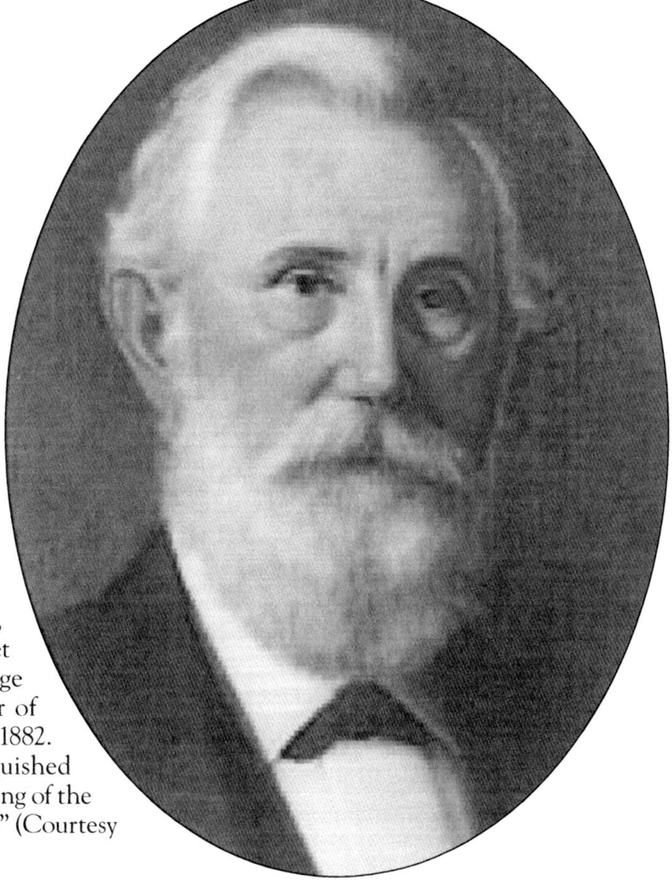

Governor of Texas Oran Milo Roberts came to San Augustine in 1841, intrigued with the unlimited possibilities available to enterprising young men in the new Republic of Texas. His spectacular rise to prestigious offices in the political life of both the Republic and the State of Texas are unequalled. In *Two Centuries in East Texas*, the Reverend George L. Crocket said of Roberts, "In 1878, Judge Roberts was elected Governor of Texas and served two terms until 1882. His administration was distinguished among other things by the building of the great new state capitol at Austin." (Courtesy of Judge Charles Mitchell.)

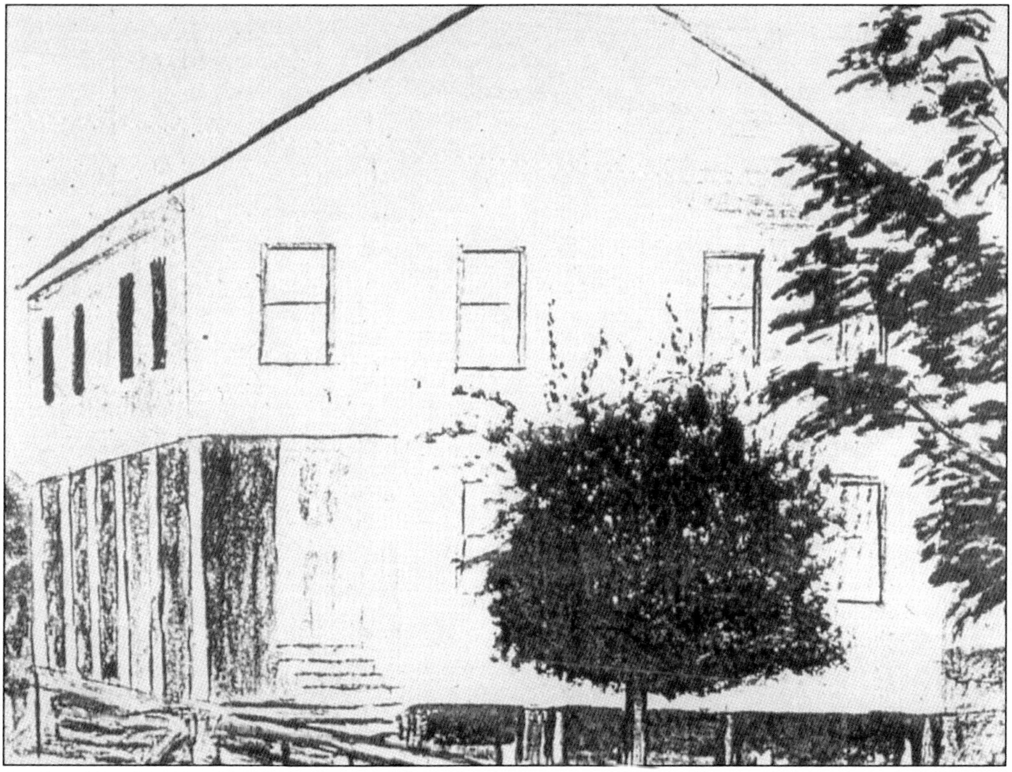

Redland Lodge No. 3 was one of the first three Masonic Orders founded in Texas in 1837 and was originally named William McFarland Lodge. McFarland was a well-respected citizen whose son Thomas McFarland surveyed the town site of San Augustine. This sketch by an unidentified artist portrays the first Lodge Hall, occupied by the Masons in 1840. (Courtesy of Redland Lodge No. 3; photograph by the author.)

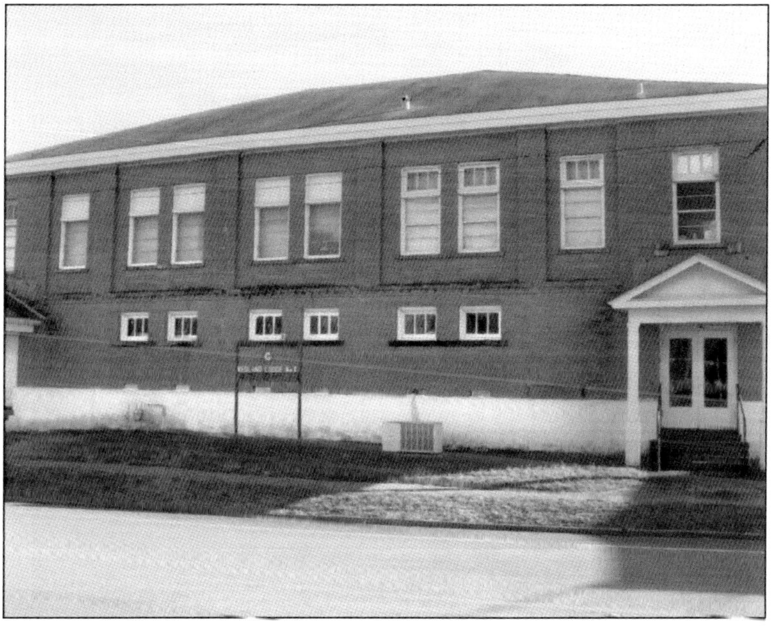

The two-story brick building for Redland Lodge No. 3 was constructed between 1907 and 1909 and houses a fine collection of museum-quality memorabilia dating to the 1830s. The historic building also provides meeting space for Shrine and Eastern Star members. (Photograph by the author.)

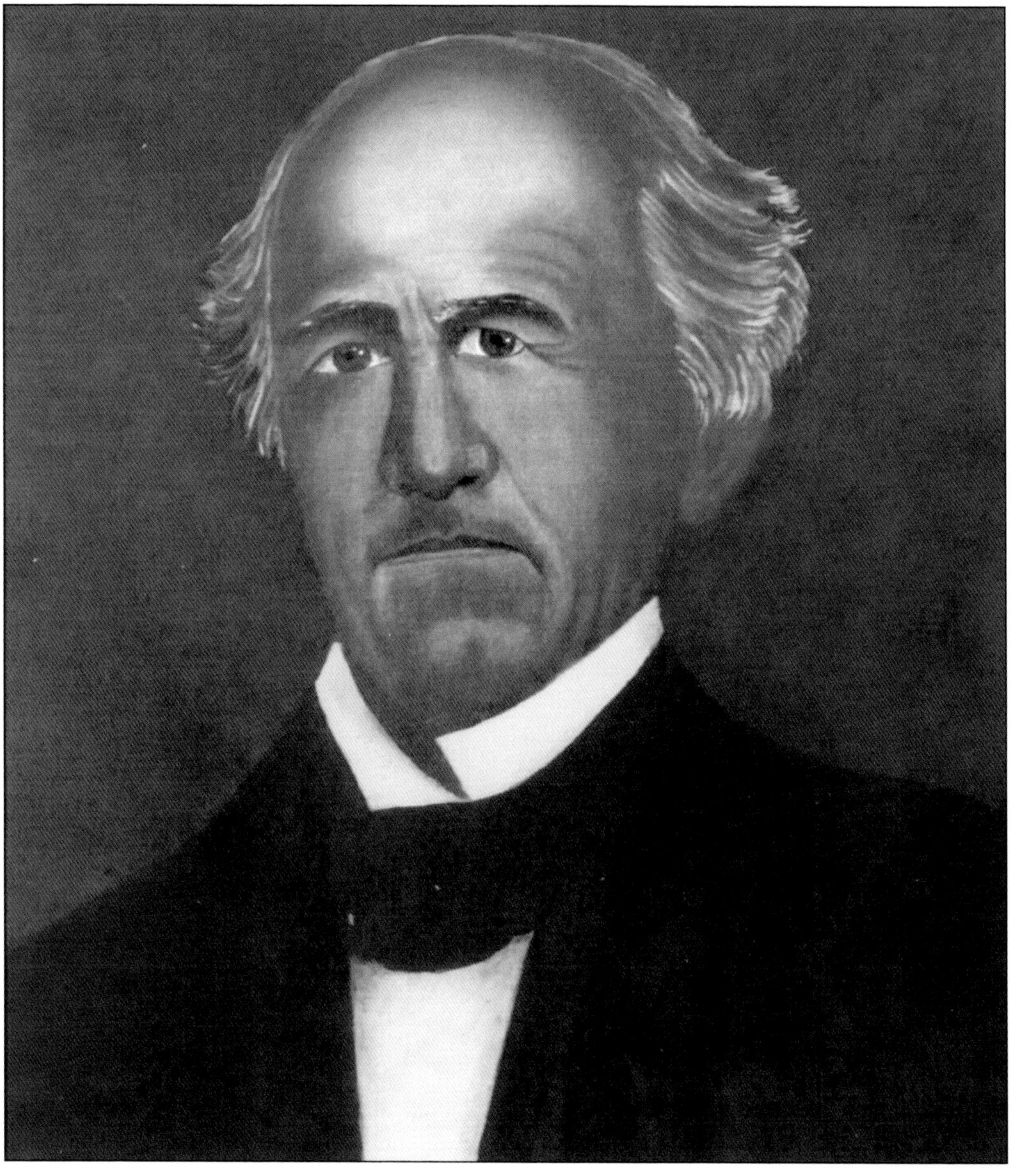

Lodge minutes show that on March 17, 1838, president of the Republic of Texas Sam Houston was heartily welcomed when he appeared at the Masonic meeting in San Augustine. This oil portrait of Sam Houston at age 63 was painted by Penelope Thomas, daughter of I. D. Thomas, a close friend of Houston. Penelope was the aunt of world-renowned artist S. Seymour Thomas, who recognized and cultivated his extraordinary talent while he was very young. This original painting is in the Seymour Thomas Art Collection housed in the Cullen House Museum. Interestingly, Farm Security Administration's Russell Lee photographed this unusual portrait in 1939 when it hung in the lobby of First National Bank. Seymour Thomas is especially remembered for his larger-than-life portrait of Gen. Sam Houston on his horse, which hangs prominently in the Monument Museum at the San Jacinto Battleground. According to James David Carter, author of *Masonry in Texas*, many of the slain heroes of the Alamo massacre on March 6, 1836, were Masons, including "James Bowie, William B. Travis, Almaron Dickenson, John C. Clarke, James Bonham, and David Crockett." (Courtesy of Ezekiel Cullen Chapter, Daughters of the Republic of Texas.)

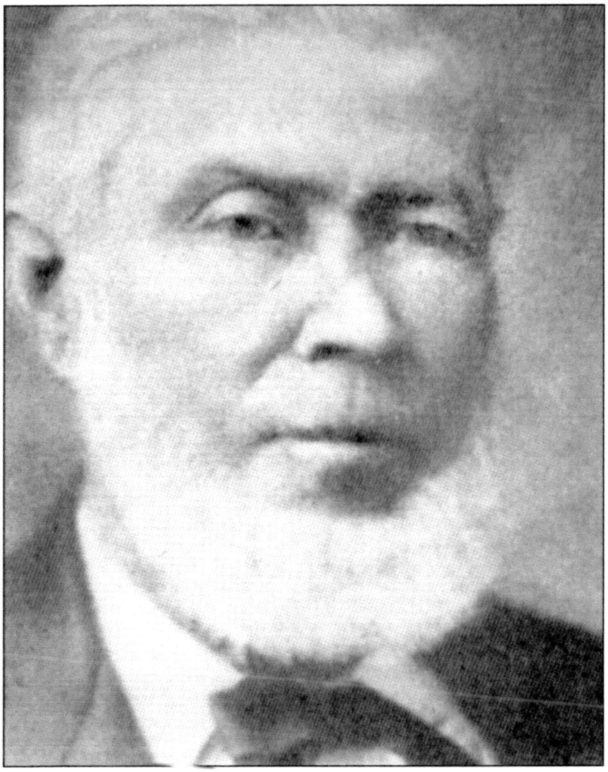

Stephen W. Blount is one of the colorful men in the history of Redland Lodge No. 3 and one of its charter members. He represented San Augustine in the Convention of 1836 at Washington-on-the-Brazos and signed the Texas Declaration of Independence along with Edwin O. LeGrand, San Augustine's other delegate. He became the first county clerk of San Augustine County in 1846 and was postmaster. During the Civil War, he was fiscal agent for the Confederate States of America. (Courtesy of Redland Lodge; photograph by the author.)

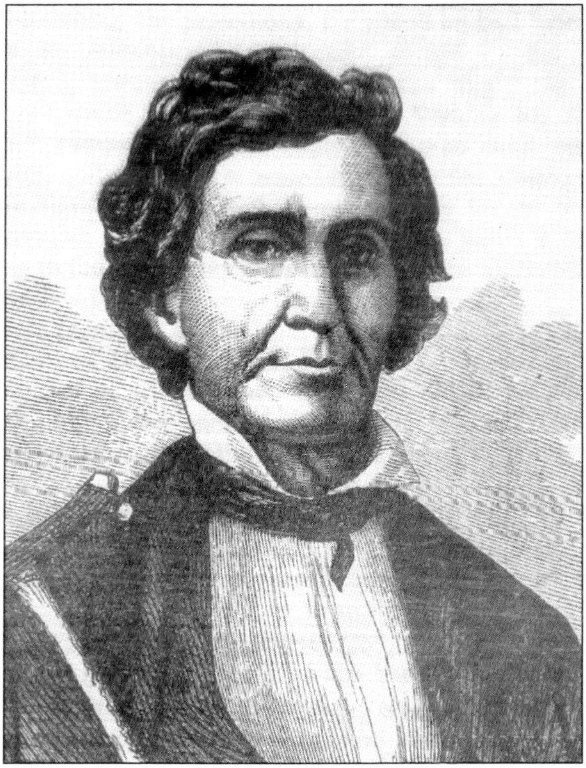

Another famous Mason was Judge Robert M. Williamson. Called "Three-Legged Willie," he was both eccentric and brilliant. Admitted to the bar at age 19, he became a talented, persuasive orator, an outspoken judge, and at the same time, a favorite of the people. One of Judge Williamson's legs was useless below the knee. He strapped it up behind him and replaced it with a wooden leg to walk on, thus the nickname. Noah Smithwick, a contemporary of Williamson and author of *Evolution of a State*, told of being awakened in the middle of night by someone calling to him from the street, "O Smithwick, here's a man with a broken leg." It was Willie, who had broken the wooden leg during a long night of dancing. "I took the fractured limb to my (blacksmith) shop and braced it up so that it was as good as new, and the judge went on his way rejoicing." (Author's collection.)

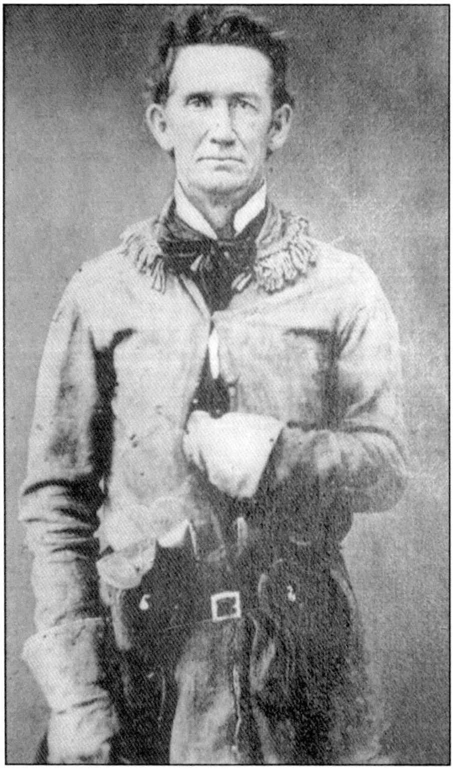

Mason John S. "Rip" Ford came to San Augustine soon after Texas Independence in 1836 and established a medical practice. In addition, he was a playwright who performed with the San Augustine Thespian Corps, a group organized in 1838. Colonel Ford wrote two comedies entitled *The Loafer's Courtship* and *The Stranger in Texas*, a play based on the author's observation of life in the Republic. He later moved to Austin and enjoyed a varied career as newspaper editor, lawyer, politician, and a Texas Ranger. As a colonel in the Confederacy, he led his forces to victory in the May 1865 Battle of Palmito Ranch. It was too late, however, to affect the outcome of the Civil War, as Gen. Robert E. Lee had surrendered a month earlier. (Courtesy of Richard Murphy.)

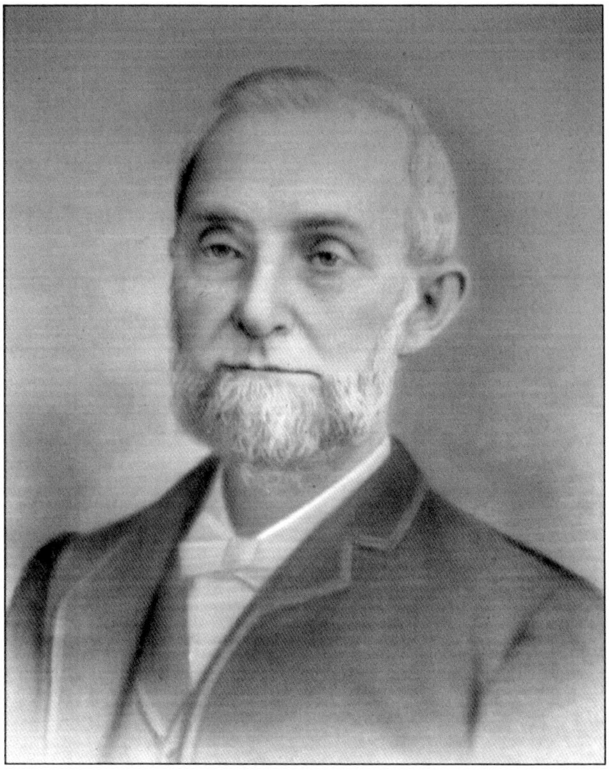

A charter member of Redland Lodge, Franklin Barlow Sexton became Grand Master of the Grand Lodge of Texas in 1854. Sexton was one of the first graduates of Wesleyan College and received his legal training from the prominent lawyers of San Augustine. He and his wife, Eliza Richardson, were parents of 12 children. Sexton served in the Confederate House of Representatives during the Civil War. When the new state capitol building was approved for construction, Sexton was selected to deliver an address during the cornerstone ceremony. (Courtesy of Redland Lodge; photograph by the author.)

The Old Town Well is a San Augustine landmark. It was dug in 1860 and is 27 feet deep. For many years, its refreshing water served local citizens and travelers along El Camino Real. Later a building was constructed around the well. When pharmacist and county judge R. N. Stripling (pictured) moved his drugstore to the location, he cleaned and restored the well. Visitors to the nostalgic old well are always welcome and often drop in coins for good luck. The San Augustine County Historical Society now owns the historic Stripling building, where indexed and digitized county records are available to researchers. Grants from the Summerlee and Gill Foundations provided funding to the San Augustine County Historical Society for the records project. (Courtesy of Mary Jane Stripling.)

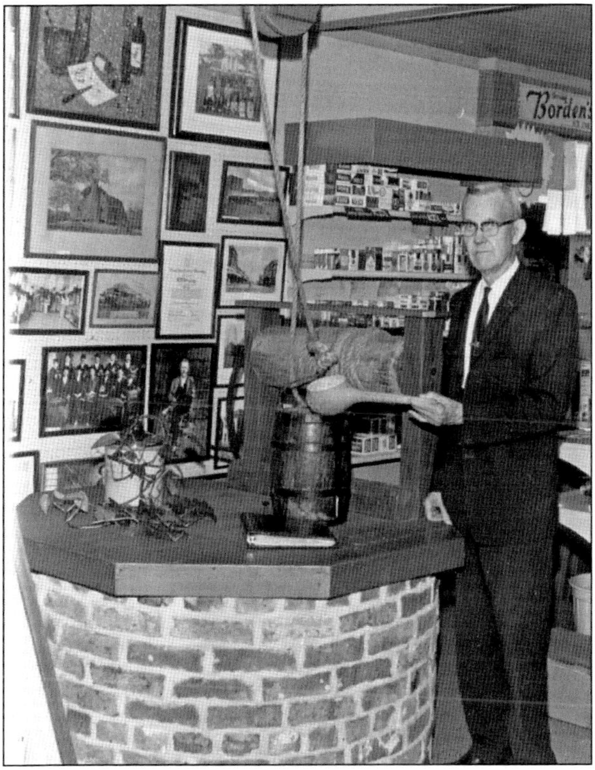

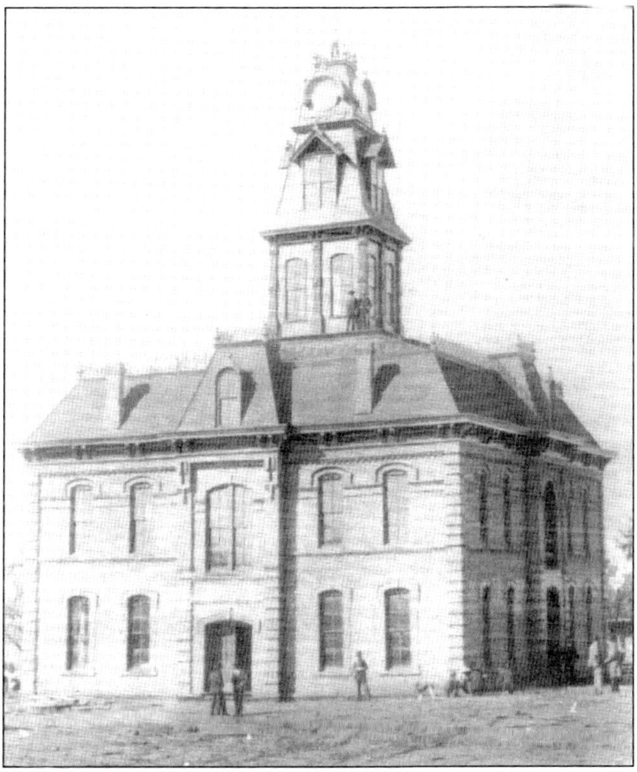

After the customhouse was no longer used as the county courthouse, a new building was constructed on the courthouse square in 1854. No sketch or photograph of this building exists today. Pictured is the second courthouse constructed on the square in 1884 with brick made near the Ayish Bayou in San Augustine. Columbus Murphy was employed to paint the trim around the windows and roof for $75. No being told the colors to use, Murphy decided to paint the roof red, much to the surprise of the citizens. This structure did not prove to be substantial and was replaced in 1927 by the current San Augustine County Courthouse. (Courtesy of Carol Wayne Vaughn.)

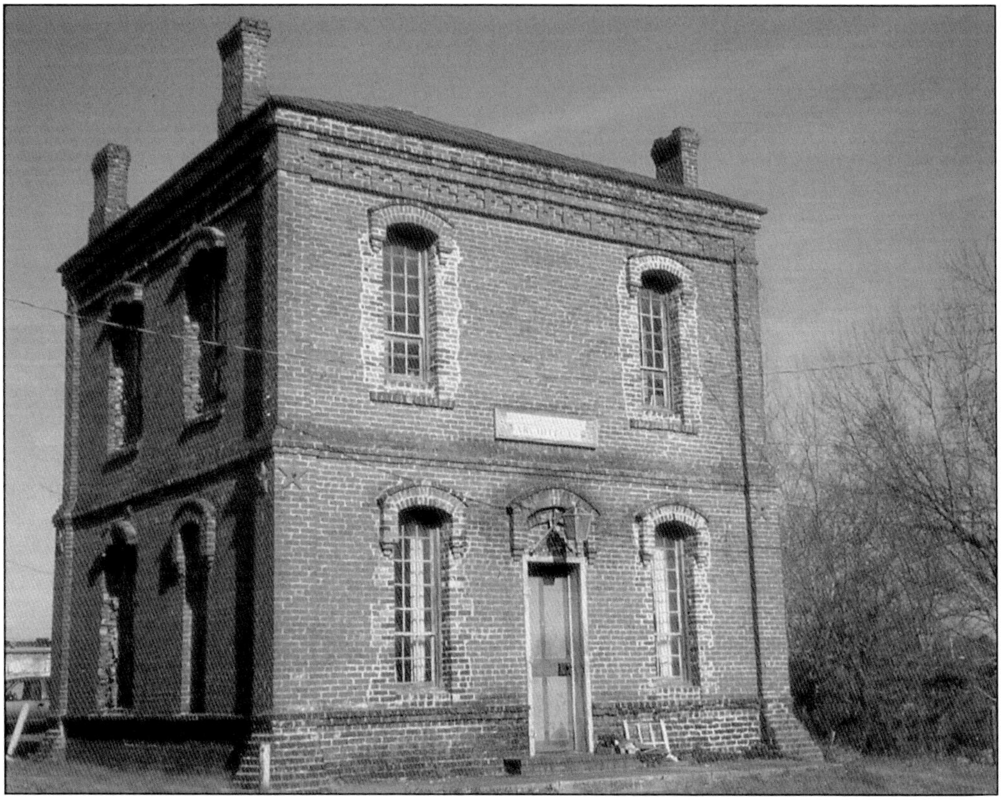

The old San Augustine County Jail was built in 1883. For reasons known only to that generation of county officials, bars from this jail were pulled out and used for the new jail built on the courthouse square in 1919. The architectural offices of Raiford Stripling and his son Ray R. Stripling were housed in the old jail for many years. Stripling replaced the brick around the windows. (Photograph by the author.)

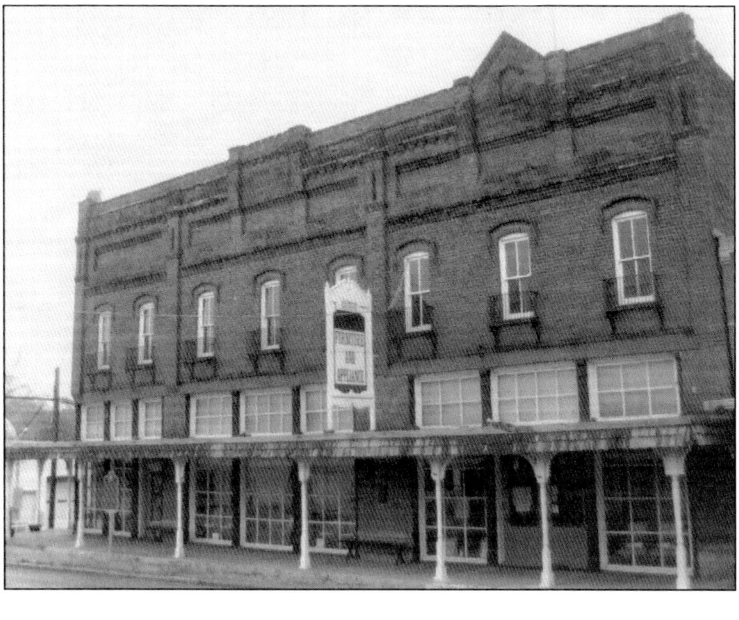

The Hollis Building, constructed in 1884, was the only substantial structure that survived the 1890 fire in downtown San Augustine. (Photograph by the author.)

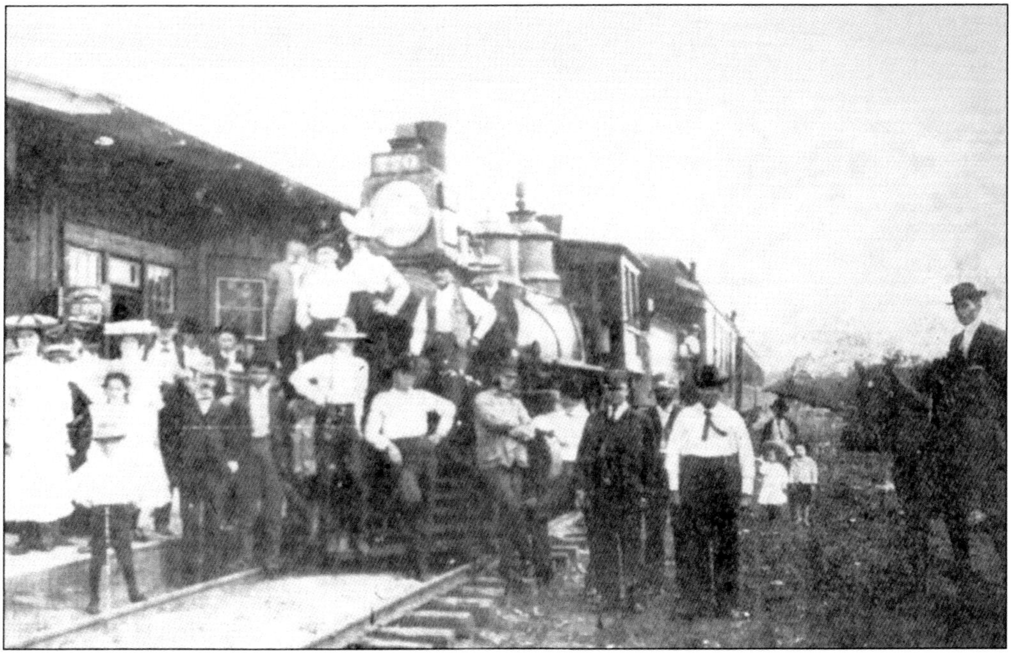

The Atchison, Topeka, and Santa Fe Railway Company (ATSF) had its beginning as the Gulf, Beaumont, and Great Northern Railway, extending its track from southeast Texas to San Augustine in 1902. The inception of the railway system brought economic renewal to San Augustine County and other sections of previously isolated East Texas. The first train into San Augustine in 1903 was welcomed by a large group of excited citizens. Notice the original depot at the top of the photograph. (Courtesy of Richard Murphy.)

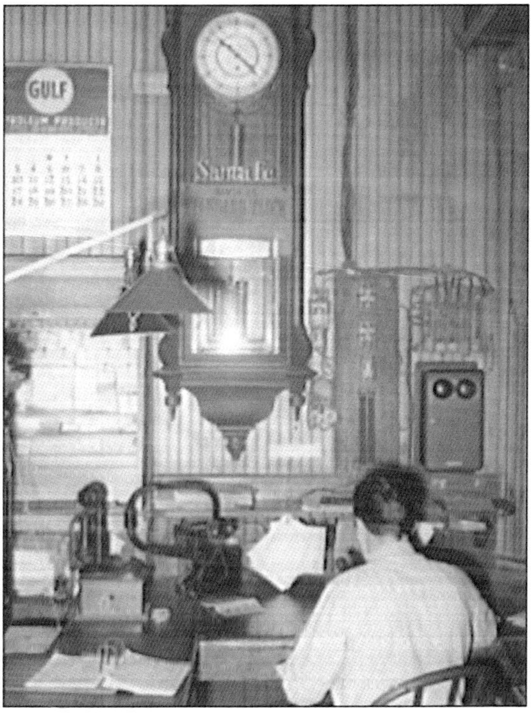

The spacious Atchison, Topeka, and Santa Fe depot stood beside the railroad track in San Augustine from 1902 until 1985. The interior office space was always a place of interest to passengers, with its up-to-the-minute clock and its busy atmosphere. In this 1939 photograph, U.S. Farm Security Administration photographer Russell Lee captured the depot agent at work. (Russell Lee, FSA, 1939, Library of Congress.)

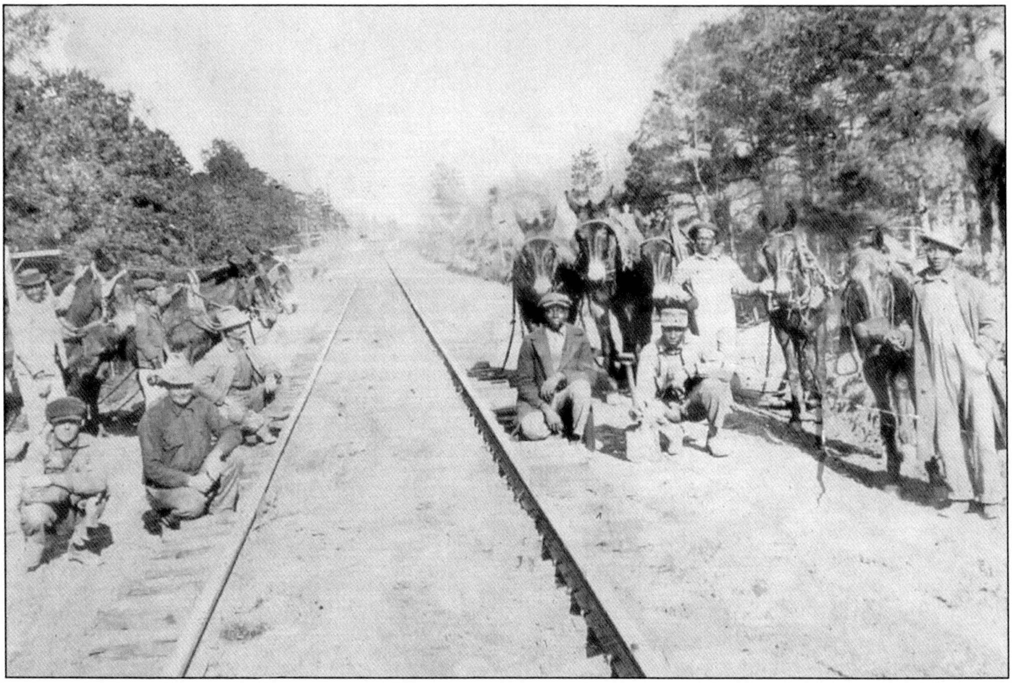

In 1905, railroad workers, called a "Section Crew," laid an extension of railroad track north from San Augustine, past Bland Lake, and on toward Center, Texas. (Author's collection.)

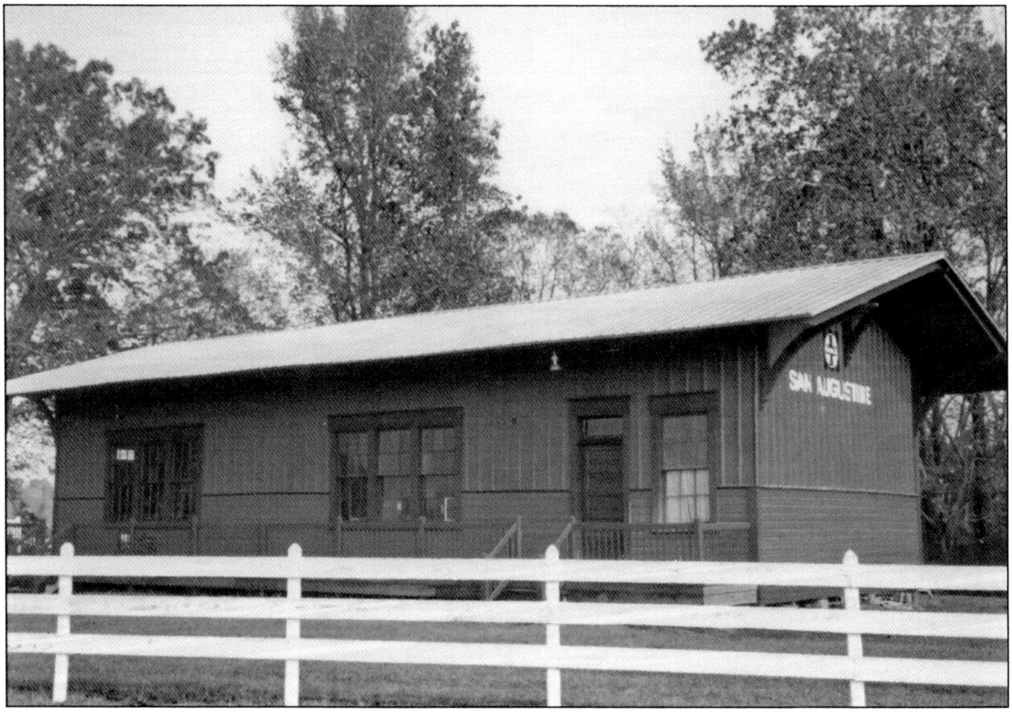

When the Atchison, Topeka, and Santa Fe Railway decided to sell its San Augustine depot in 1985, it was purchased by John and Lucy Mitchell, who moved the historic building to their farm and restored it as a railroad museum. (Photograph by the author.)

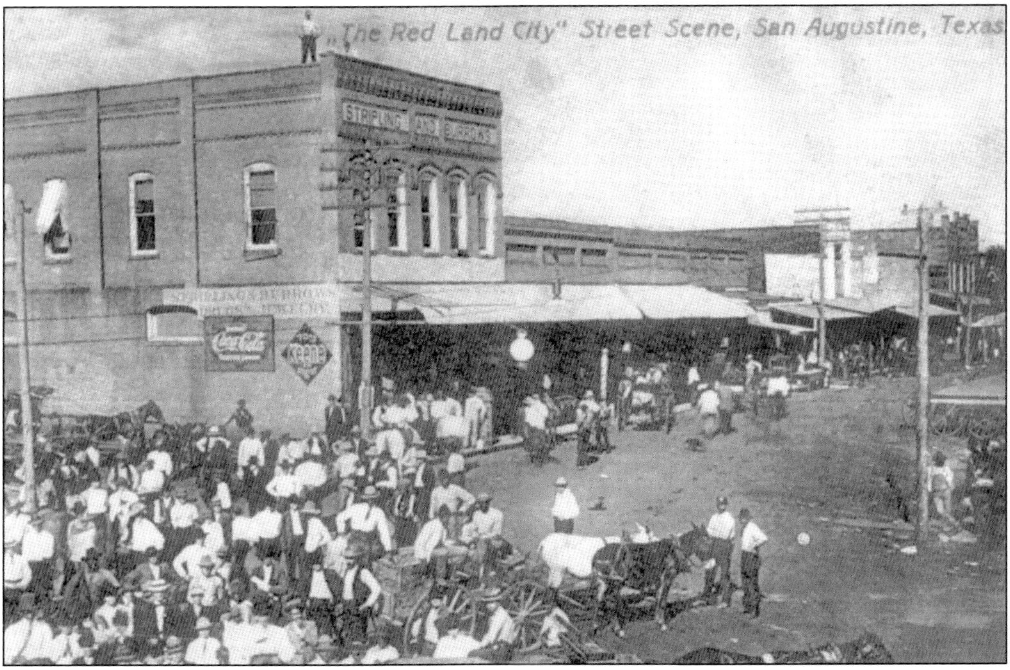

San Augustine was called "Redland City" by many residents in 1901, and the county and surrounding area was known as "The Redlands" due to the iron-rich crimson soil. (Courtesy of Nelsyn Wade.)

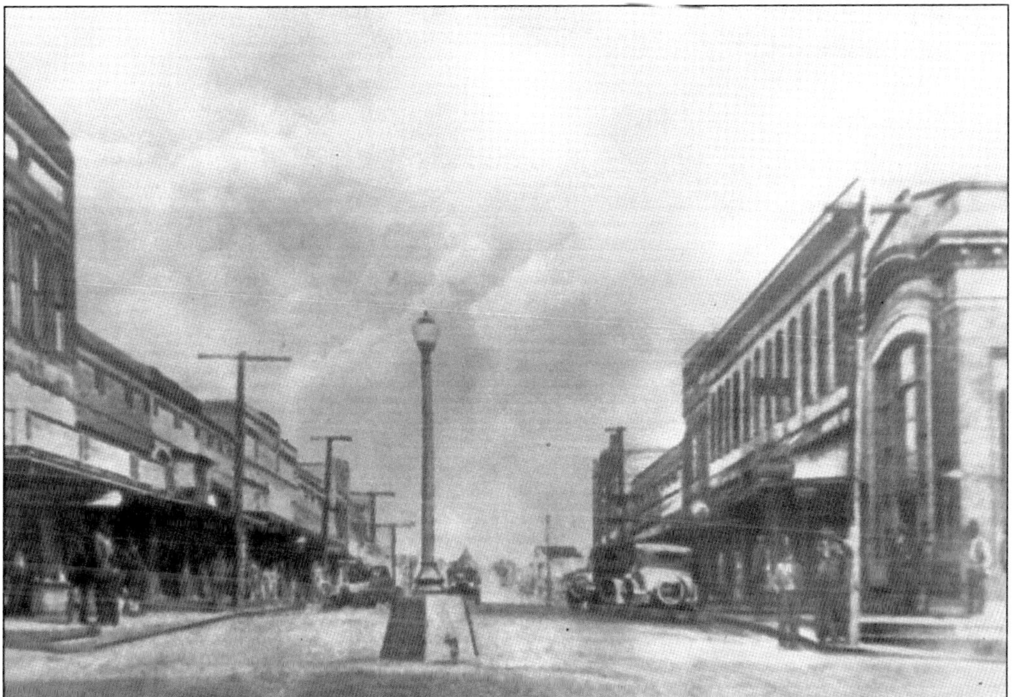

Early downtown San Augustine had a lantern-style gaslight pole in the middle of the street around 1912. (Courtesy of Nelsyn Wade.)

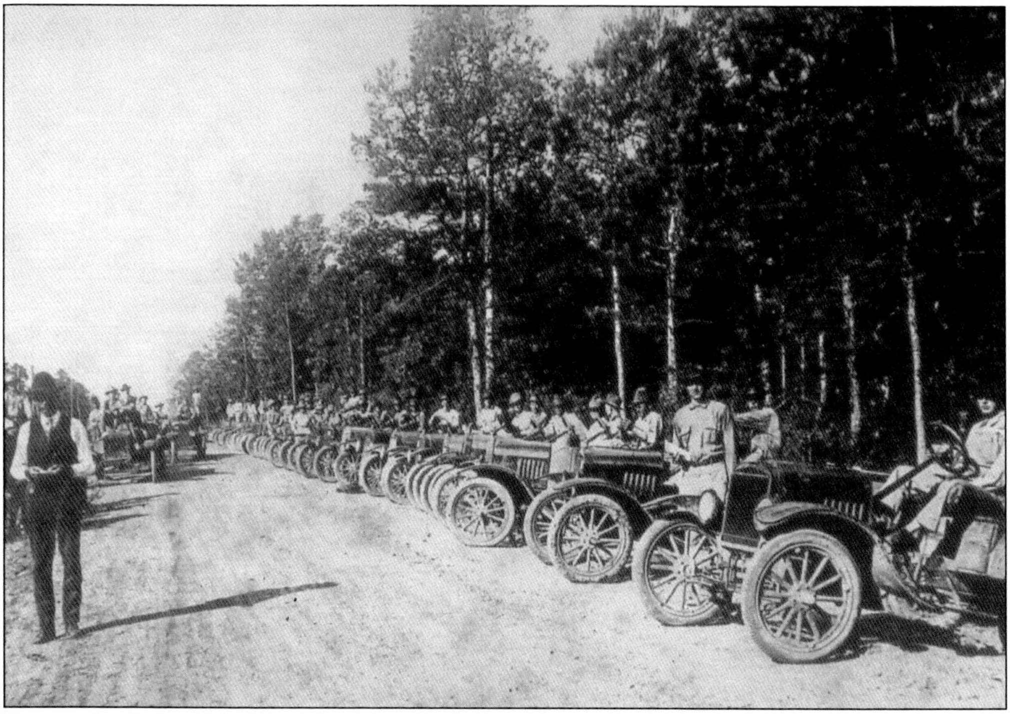

During the flurry of 1920s road construction in San Augustine County, Ford trucks were parked in perfect alignment along the road for this photograph. (Author's collection.)

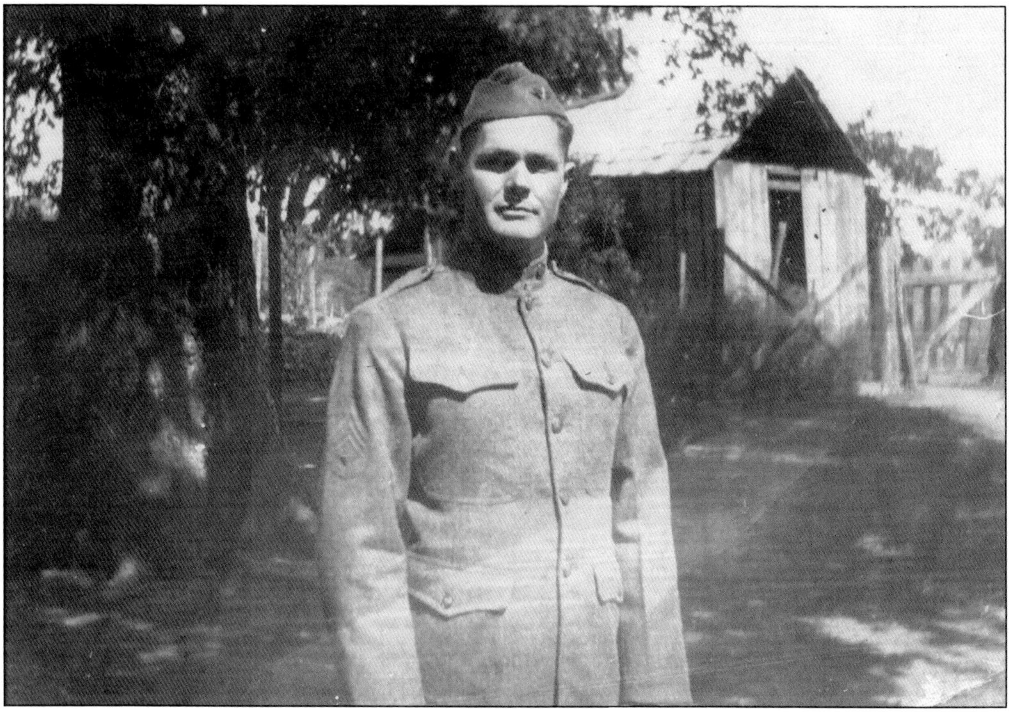

John Thomas Bodine fought in France during World War I. When he returned home, he became a farmer and raised nine children on the Bodine family land. (Courtesy of Al Broden.)

Tom Gamble, pictured at right, served with distinction in World War I. Other San Augustine men who bravely fought in World War I included, among others, Ivy Lewis, Will Wade, Dr. Charles Haley, George Ford, Drew Wade, Jim Brown, and Abbie Whitton Sr. A tall marker on the San Augustine County courthouse square, erected by Post 387 of the American Legion, records the names of San Augustine County men who died in the service of their country during World War I, World War II, Korean War, and Vietnam. This monument, shaded by large pecan and crape myrtle trees, is a stark and constant reminder of the high cost of freedom. (Courtesy of Verline Gamble Stewart.)

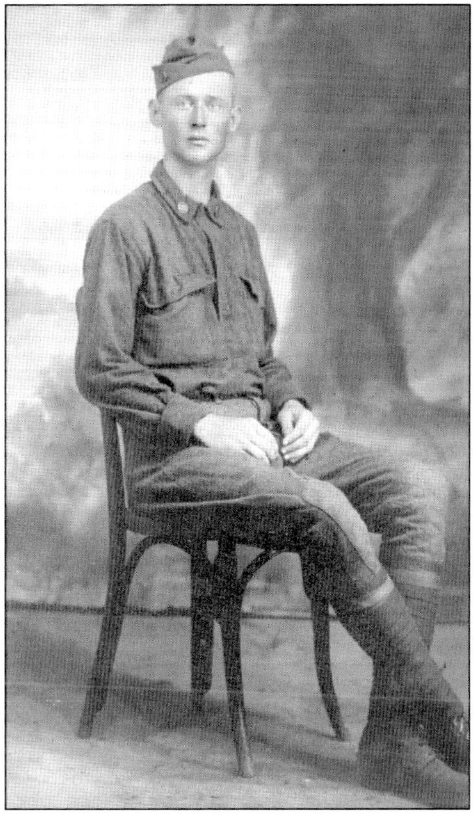

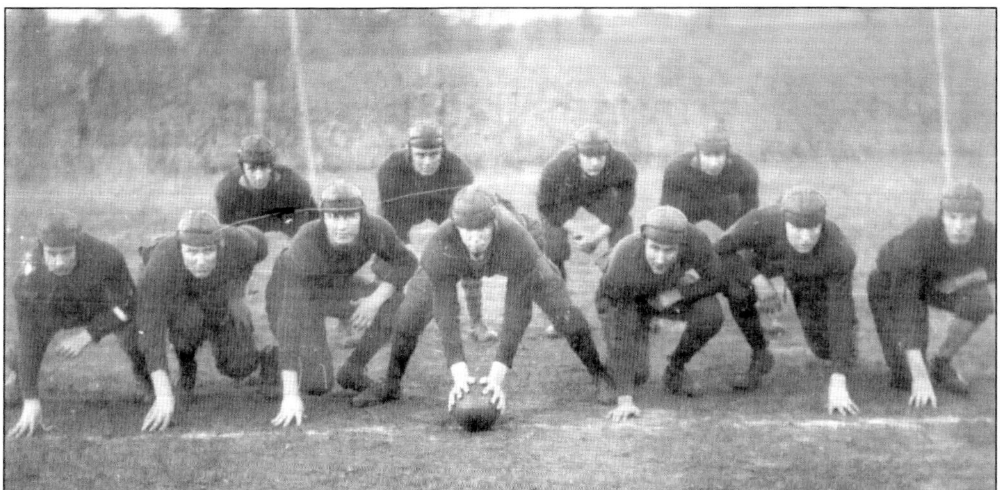

The 1921 San Augustine High School football team was called the Tigers. Pictured are, from left to right, (first row, the line) right end Logan Palmer, right tackle Elbert Thomas, right guard Jewett Enlowe, center Frank Miller, left guard Paul Whitton, left tackle Link Jeanes, and left end Albert Murphy; (second row, backfield) right halfback Franklin Blount, fullback Lister Smith, quarterback Oran Baggett, and left halfback Foster Davis. Sometime later, the San Augustine County schools named their mascots for all sports the San Augustine Wolves and the Broaddus Bulldogs. (Courtesy of Richard Murphy.)

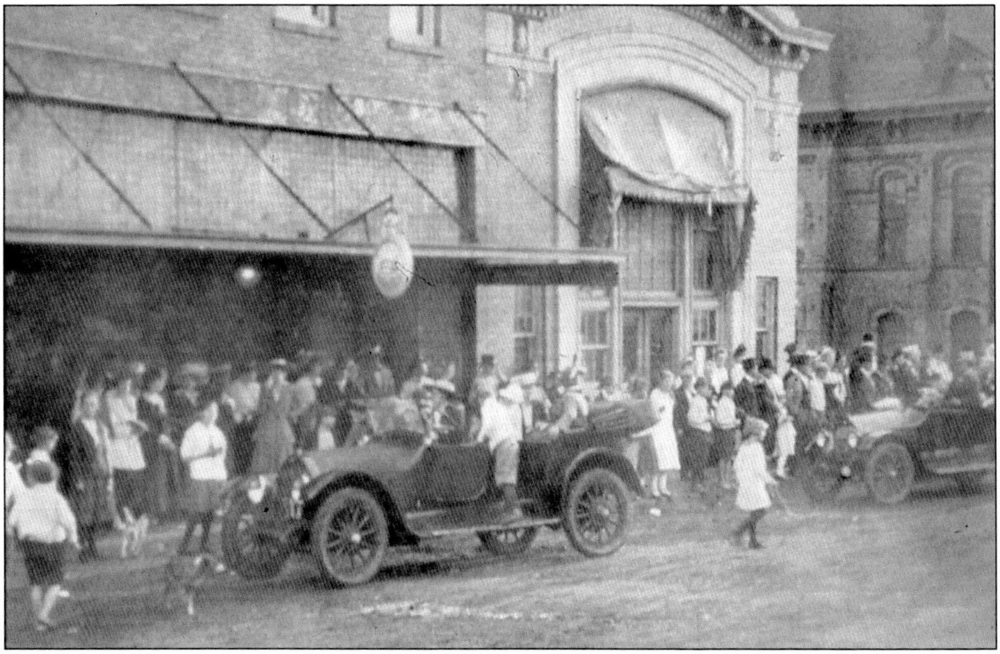

Early San Augustine photographs usually show large crowds milling about, always in close proximity to one another. It is obvious that people came to town in large droves to any event and for any reason during the early 1900s. This is the First National Bank in 1920, with the 1884 San Augustine County Courthouse in the photograph on the far right. (Author's collection.)

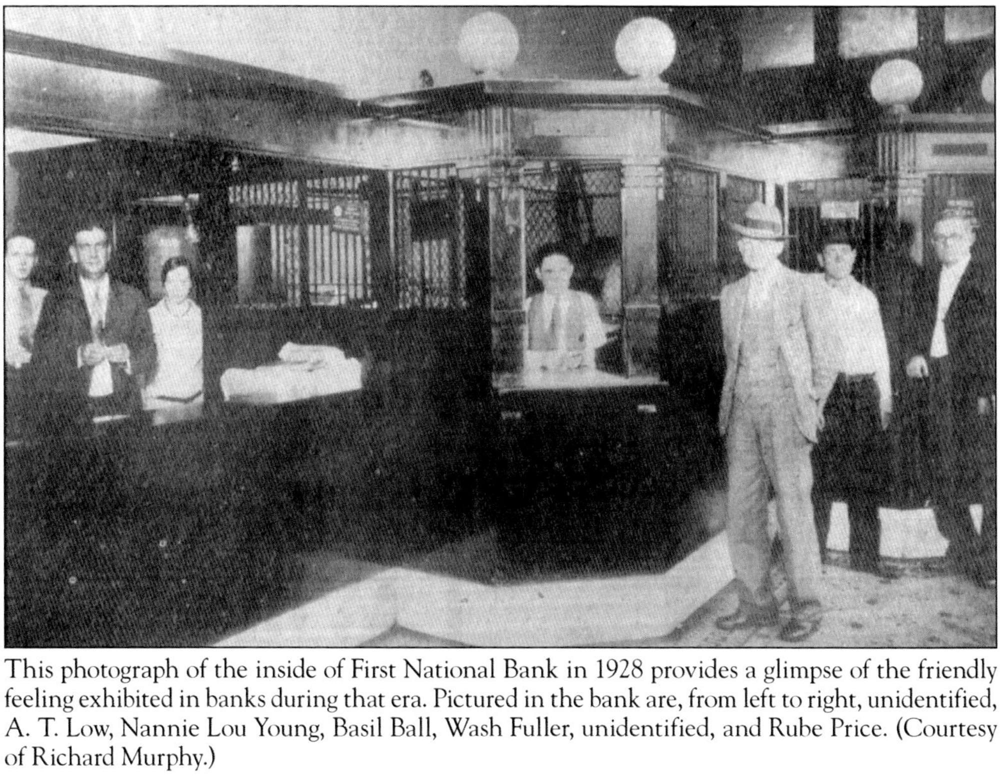

This photograph of the inside of First National Bank in 1928 provides a glimpse of the friendly feeling exhibited in banks during that era. Pictured in the bank are, from left to right, unidentified, A. T. Low, Nannie Lou Young, Basil Ball, Wash Fuller, unidentified, and Rube Price. (Courtesy of Richard Murphy.)

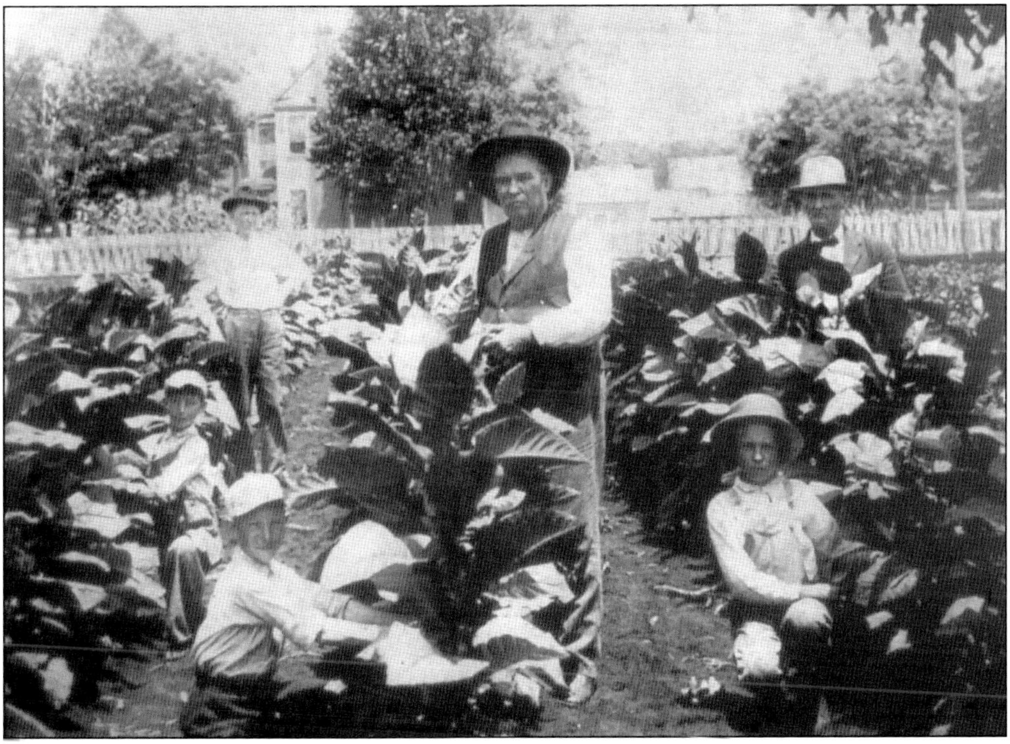

In the 1920s, J. A. Blohm, a tobacco culturist, migrated to San Augustine and began growing exceptional tobacco in the rich red soil. His warehouse and office were on the east side of the courthouse square, where the tobacco leaves were hung up to dry. Blohm painstakingly rolled the cigars layer by layer. They were then placed in molds and cut to the proper length. After aging, they were boxed for shipping throughout Texas and Louisiana. The diminutive J. A. Blohm (standing at right) is pictured with Lafayette "Pet" Sharp (center), among others, in the latter's tobacco patch. (Courtesy of Jerry Payne.)

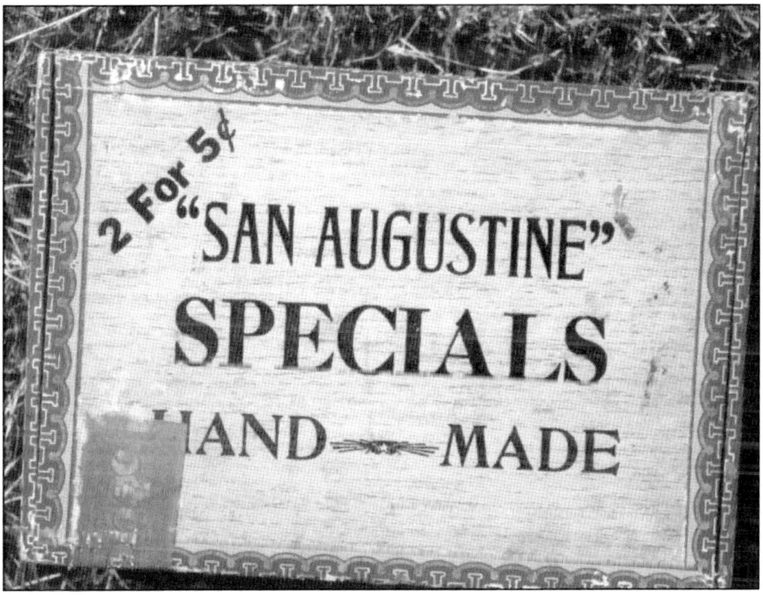

J. A. Blohm's famous San Augustine cigars were placed in these colorful wooden boxes for shipping and display. (Courtesy of Jerry Payne.)

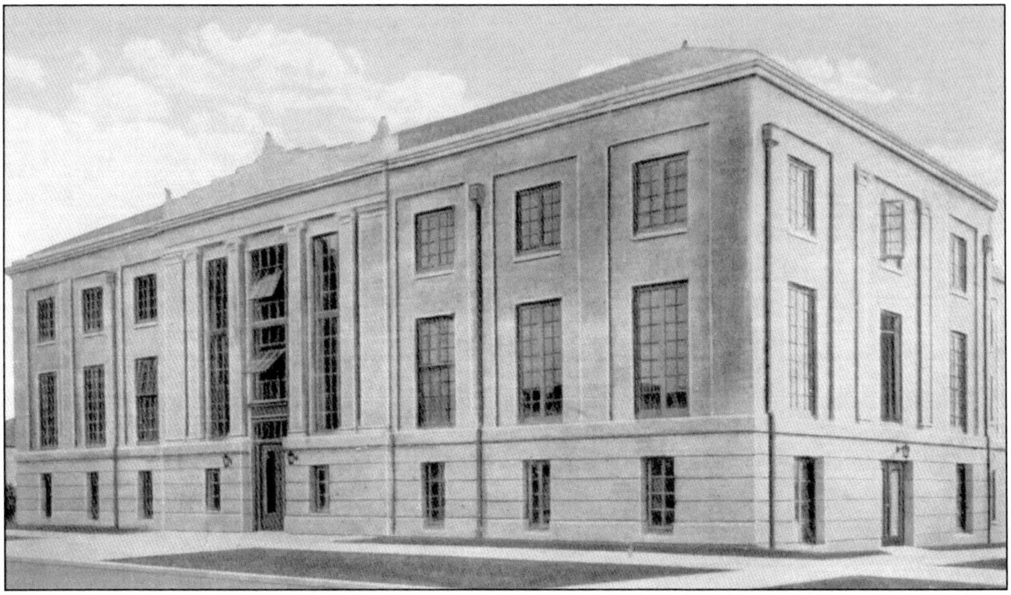

This image of the new 1927 San Augustine County Courthouse is from a postcard widely circulated during the early 1930s. A restoration of the 83-year-old building began in 2009 and was completed in August 2010. Beginning in the year 2000, San Augustine Garden Club spearheaded the drive to restore the courthouse through Texas Historical Commission's Courthouse Preservation Program with the approval of county officials. The organization also raised the local matching funds for the project. (Courtesy of Mary Jane Stripling.)

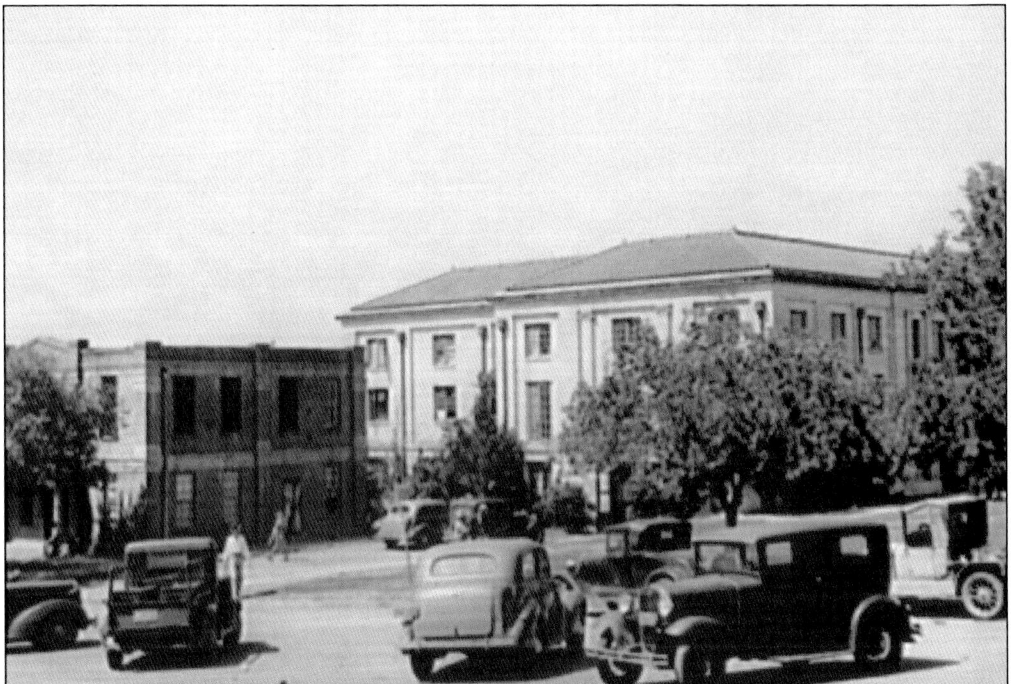

This view of the 1927 San Augustine County Courthouse and the 1919 jail was photographed from the east side of the courthouse square. (Russell Lee, FSA, 1939, Library of Congress.)

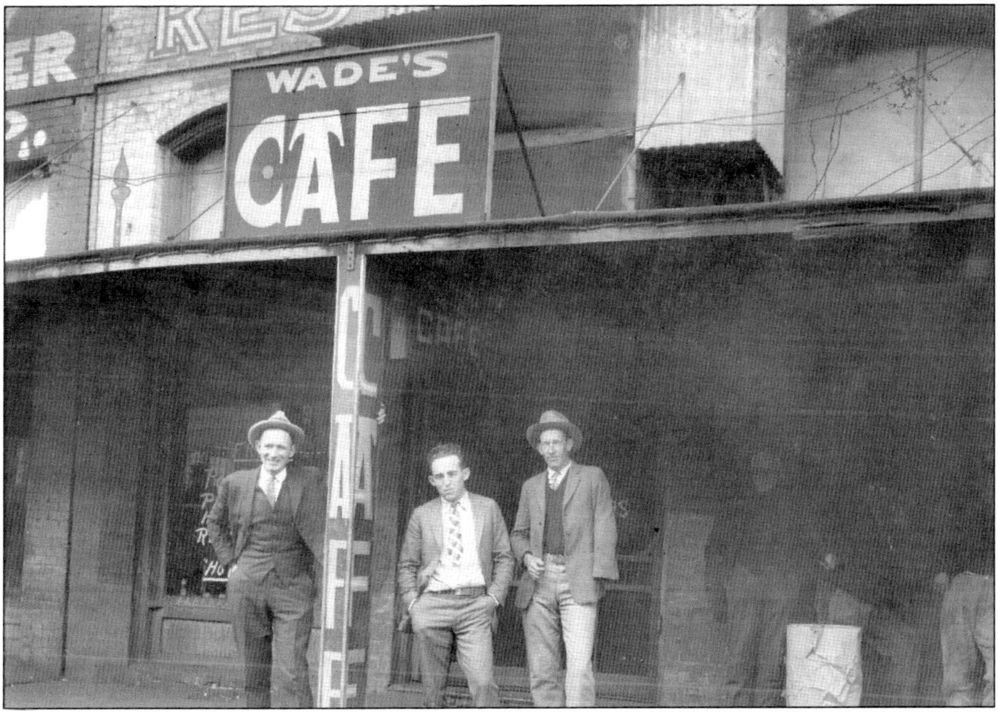

Wade's Café was later called City Café. This photograph is from the mid-1930s. (Courtesy of Nelsyn Wade.)

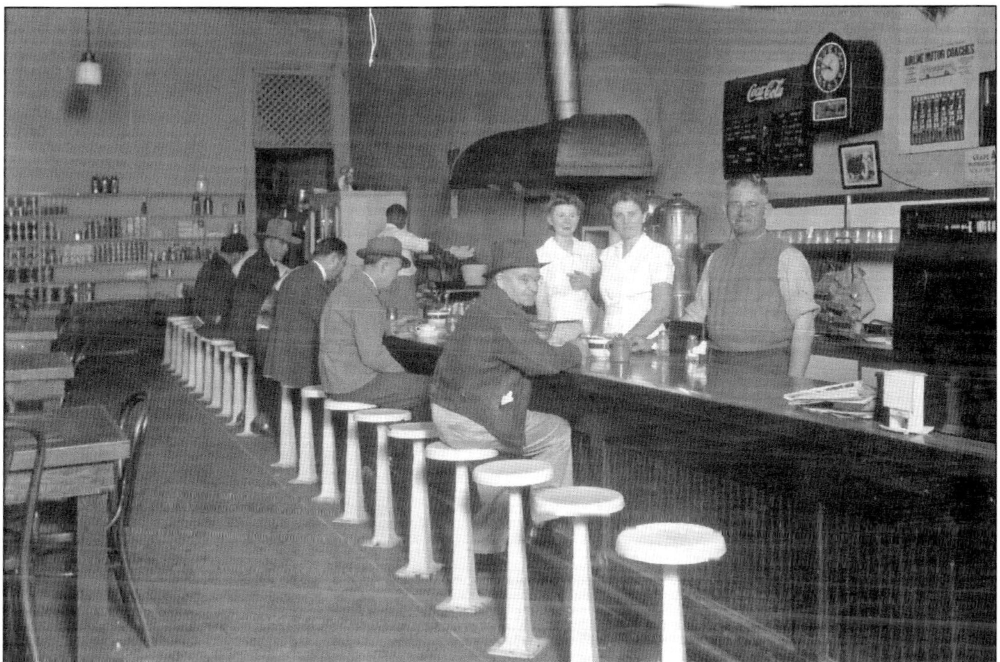

For nearly three decades, Wade's City Café served San Augustinians with delicious home-style cooking. Owner Will Wade is pictured in the foreground in this 1941 photograph. (Courtesy of Nelsyn Wade.)

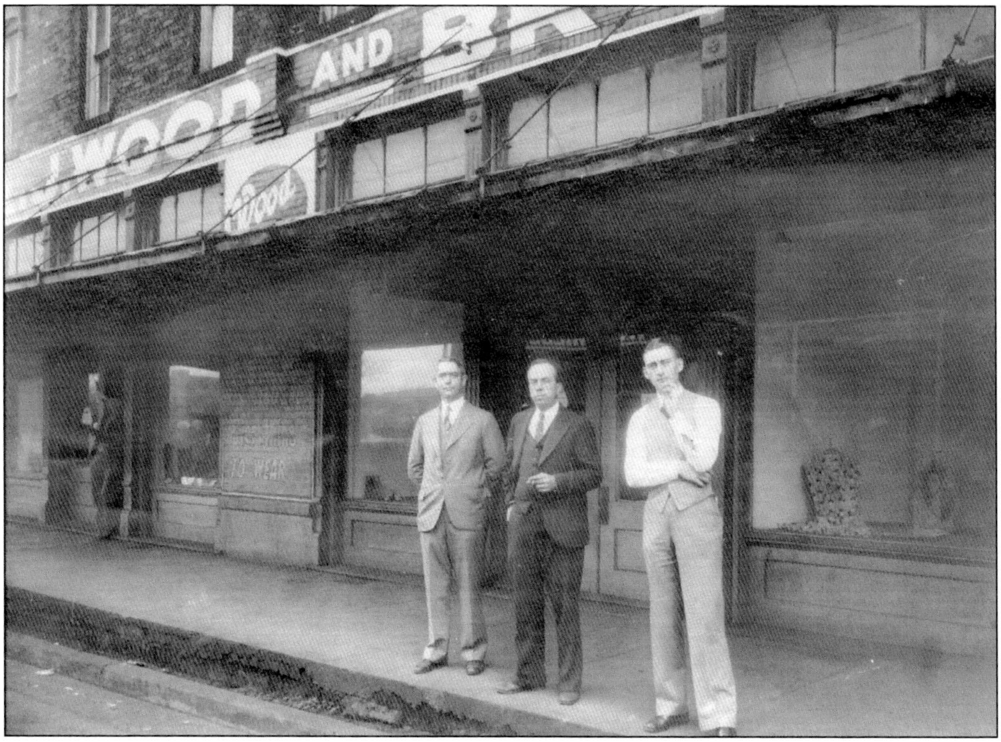

A. J. Wood and Brothers was a department store that opened for business in the 1920s. This photograph was taken in 1932. Pictured from left to right are Price Wood, Melville Ingram, and Jack Wood. (Author's collection.)

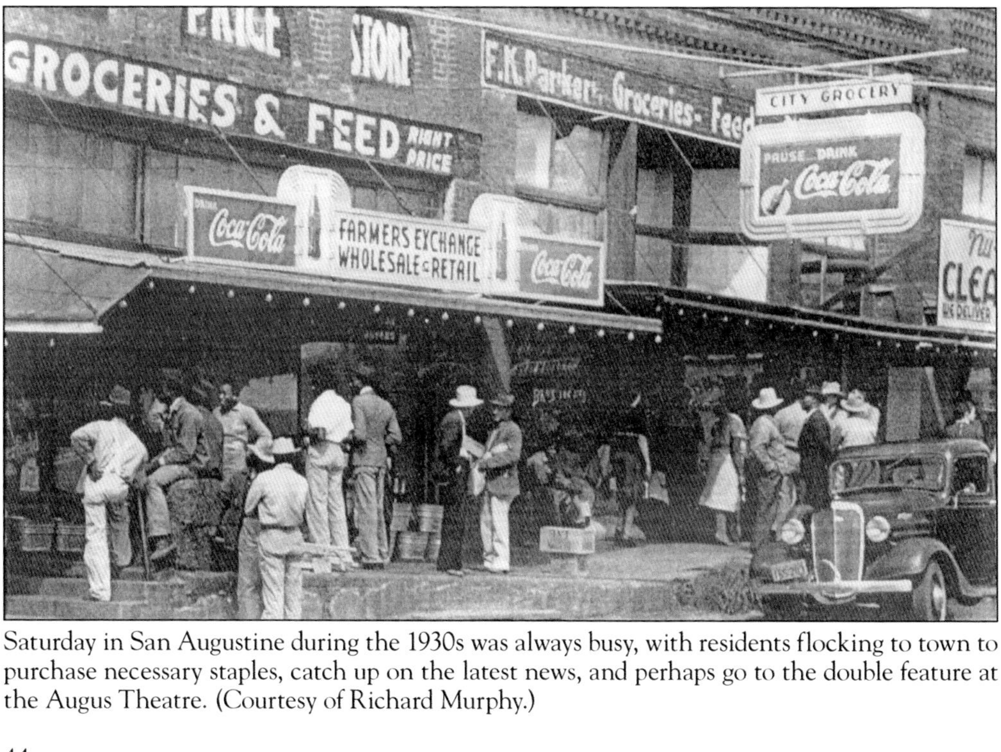

Saturday in San Augustine during the 1930s was always busy, with residents flocking to town to purchase necessary staples, catch up on the latest news, and perhaps go to the double feature at the Augus Theatre. (Courtesy of Richard Murphy.)

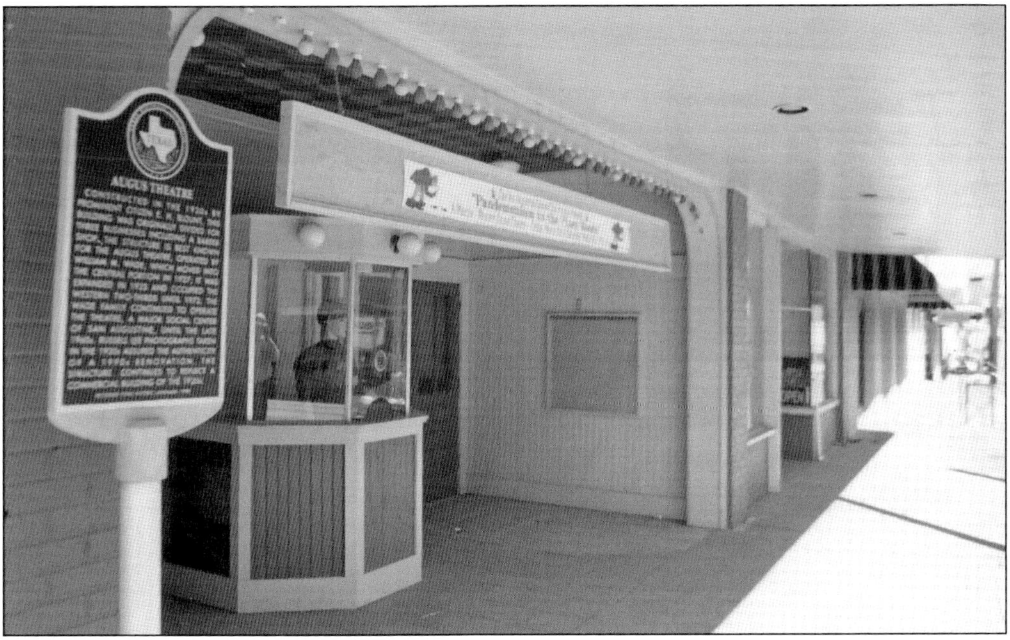

The Augus Theatre, owned by the San Augustine County Historical Society (SACHS), was constructed in the early 1920s and used for a variety of purposes until 1927, when Will and Atheniar Wade opened a movie house there. They operated it until their retirement in 1970. Ray R. Stripling assisted the SACHS with its complete restoration as a live theater and museum complex during the late 1990s. (Photograph by the author.)

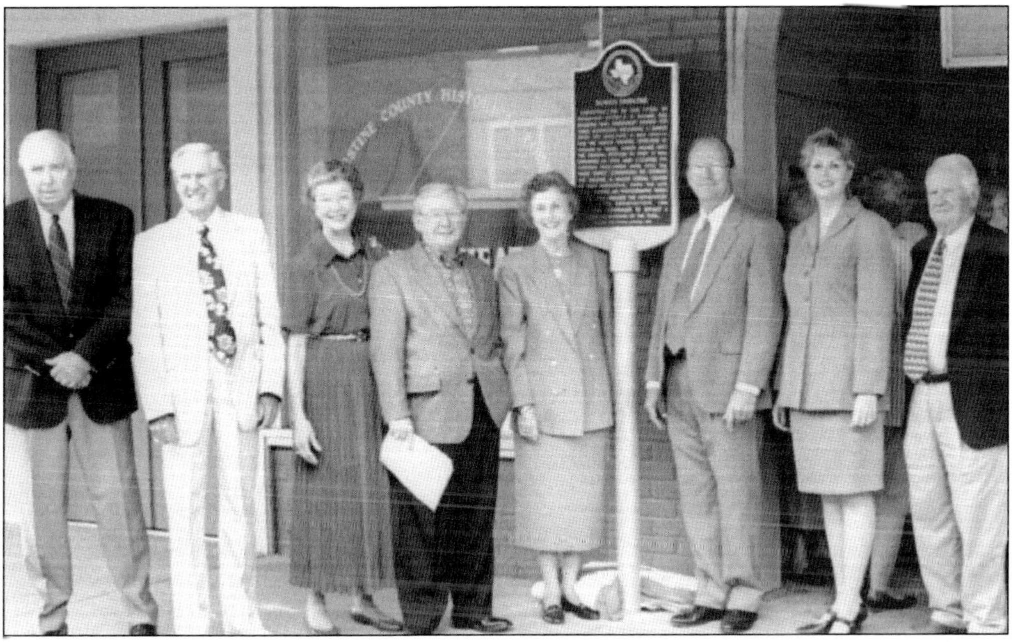

Participating in the Recorded Texas Historic Landmark dedication ceremony of the Augus Theatre in 1999 were, from left to right, John Oglesbee, Dr. Lewis McAdow, Julia Wade, Bob Bowman of the Pineywoods Foundation, McXie Martin, Alfred Broden, Charlotte Davis, and Kenneth Skillern. (Courtesy of *San Augustine Tribune*.)

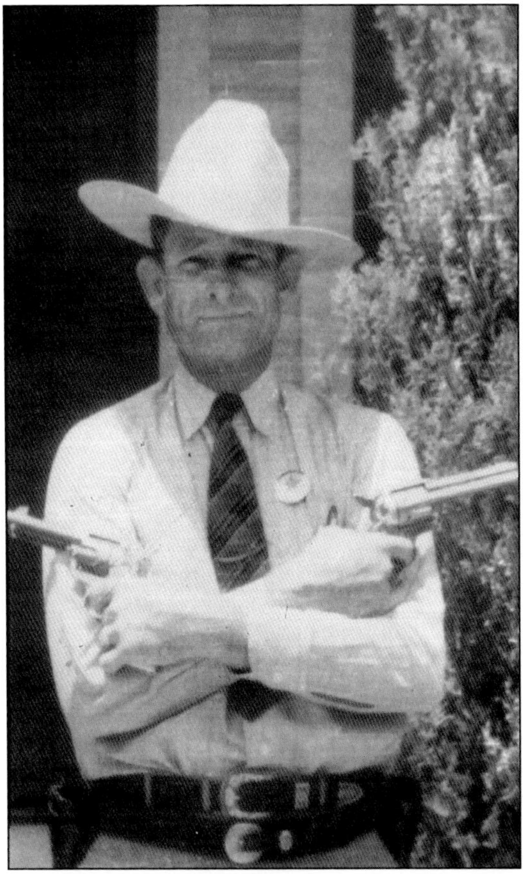

Texas Ranger Leo Bishop was presented with two Colt revolvers given to him in appreciation for his outstanding record of service to the citizens of San Augustine County in 1937. The citizens of San Augustine County once again felt safe in their community and county and gave Ranger Bishop, Ranger Dan Hines, and Capt. J. W. McCormick each a brace of engraved pistols to demonstrate their thanks. Each of the three sets of pistols was engraved with the recipient's name as follows: "Grateful citizens of San Augustine to Leo Bishop, Ranger." (Courtesy of Richard Murphy.)

The U.S. Post Office was located on the west side of the courthouse square at the time this photograph was taken during the 1940s. Postmaster Atheniar Wade (left) and Erna Eddings (right) are standing in front of the building, with a reflection of the courthouse in the plate glass window. (Courtesy of Nelsyn Wade.)

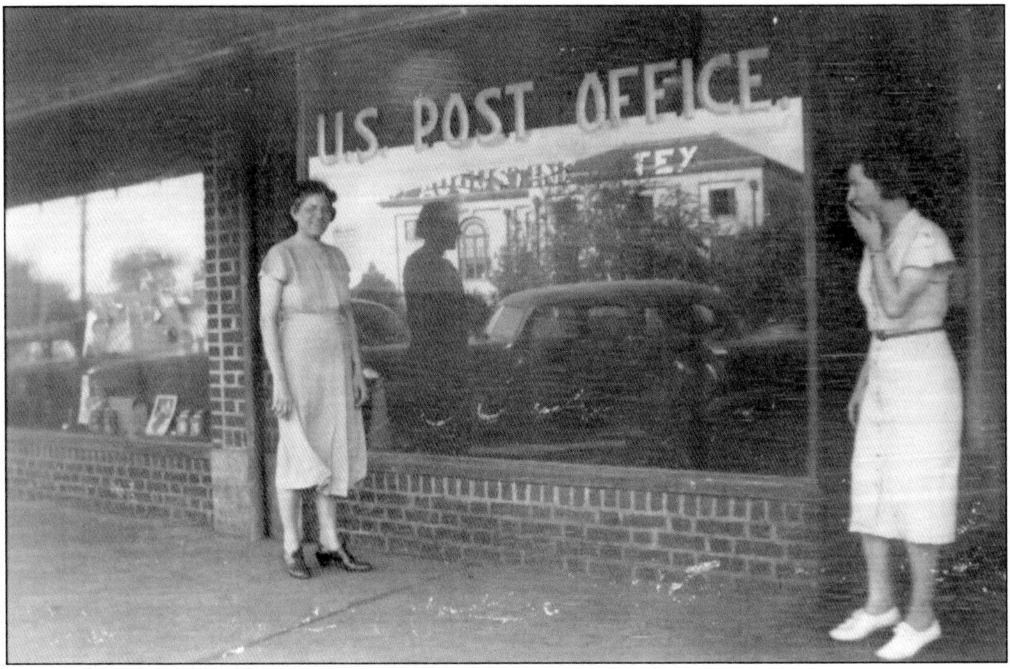

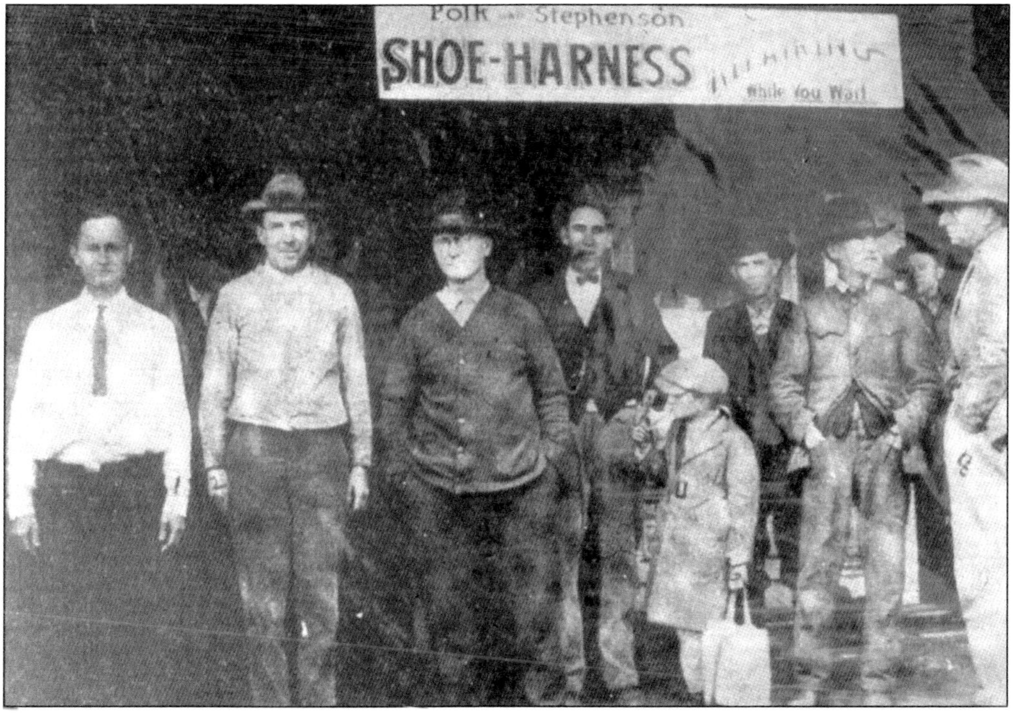

John Polk and Winfred Stephenson operated this thriving business on the north side of the San Augustine County courthouse square. (Author's collection.)

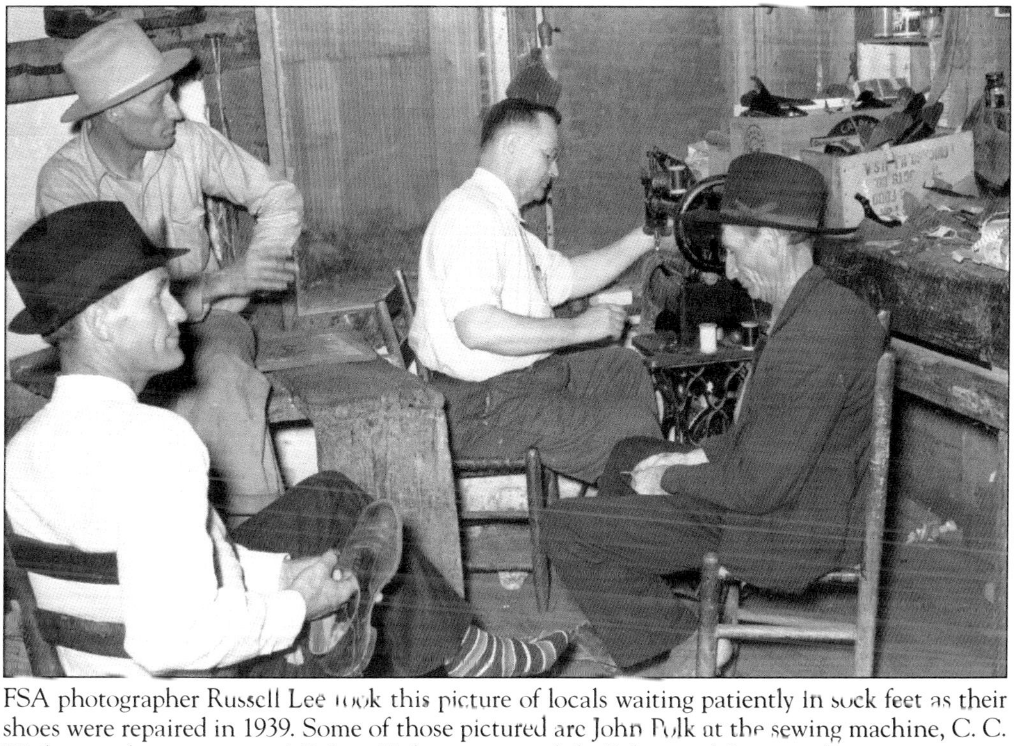
FSA photographer Russell Lee took this picture of locals waiting patiently in sock feet as their shoes were repaired in 1939. Some of those pictured are John Polk at the sewing machine, C. C. Withers with cigarette, and Calvin Holt at extreme left. (Library of Congress.)

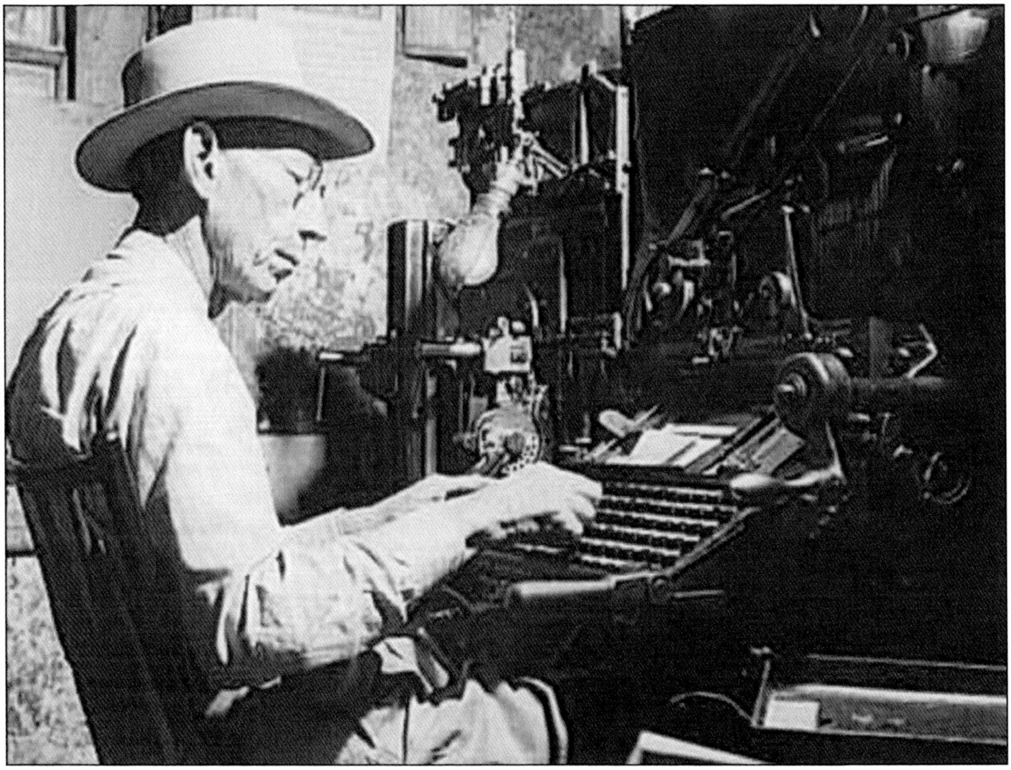

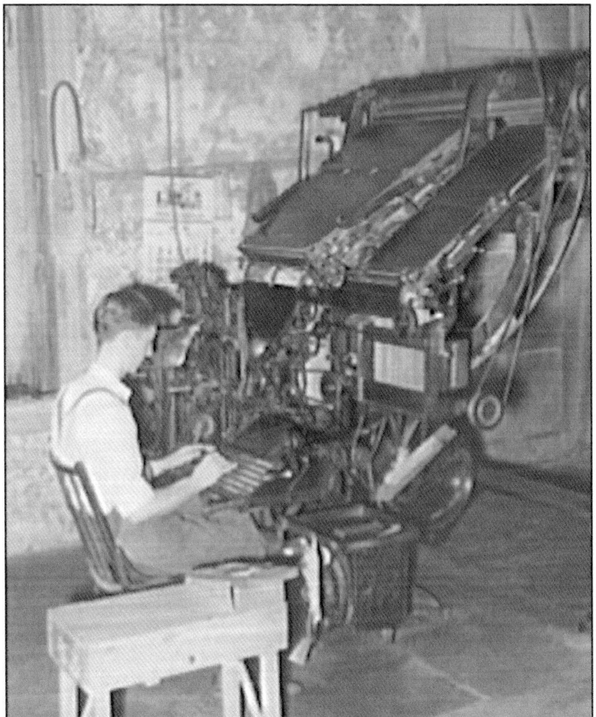

San Augustine Tribune publisher/ editor Webster Hays began publishing the historic newspaper in 1916. It has served San Augustine County residents and subscribers from all over the world for 94 years. (Photograph by Russell Lee, FSA, 1939, Library of Congress.)

Typesetting was a tedious task for Arlan Hays as he prepared the next issue of the weekly *Tribune*. Thanks to modern technology, those days are long over. The antique machine is still owned by the newspaper as a relic of the past. (Photograph by Russell Lee, FSA, 1939, Library of Congress.)

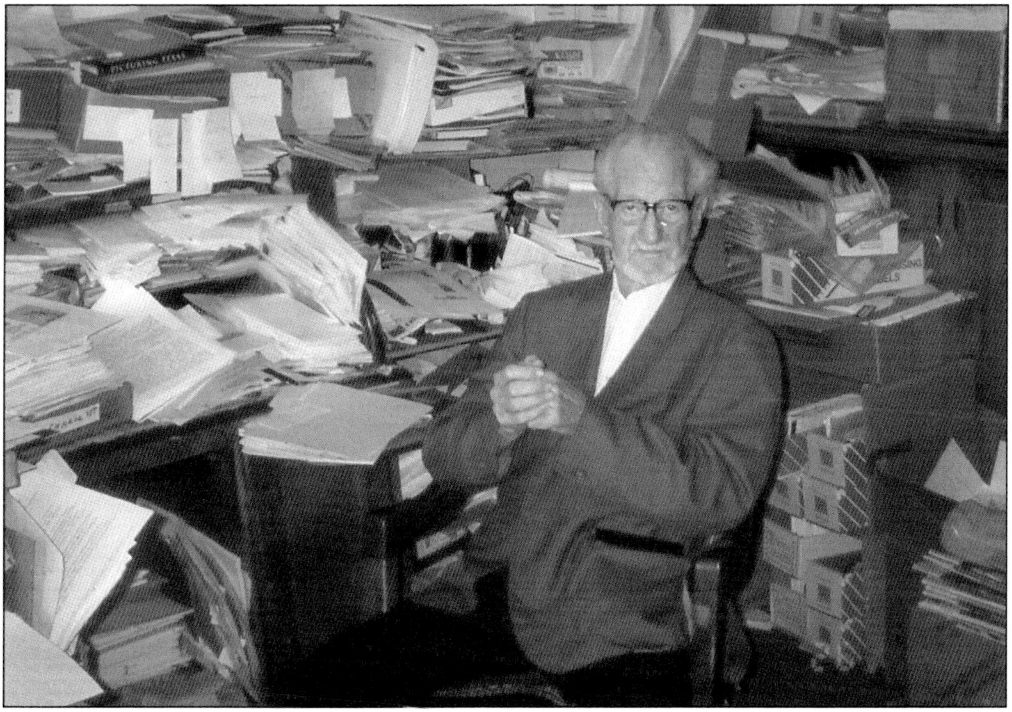

San Augustine Tribune publisher/editor Arlan Hays was still going strong in the year 2000. His son Stephen Hays is continuing the family tradition. (Photograph by the author.)

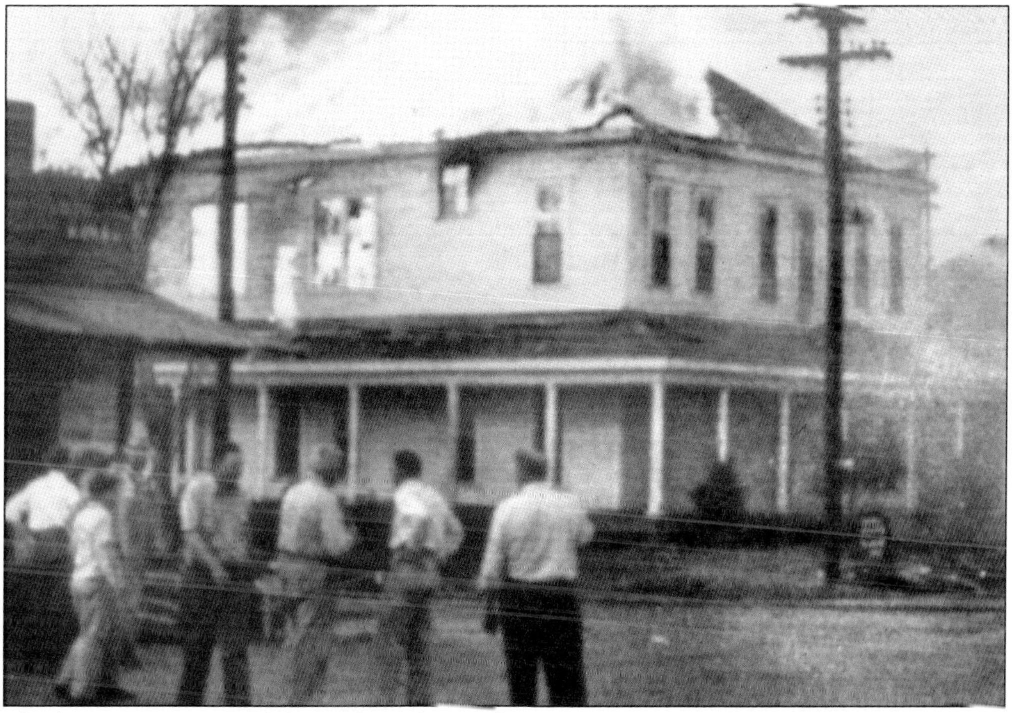

The historic Moss Hotel, located on the southeast corner facing the courthouse square, was destroyed by fire in 1946. (Courtesy of Jerry Payne.)

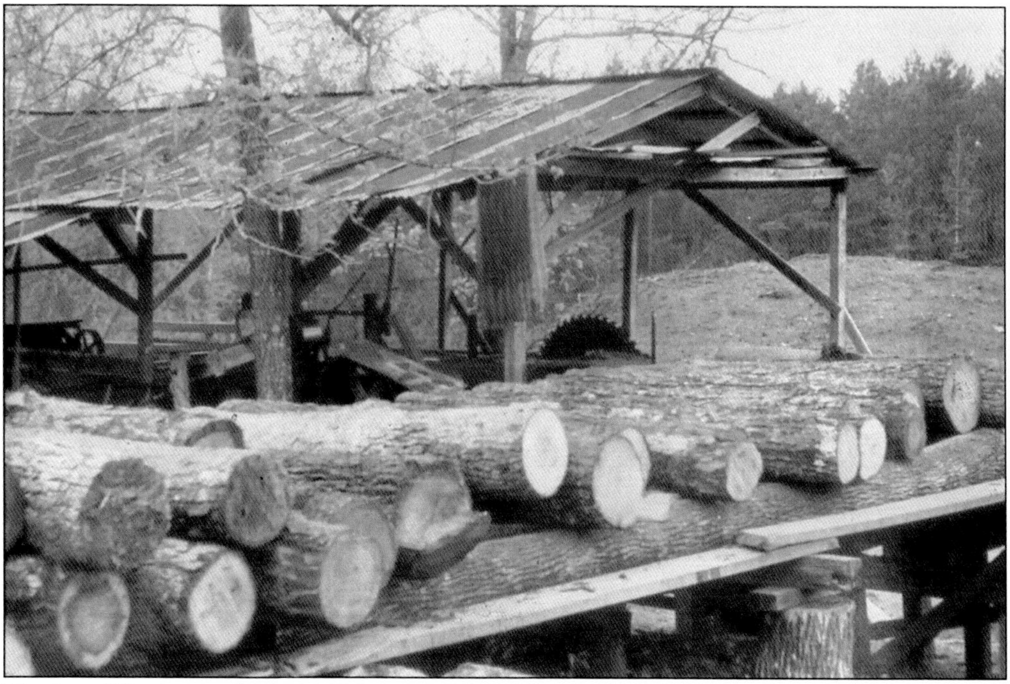

The Lon Ware sawmill was a classic example of the small log mills, often called "peckerwood mills," and were scattered throughout San Augustine County in the 1930s and 1940s. (Courtesy of Leeon Ware.)

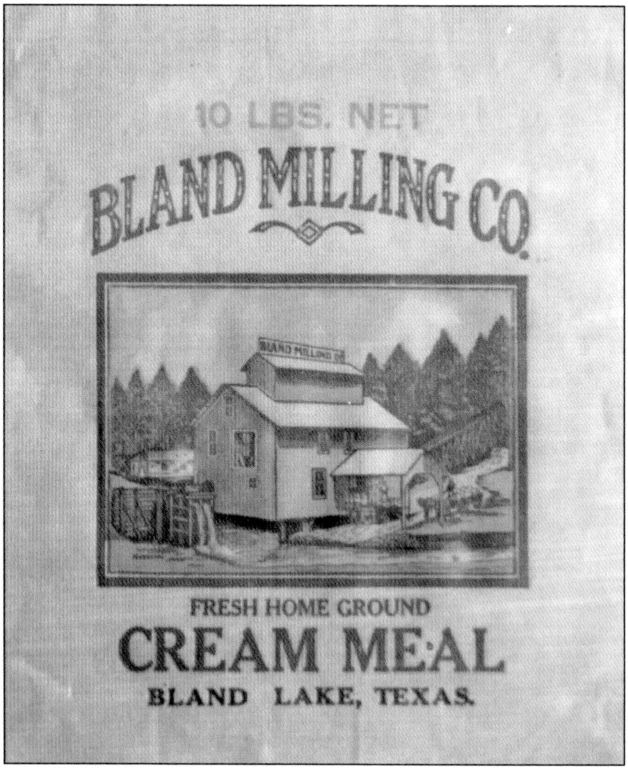

The community of Bland Lake, 5 miles due north of the city of San Augustine, is adjacent to the headwaters of the Ayish Bayou. In the 1890s, Calvin Bland and his son Jeff built a dam on the bayou and created Bland Lake to power their sawmill. Several years later, a gristmill for grinding corn was constructed on the lake. This sack from Bland Milling Company pictures the gristmill powered by the water of Bland Lake in northern San Augustine County. (Courtesy of A. E. (Jake) Whitton.)

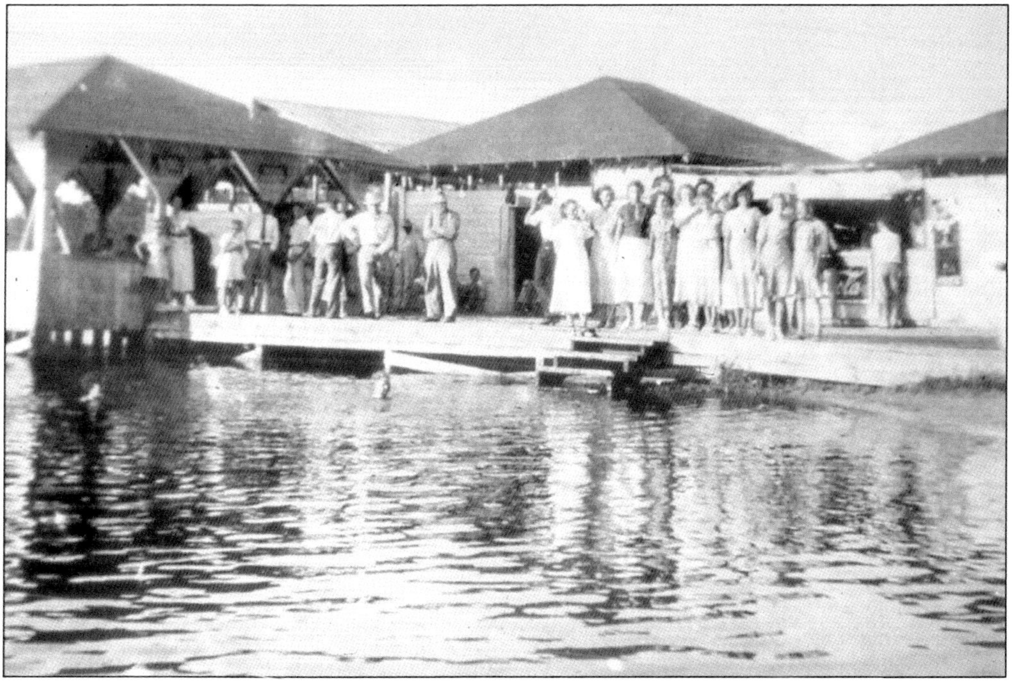

A crowd of young people was always gathered on the pavilion at Bland Lake. Locals bought season swimming tickets for $1. Day rates to swim, slide, or rent a bathing suit were 25¢. A jukebox provided music for dancing. (Courtesy of Richard Murphy.)

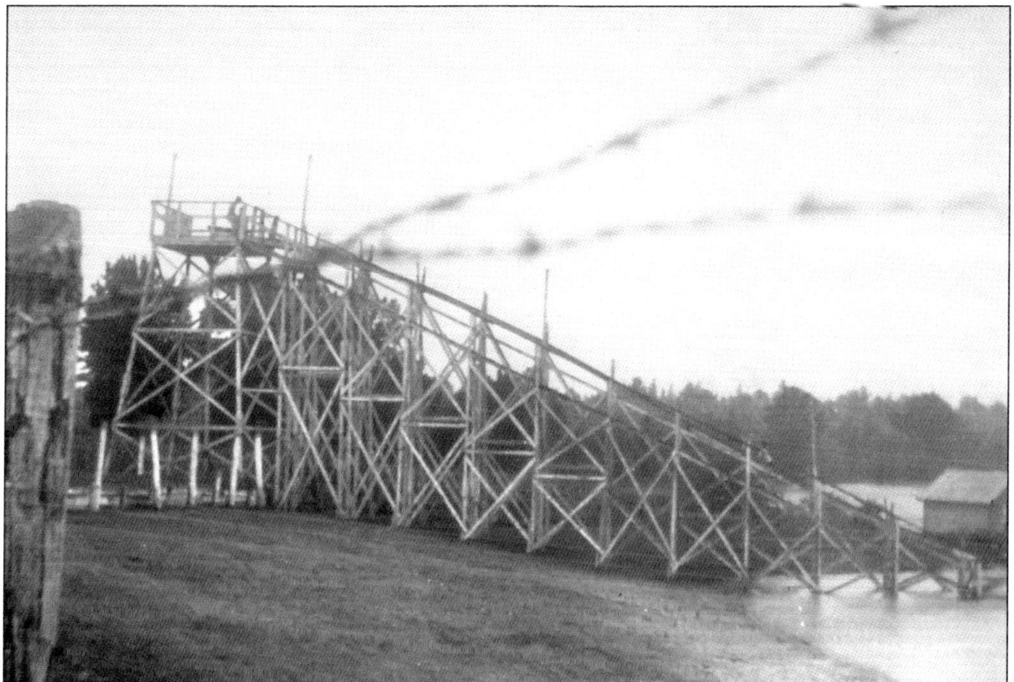

The San Augustine version of excitement was a ride down the giant slide, called the "chute de chute" on the edge of Bland Lake. (Courtesy of Richard Murphy.)

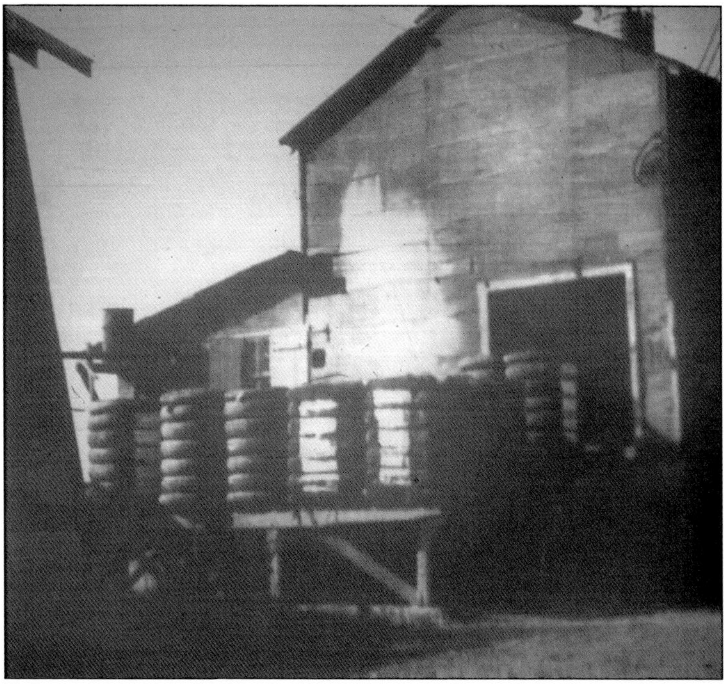

Cotton reigned supreme as the cash crop for San Augustine County farmers during the 1930s, 1940s, and early 1950s. Cotton gins owned by Oscar Belser, J. M. Langston, Percy McLemore, Frank Thompson, J. O. Payne, Vestal Polley, Olan Chambers, Buster Henry, Ebb Sowell, Oscar Buckner, Warren Wall, Joe Harris, Buck Griffin, and J. W. Blackstock dotted the countryside. There were three generations of Fussell family gins, the first as early as 1899. (Courtesy of Holly Fussell Flynt.)

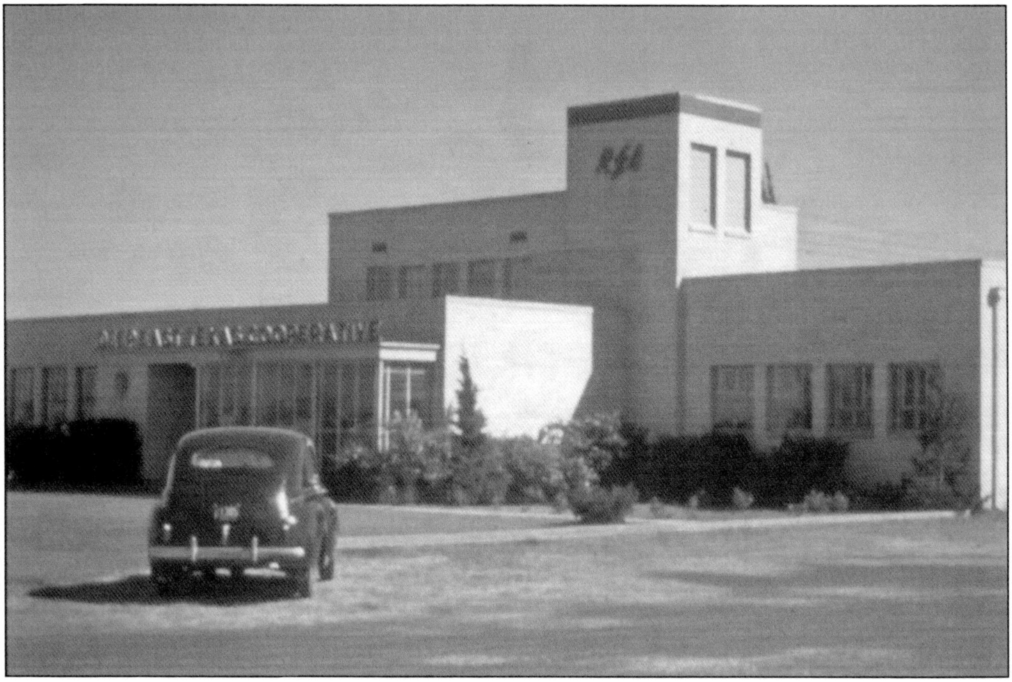

This photograph of the Deep East Texas Electric Cooperative (DETEC) is from around 1944. DETEC was chartered on January 14, 1938, with its headquarters located in San Augustine, Texas. Pres. Franklin D. Roosevelt signed a bill in 1935, which allowed nonprofit electric cooperatives to be formed for the purpose of bringing electricity to rural areas across the nation. Today eight counties are served by DETEC: San Augustine, Nacogdoches, Shelby, Newton, Panola, Jasper, Sabine, and Rusk. (Author's collection.)

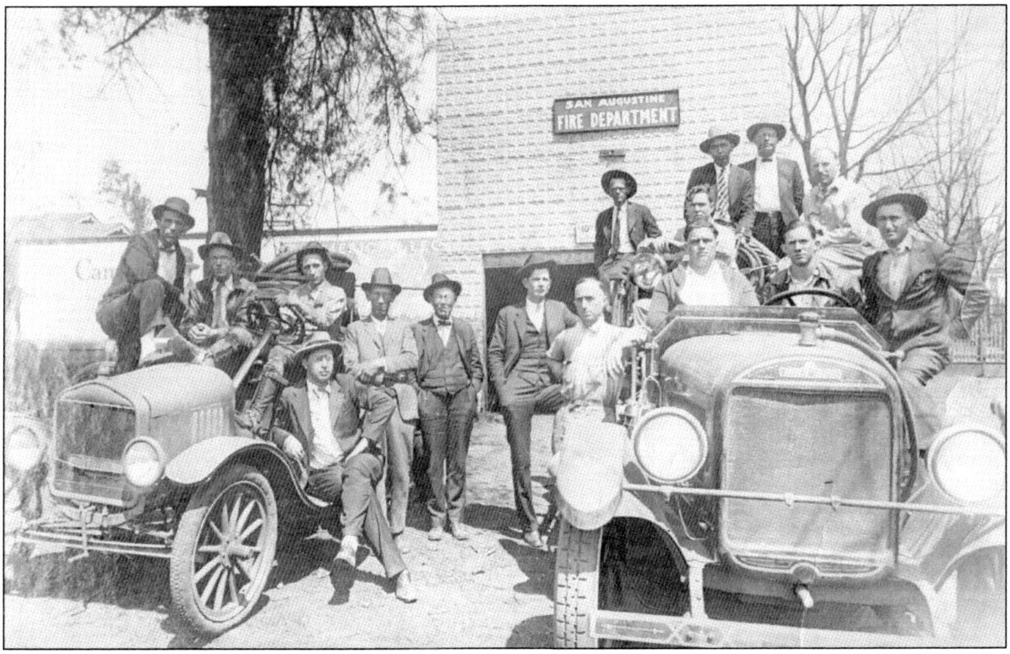

The San Augustine Volunteer Fire Department (SAVFD) in 1929 is a far cry from the SAVFD today. The well-trained firemen take calls all over San Augustine County and have won numerous awards for their professionalism and safety achievements. One aspect of the fire department appreciated most by local historians is the care taken in protecting irreplaceable historical homes and places. (Courtesy of Charles Bradberry and Jerry Payne.)

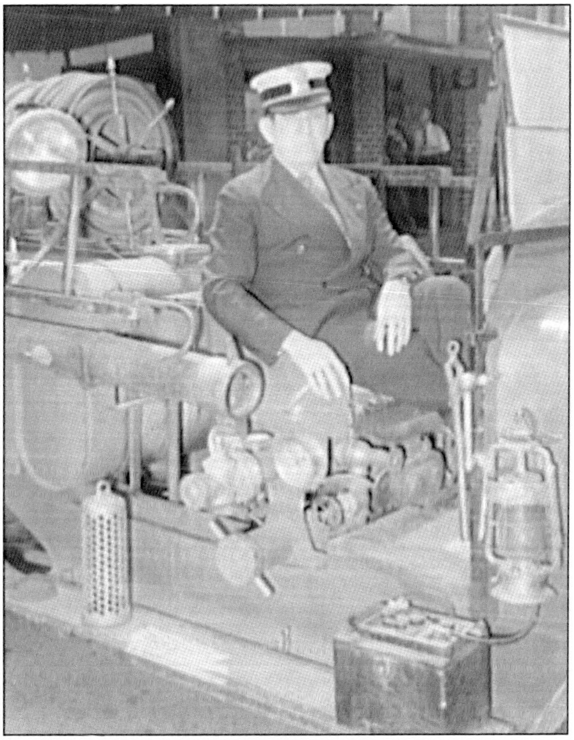

Herman Clark, owner of Clark Downs Department Store, was fire chief in 1939. Note the lantern hanging toward the front of the fire truck. Looking at images of San Augustine's firefighting equipment from 70 or 80 years ago gives a new appreciation for the capabilities of the volunteer fire department today. In 2010, there are rescue trucks with jaws-of-life sets, grass trucks, several tankers and a pumper, two thermal imaging cameras, and 30 new sets of Buncker gear. (Photograph by Russell Lee, FSA, 1939, Library of Congress.)

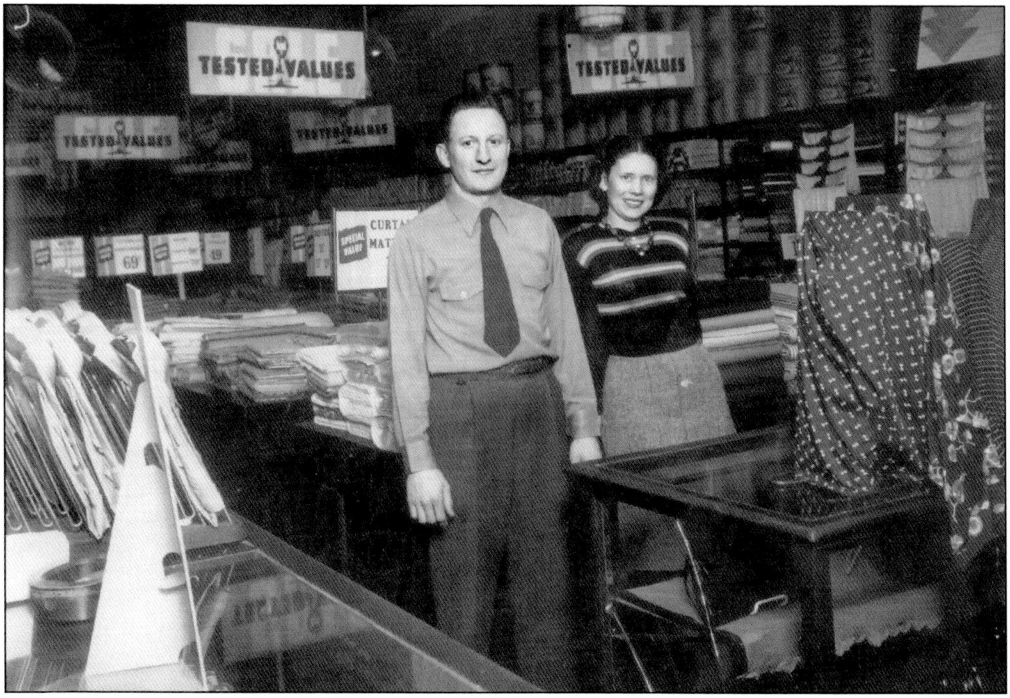

Woodrow Mathews and Mildred Mathews are shown inside the J. P. Mathews Department Store in the 1930s. (Courtesy of Martha Mathews Butts.)

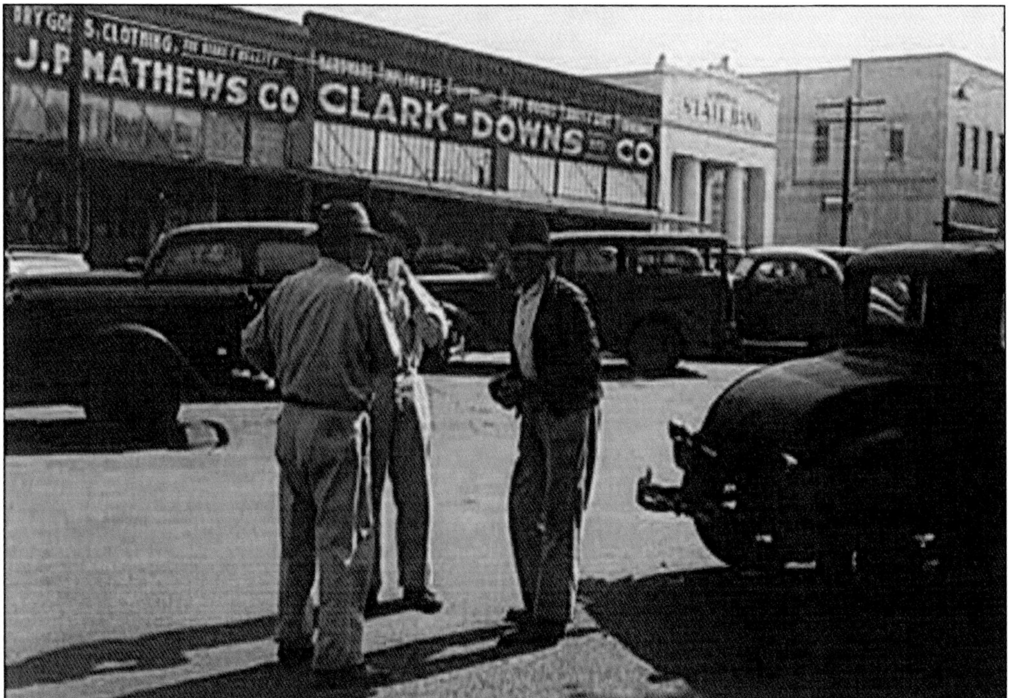

Downtown San Augustine was bustling with activity during the World War II years. (Photograph by John Vachon, Office of War Information [OWI], 1943, Library of Congress.)

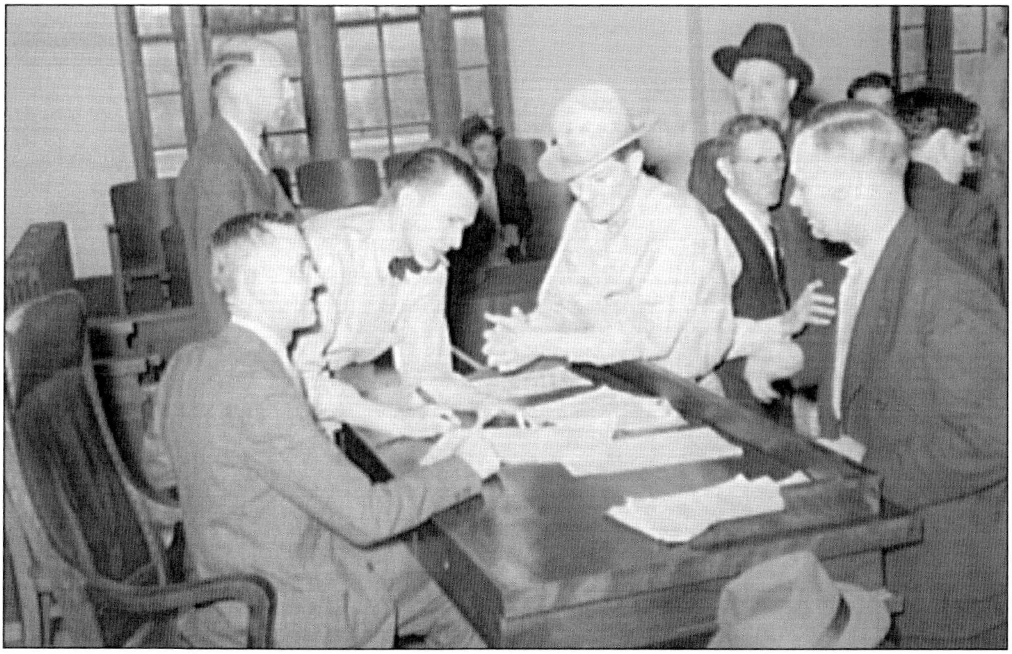

Judge R. N. Stripling and J. P. (Pete) Mathews (left) discuss ways to continue Works Progress Administration (WPA) road improvements in San Augustine County in 1943 as Burl Harvey (right) looks on. B. J. Butts is standing in the background (top left). (Photograph by John Vachon, OWI, 1943, Library of Congress.)

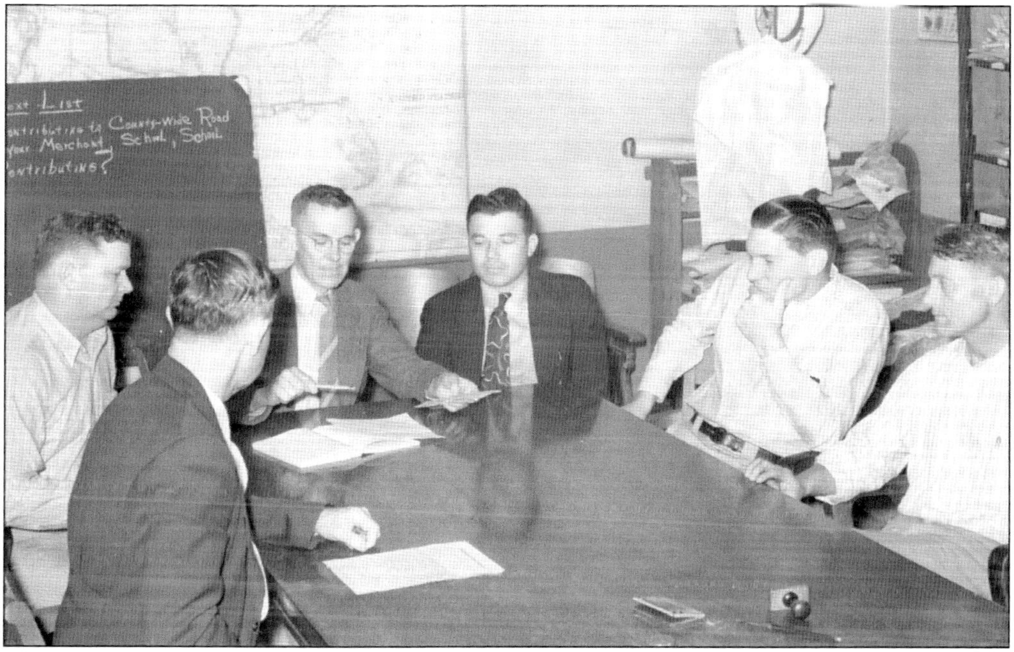

This is a meeting of county commissioners in 1943 with, from left to right, county school superintendent Gilbert Mathews, unidentified, county judge R. N. Stripling, county treasurer McNeil Sanders, and county commissioners Burl Harvey and Jay Gardner. (Photograph by John Vachon, OWI, 1943, Library of Congress.)

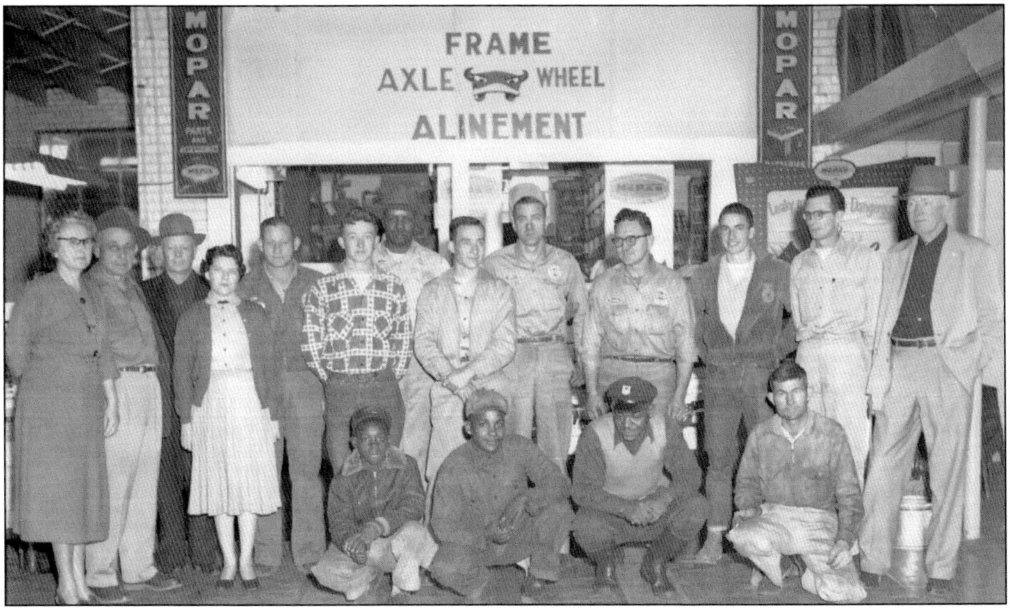

Bickley Motor Company owners and employees posed for this picture in the 1950s. Pictured from left to right are (first row) John Johnson, Joe Montgomery Jr., Tootsie Hoyt, and Sid Leach; (second row) Pearl Bickley, P. B. Bickley, E. T. Killion, Ruby Lillian Bickley, Joe Bickley, Oran Davis, Charlie Weathered, Wilburn Davis, Joe Fitts, Freddie Leak, Buck Sowell, Fred Murphy, and D. G. Butts. (Courtesy of Joe Bryan and Nancy Bickley.)

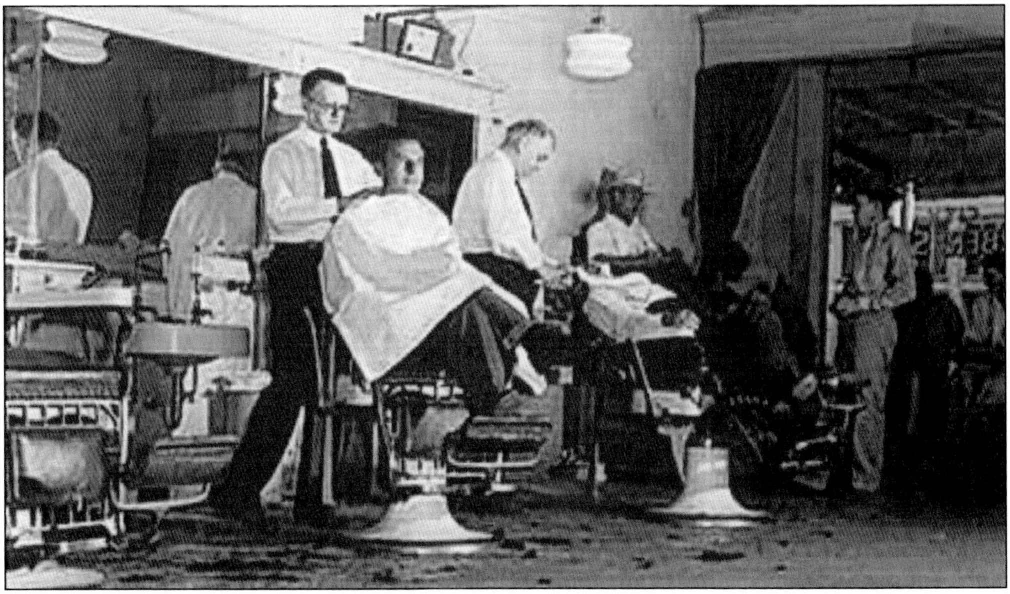

Drew Wade (left) and Beet Price (center) were the barbers in downtown San Augustine's City Barbershop. A back room pool table provided entertainment while men waited for haircuts, and tubs for baths were available. Billy Singleton (right) was employed in the barbershop, but his primary interest was boxing. He went to Shreveport and elsewhere for boxing matches, and on one occasion defeated heavyweight boxer Maxie Rosenblum. (Photograph by John Vachon, OWI, 1943, Library of Congress.)

L. W. (Casey) Jones, pharmacist at Rushing's Drug Store, invented his famous "Grapefruit Hiball" in the 1940s. The popular and refreshing drink continues to be a favorite at the successor firm, San Augustine Drug. Casey Jones was also well known for his beautiful tenor voice and his penchant for fox hunting. His wife, Eva McDaniel Jones, was a master gardener whose vegetables and roses were legendary. She was also a talented artist whose oil paintings rivaled those of Grandma Moses. (Courtesy of *San Augustine Tribune*.)

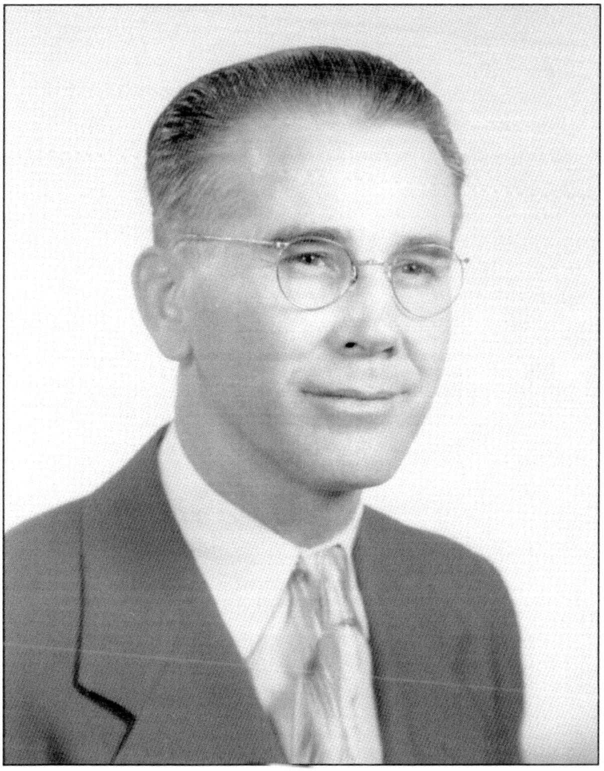

The drugstore's soda fountain, pictured here in 1943, shows a man enjoying one of Casey Jones's "Grapefruit Hiballs." (Photograph by John Vachon, OWI, Library of Congress.)

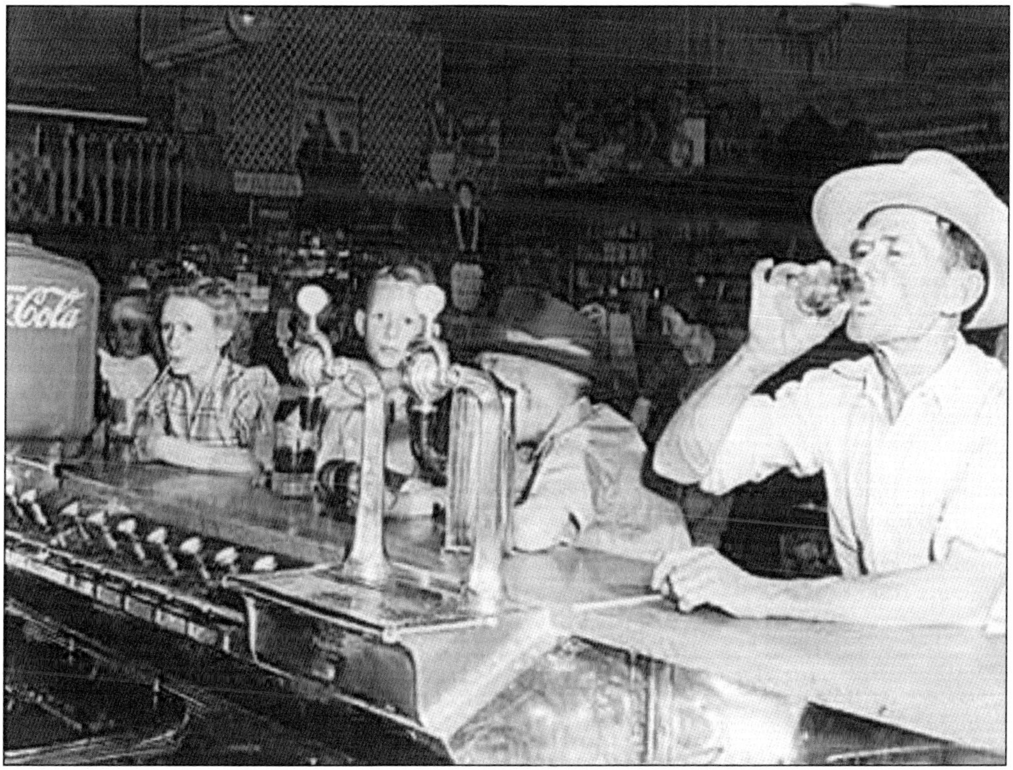

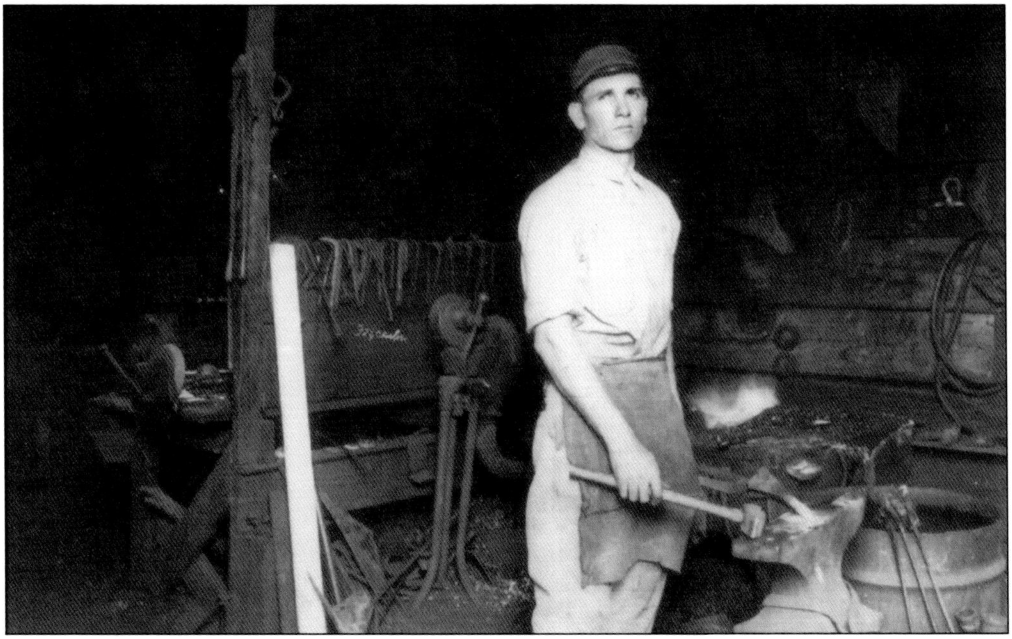

Darrell Curgas Hall's blacksmith shop was on the west side of the courthouse square from 1921 to 1947 before moving to a new location east of town. Hall's father, James Roselle Hall, bought the shop in 1920 from Harry Hawk. The shop had been in operation since the mid-1800s. D. C. Hall was a skilled wheelwright, creative metalwork designer, and expert craftsman who built wagon wheels, pulpwood hooks, plows, and everything to serve the needs of the farmer. He operated his blacksmith shop until 1977. After his death, his shop was moved in its entirety to the John Jay French Museum in Beaumont, Texas. (Courtesy of Gwendolyn Hall Odom.)

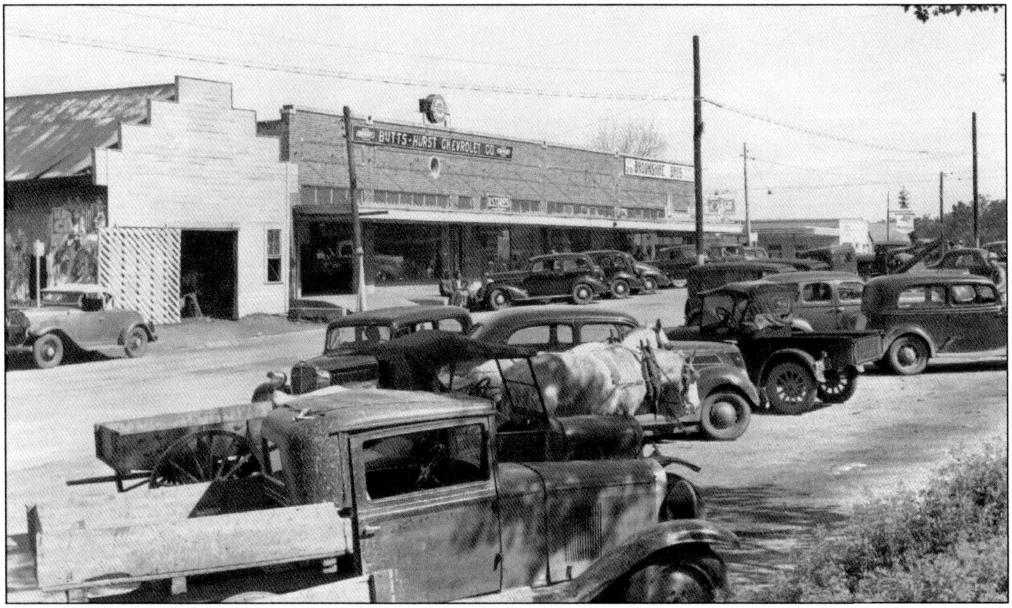

Street repairs around the courthouse square in 1939 show Butts-Hurst Motor Company (right) and D. C. Hall's Blacksmith Shop (left). (Photograph by Russell Lee, FSA, 1939, Library of Congress.)

Three

CHURCHES IN THE WILDWOOD

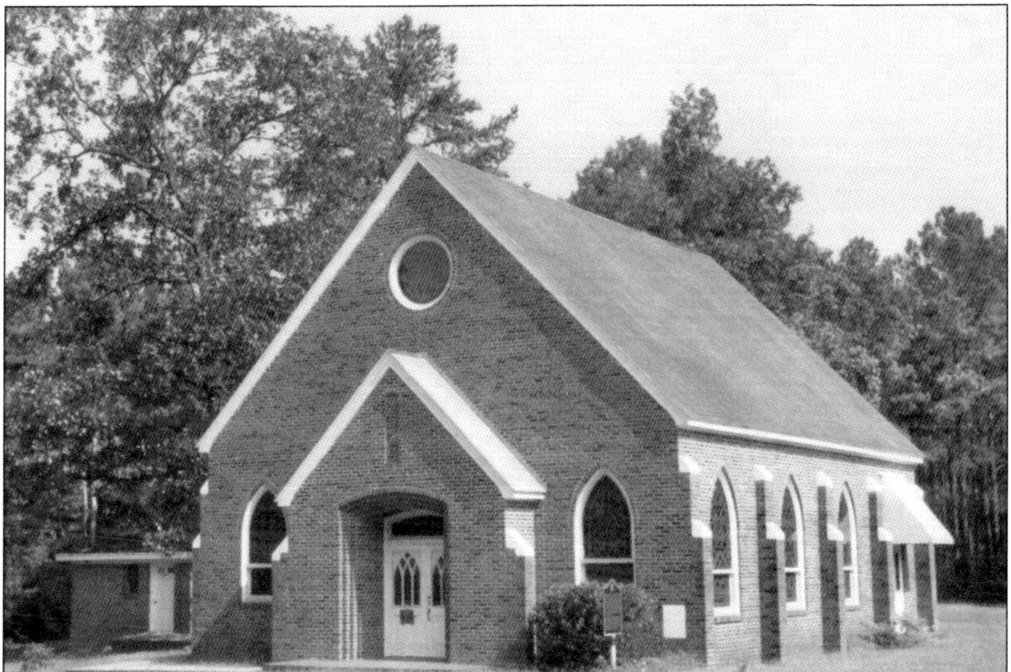

McMahan Chapel is located 2 miles south of Highway 21 (El Camino Real) between San Augustine and Geneva, Texas. It is both the First Protestant and the First Methodist Church in Texas, founded in 1833 as a "class meeting" since the Protestant religion was not allowed in Mexican Texas at that time. The current chapel, built in 1949, is the third sanctuary on the site and features magnificent stained-glass windows placed in honor of early members of the church. The large tombstone behind the pulpit is that of the Reverend Littleton Fowler, one of the first three missionaries to Texas in 1838, who requested that he be buried there upon his death. A museum and events center named in honor and memory of Jack and Charlsie Maund is adjacent to the church. The adjoining cemetery has graves of many early leaders of Methodism and is in itself a record of early Texas religious history. Designations include Recorded Texas Historic Landmark (RTHL) and National Register of Historic Places (NR). (Photograph by the author.)

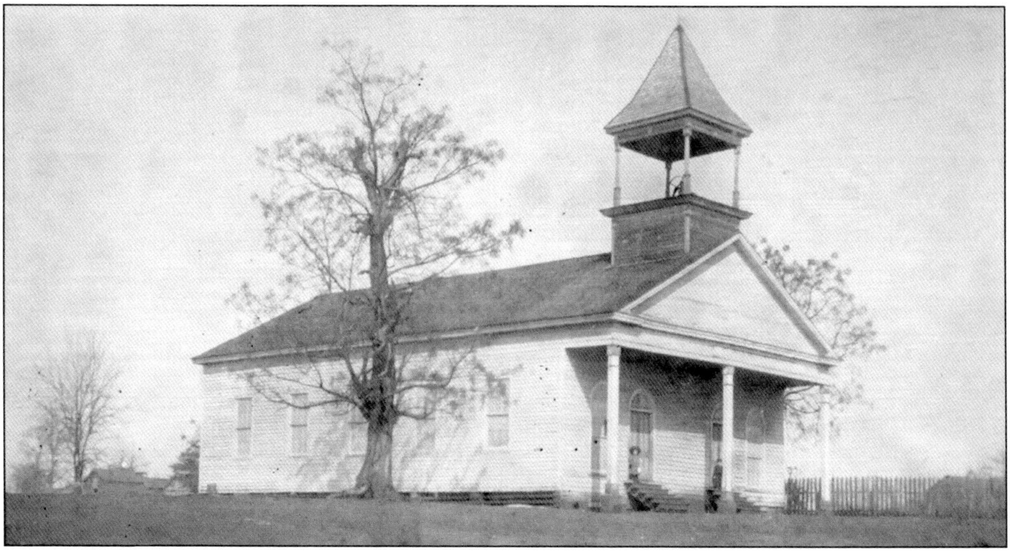

In October 1837, the Reverend Littleton Fowler came to San Augustine and organized the first Methodist Episcopal Church, South, in Texas. Funds were quickly raised to build a church. When the cornerstone was laid in January 1838 by the Masonic Order, 500 to 800 people were in attendance. Notables present were the Reverend Littleton Fowler, Thomas J. Rusk, John S "Rip" Ford, Samuel Doak McMahan, William Garrett, Wyatt Hanks, Philip Sublett, Alexander Horton, John M. Bradley, Thomas and William McFarland, and two signers of the Texas Declaration of Independence, E. O. Legrand and Stephen W. Blount. Master builder Augustus Phelps was employed to design and construct the new church. (Courtesy of Stephanie Kardell.)

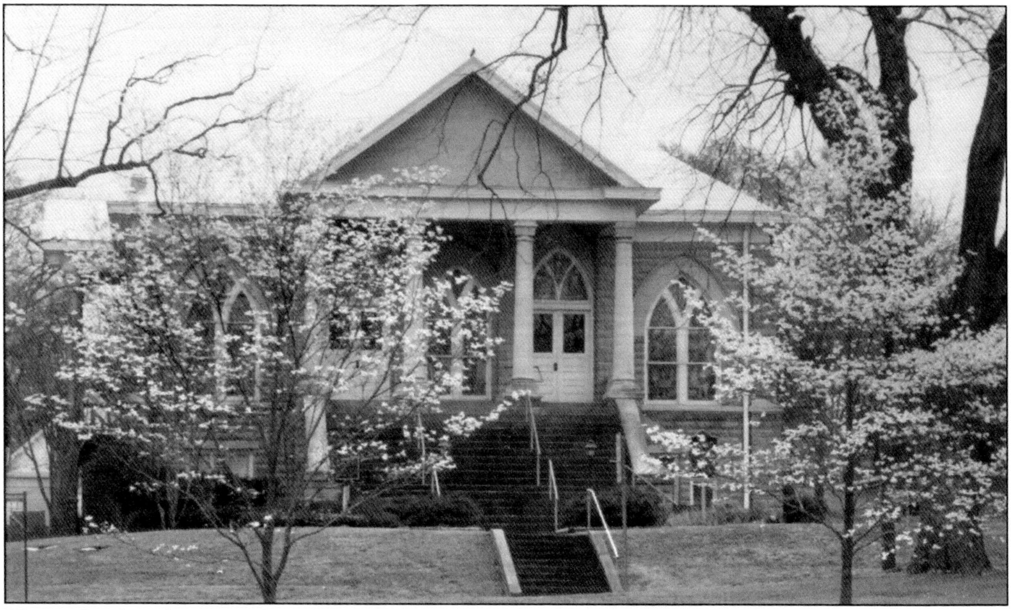

The 1838 church was replaced in 1907 with the new and current First United Methodist Church (RTHL). Columbus Cartwright gave an entire city block for the building of the new sanctuary, with the stipulation that a hitching post would always be available for the horses of worshipers. The second-floor sanctuary of the church is resplendent with beautiful stained-glass windows and original pulpit furnishings. (Photograph by the author.)

Methodism's founder, John Wesley, and his brother Charles Wesley, who wrote many of the hymns sung in churches today, are pictured in one of the stained-glass windows of the 1907 Methodist church. On February 25, 2009, a devastating fire caused massive damage to the sanctuary and youth area. Thanks to the quick response of San Augustine Volunteer Fire Department and other area firefighters, the historic windows were undamaged. They were carefully cleaned, then covered with plywood during the restoration and rebuilding of the church. (Photograph by the author.)

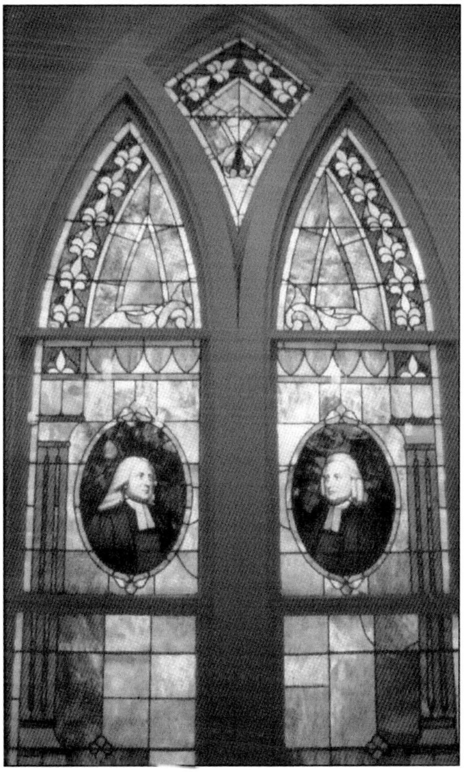

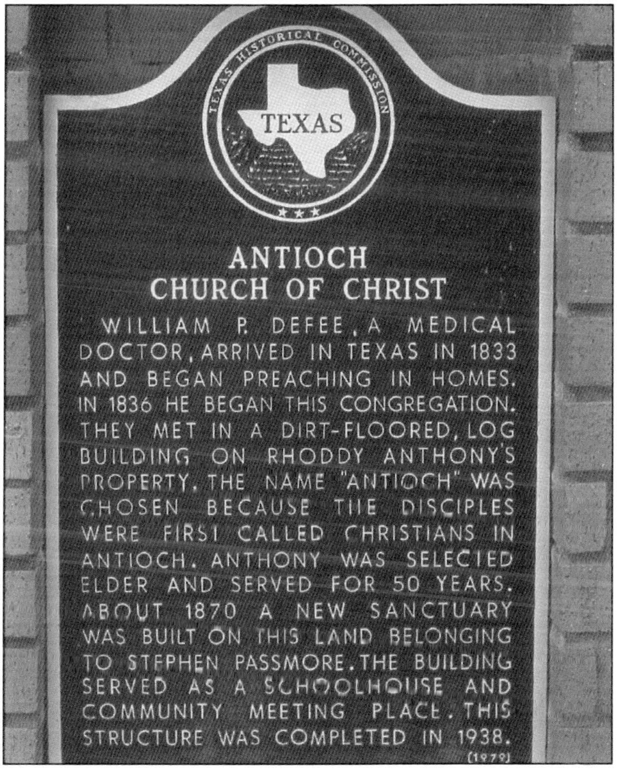

Antioch Church of Christ was organized by Dr. William P. Defee in 1833. The RTHL marker erected in front of the current sanctuary gives an excellent description of this historic church in San Augustine County. While Texas was still a part of Mexico, people of the various Protestant denominations were not allowed to establish churches. Dr. Defee began preaching in the home of elder Rodney Anthony. T. W. M. Baggett was the other elder of the church. A large cemetery adjoins the current church building, which was constructed in 1938. (Photograph by the author.)

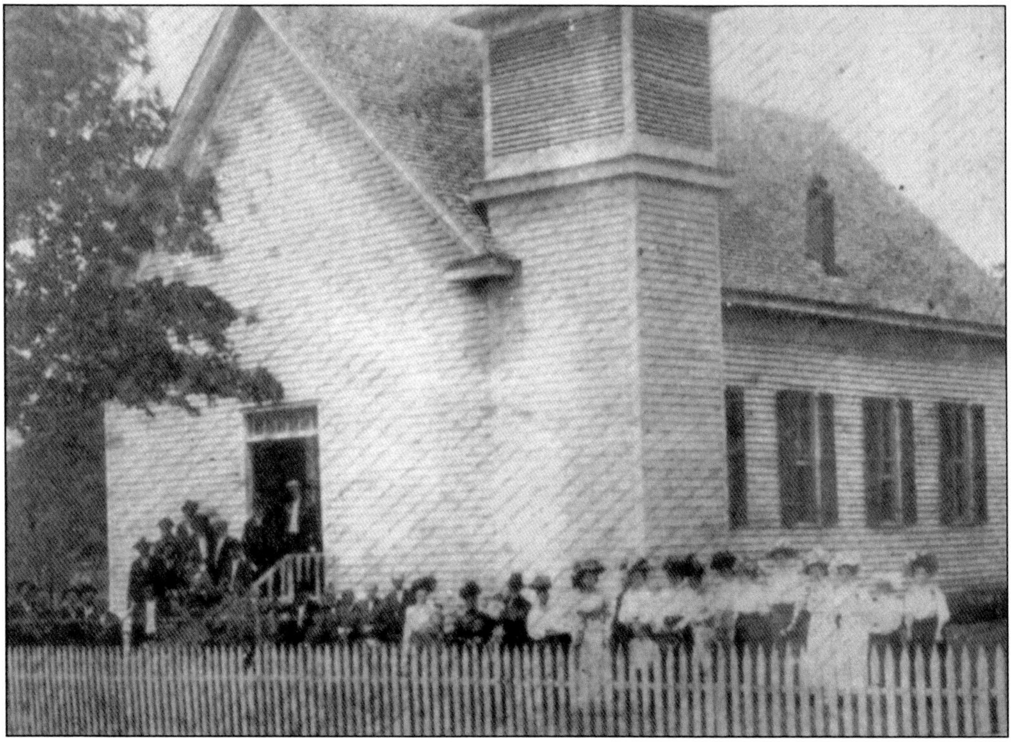

Memorial Presbyterian Church was organized in June 1838 three miles west of San Augustine by the Reverend Hugh Wilson. A few years later the congregation moved to downtown San Augustine and built the church pictured here. No "images" of Reverend Wilson exist, as he determined that the second commandment forbidding "the making of graven images" included photography and refused to have his picture taken. (Courtesy of Richard Murphy.)

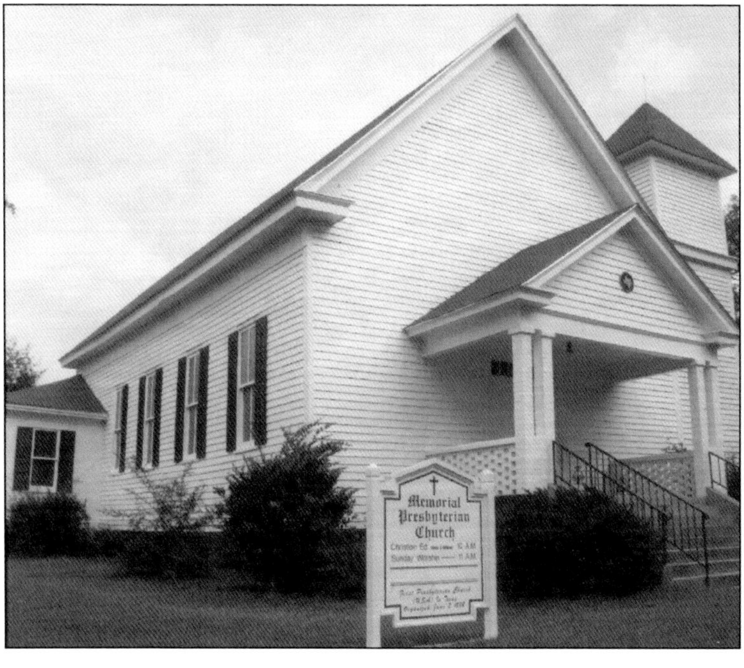

Present-day Memorial Presbyterian Church (RTHL) looks much the same today as it did 170 years ago. Built by shipbuilder-turned-carpenter Abel Coffin Ketchum, it is considered one of the most unique churches in Texas, with the inside ceiling constructed in the fashion of an inverted ship hull. (Photograph by the author.)

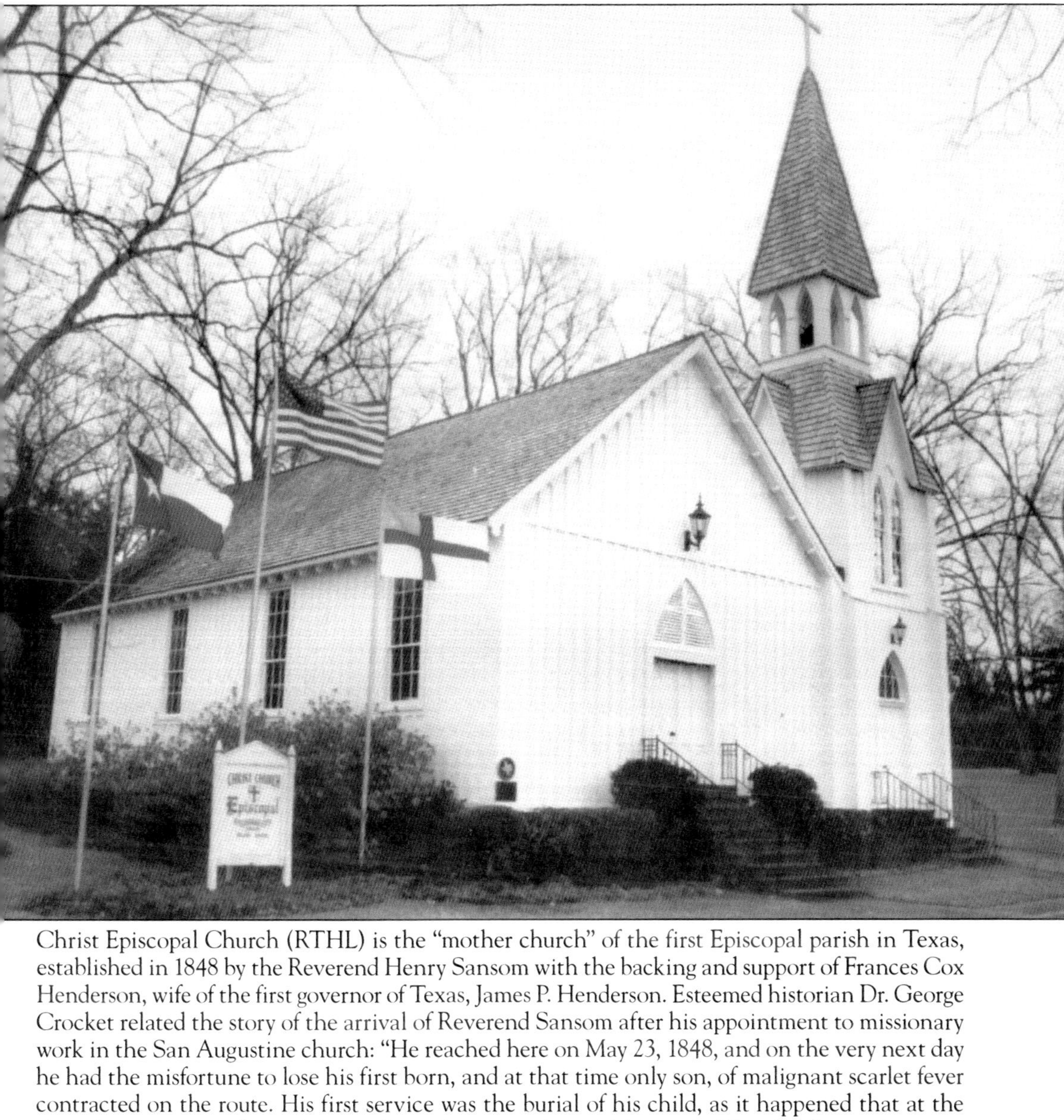

Christ Episcopal Church (RTHL) is the "mother church" of the first Episcopal parish in Texas, established in 1848 by the Reverend Henry Sansom with the backing and support of Frances Cox Henderson, wife of the first governor of Texas, James P. Henderson. Esteemed historian Dr. George Crocket related the story of the arrival of Reverend Sansom after his appointment to missionary work in the San Augustine church: "He reached here on May 23, 1848, and on the very next day he had the misfortune to lose his first born, and at that time only son, of malignant scarlet fever contracted on the route. His first service was the burial of his child, as it happened that at the time there was no other minister of any denomination within reach. The child's remains were afterward interred under the altar of the new church." The original building was destroyed in a storm. The current building was completed in 1870 and is one of the most photographed churches in Texas. The Reverend Dr. George L. Crocket served as pastor for 42 years. Many of the hand-carved furnishings inside the sanctuary are the work of Dr. Crocket. The church was restored by Raiford Stripling, and the authentically replicated interior lights were a gift of the ambassador to Australia, Edward Clark, and his wife, Anne. (Photograph by the author.)

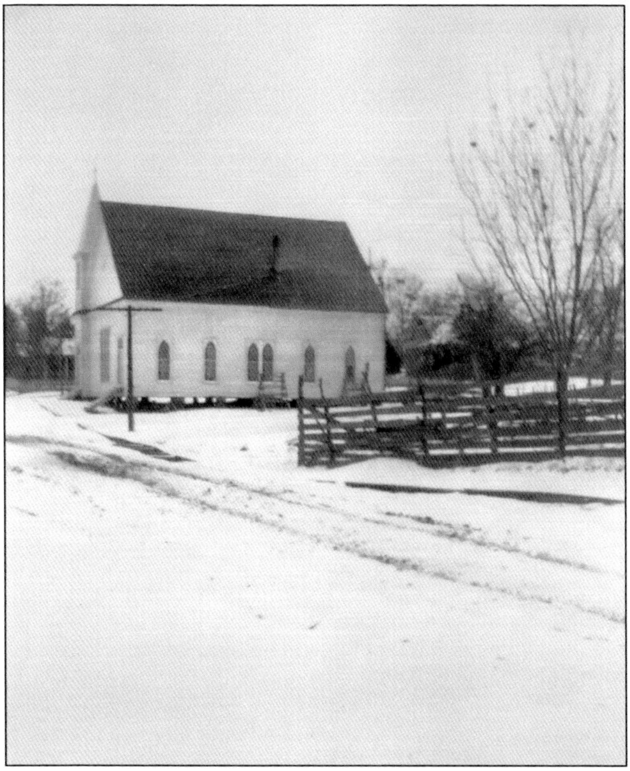

First Baptist Church was organized in 1902. Members met in a log cabin until the beautiful frame structure pictured was built later that year during the ministry of Rev. Thomas Harrell. Longtime member Eva McDaniel Jones authored a history of San Augustine's First Baptist Church entitled *From Darkness into Light*, copies of which are still available to persons interested in a detailed account of the establishment and growth of the church. (Courtesy of Stephanie Kardell.)

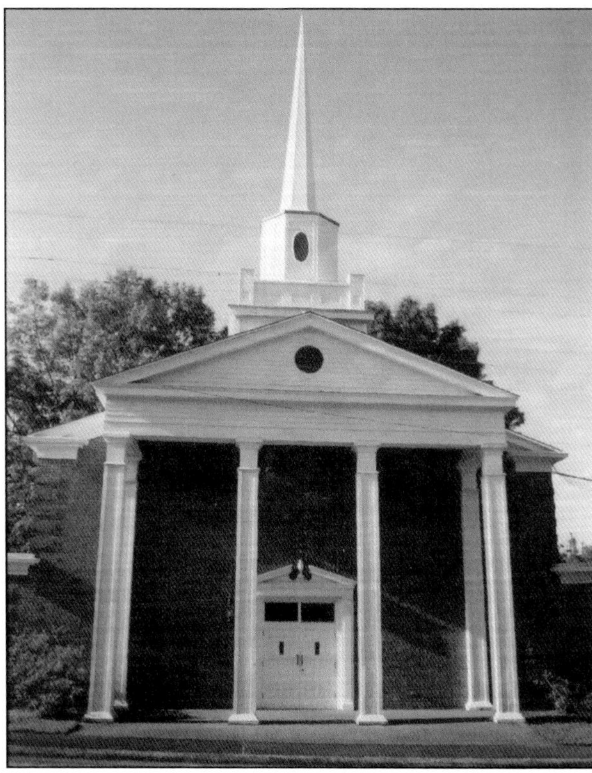

First Baptist Church today still occupies the same site as the 1902 church. Numerous churches, mostly Baptist and Missionary Baptist, dot the landscape of San Augustine County. Faithful church attendance is still a part of life in this rural eastern section of Texas, where churches such as Liberty Hill, Little Flock, New Hope, Shiloh, Holly Grove, White Rock, True Vine, County Line, Mount Dena, Bethel, and Union Grove have been in existence for generations. (Photograph by the author.)

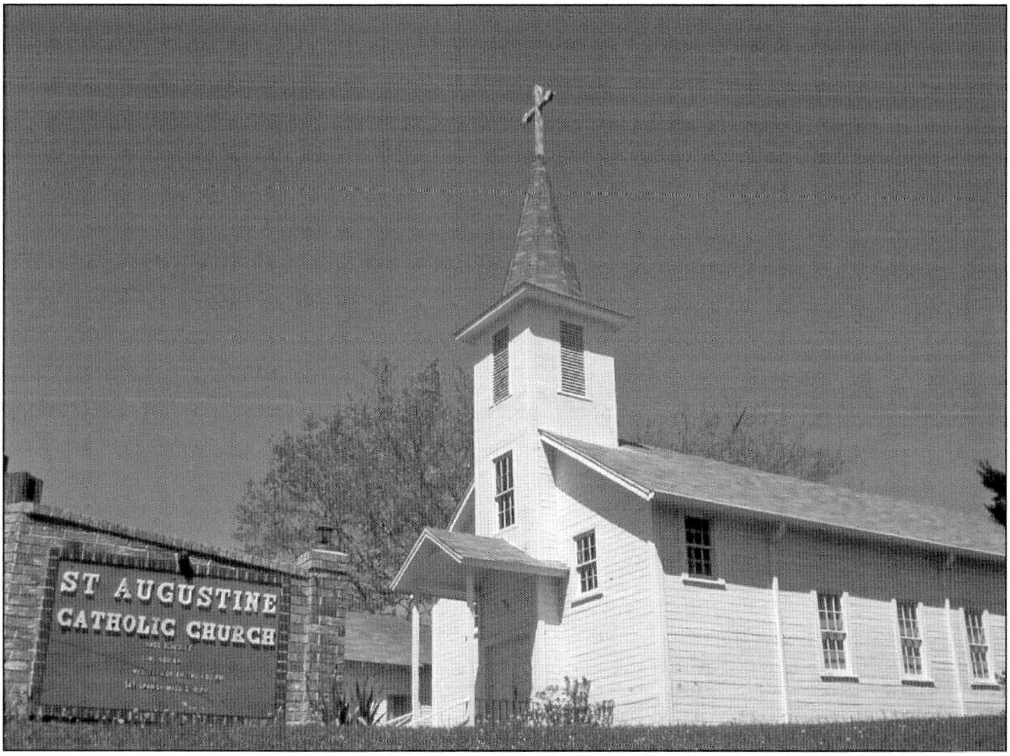

Catholicism appeared in the San Augustine vicinity in 1716 and 1717 with the founding of Mission Dolores. In 1880, land for a Catholic church was purchased, and the following year a sanctuary was constructed. In 1937, a new sanctuary, pictured here, was built at the same location. In recent years, the church has been named St. Augustine Catholic Church. (Photograph by the author.)

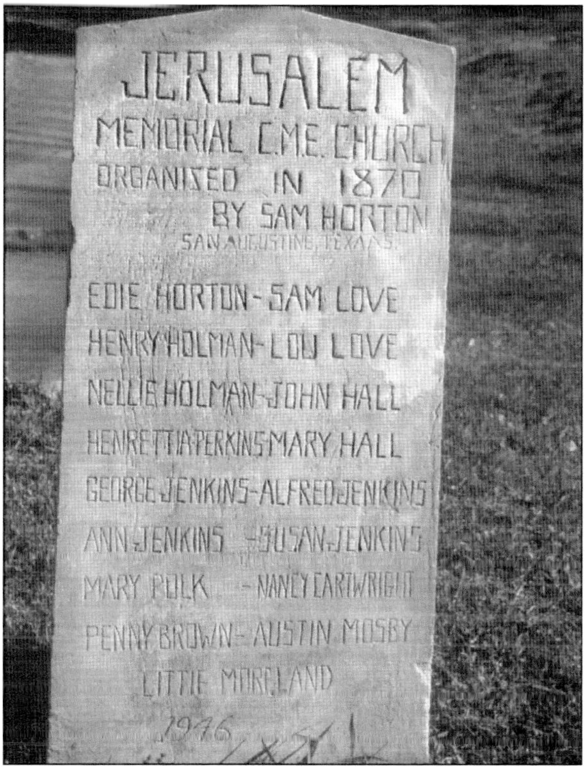

Jerusalem CME was organized in 1845 and was the first African American Methodist Church in Texas. The furniture inside the sanctuary was hand carved by Tommy Nathan. The current church was built in 1942 after the original church was destroyed in a storm. This handmade monument for Jerusalem CME indicates that the church was reorganized in 1870. (Photograph by the author.)

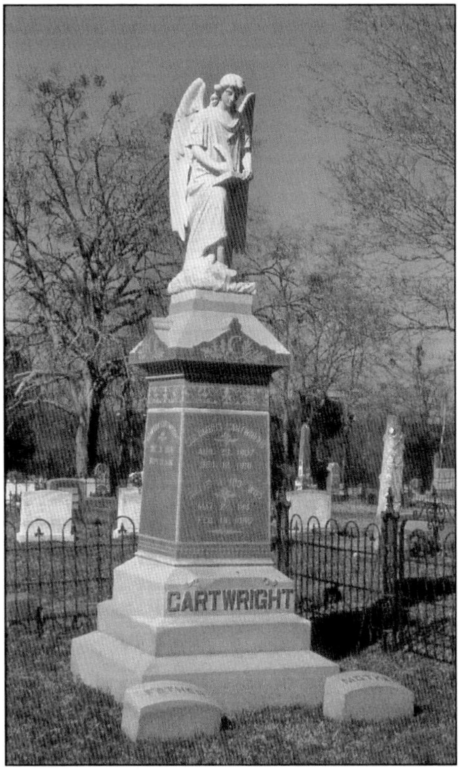

The angel at City Cemetery has been a San Augustine landmark since the late 1800s, towering over the graves of Columbus and Clinton Cartwright. The top of one wing was lost in a storm many years ago, thus "the angel with the broken wing" continued watch over the cemetery and downtown San Augustine until the wing was found buried nearby. Monument professional Kenneth Poindexter expertly reattached the wing, restoring the angel's original appearance. (Photograph by the author.)

The dedication ceremony for the Recorded Texas Historic Landmark designation of City Cemetery included, from left to right, Raiford Stripling, federal judge Joe J. Fisher, Nelda Greer Goetz, ambassador Edward Clark, Velma Birdwell, and Wilma Cartwright. The oldest grave in the cemetery dates back to the 1830s. Graves include early-day notables Col. Stephen W. Blount and the Reverend Dr. George L. Crocket. (Courtesy of *San Augustine Tribune*.)

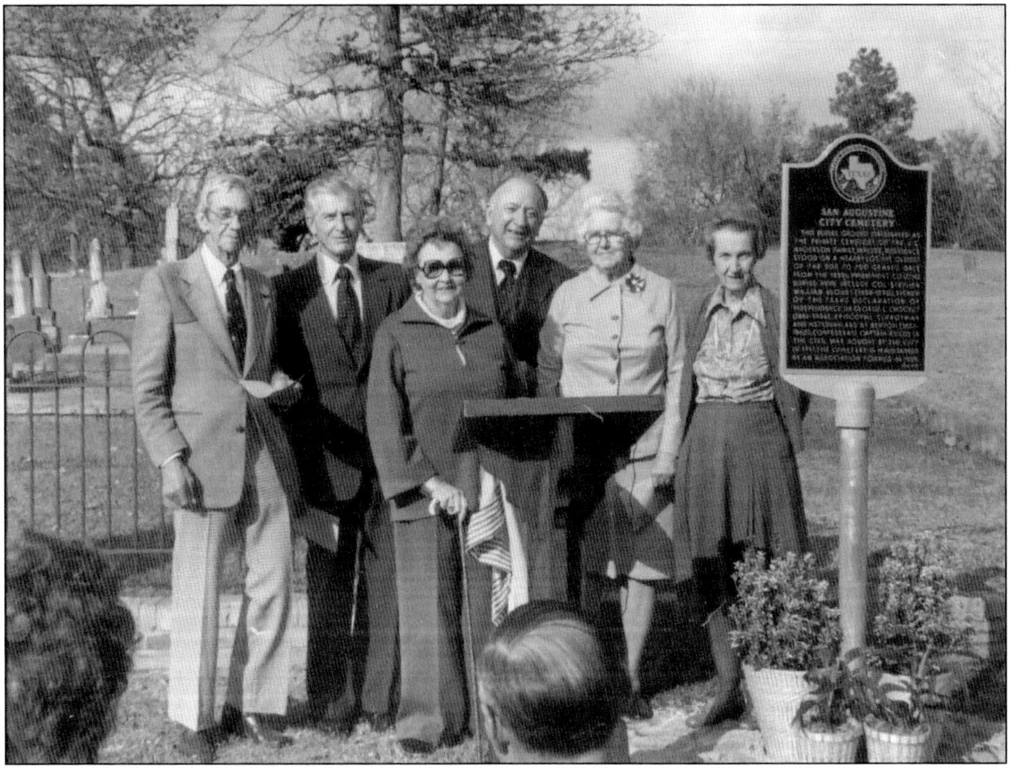

Four

A Legacy of Enduring Homes

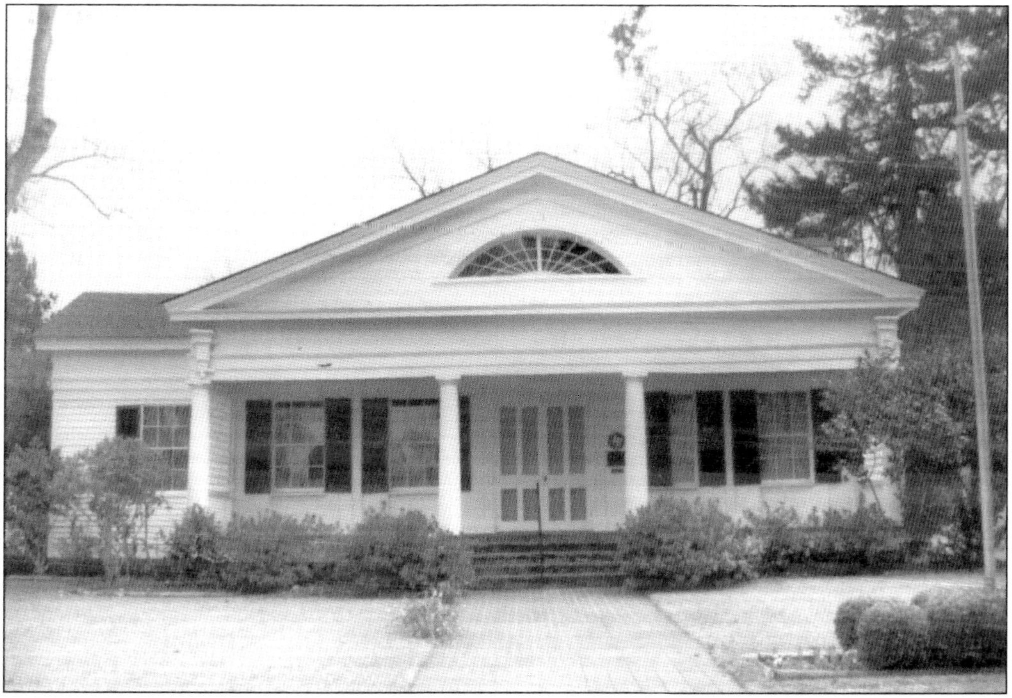

The 19th and early 20th century homes of San Augustine County provide the most visible link to the Republic of Texas to be found anywhere in the Lone Star State, thanks to the superb talents of master builders such as Augustus Phelps and carpenters/cabinetmakers W. H. and F. N. Horn. Pictured above is the Ezekiel Cullen Home built in 1839 by Augustus Phelps and restored by architect Raiford Stripling. Cullen's grandson Hugh Roy Cullen gave the house to the Ezekiel Cullen Chapter, Daughters of the Republic of Texas, in 1953. The artwork of native son S. Seymour Thomas is featured throughout the house. The Cullen Home has received both Recorded Texas Historic Landmark and National Register of Historic Places designations. All photographs in this chapter are by the author unless credited otherwise. Recorded Texas Historic Landmark and National Register of Historic Places designations of the pictured homes are shown as RTHL and NR in the captions.

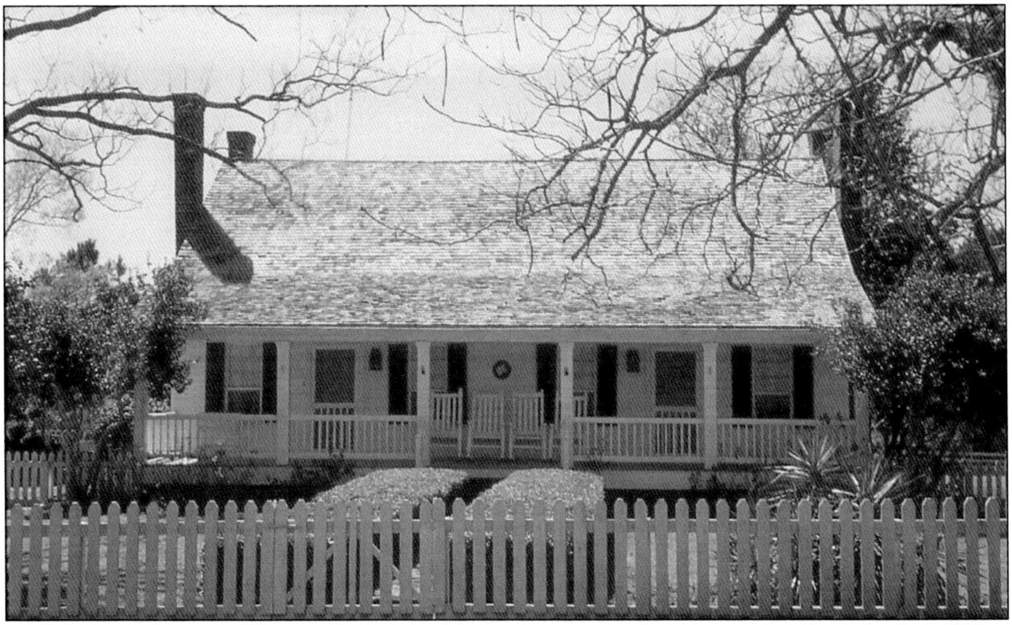

The Thomas Napoleon Bonaparte Greer House (RTHL) was built around 1838 by Augustus Phelps. This house is a fine example of a historic home in deteriorating condition that was saved through the restoration efforts of architect Raiford Stripling. Dorothy Fussell is the current owner.

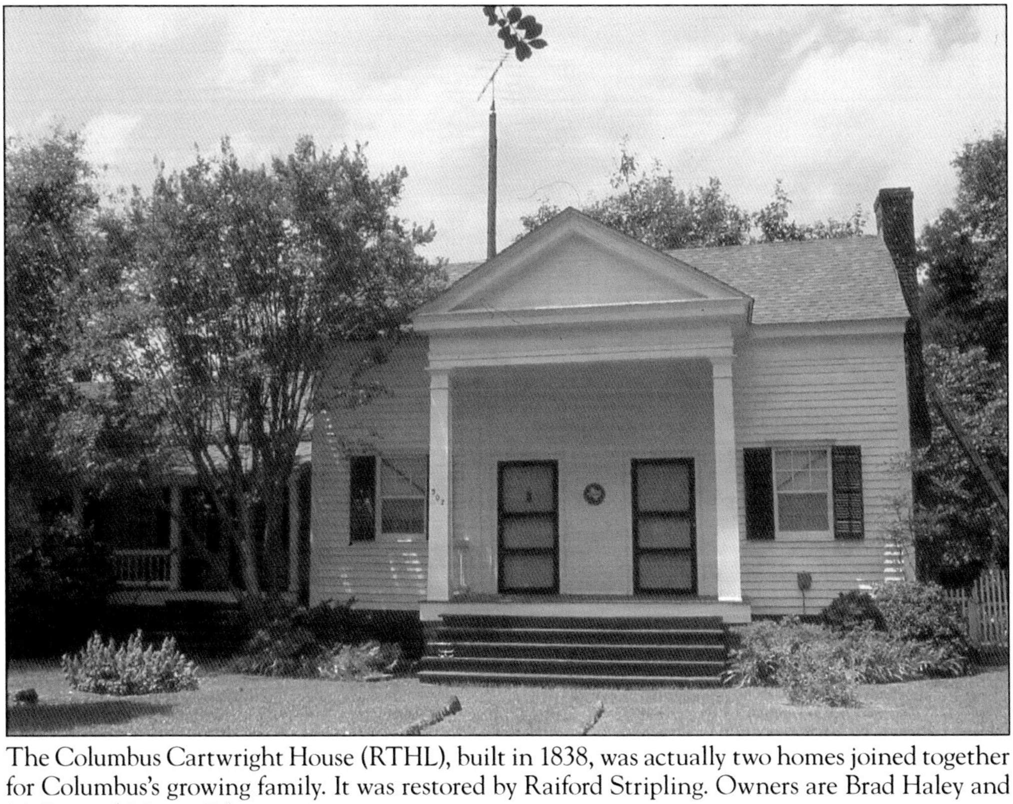

The Columbus Cartwright House (RTHL), built in 1838, was actually two homes joined together for Columbus's growing family. It was restored by Raiford Stripling. Owners are Brad Haley and Mollie and Monte Ethington.

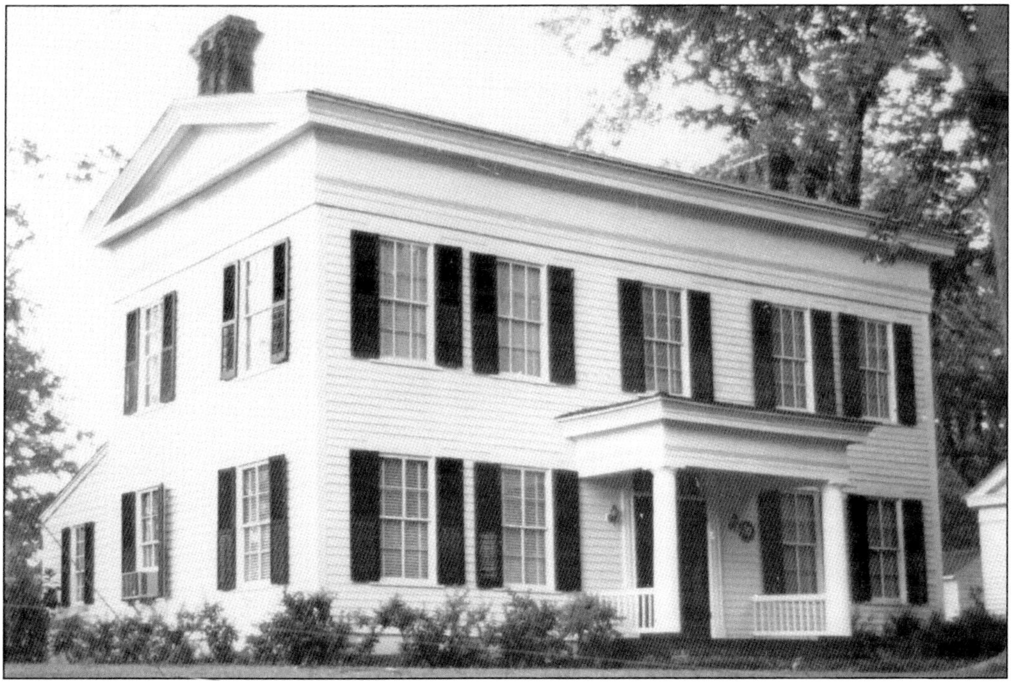

The Matthew Cartwright House (RTHL, NR) was built by Augustus Phelps in 1839 and restored by Raiford Stripling. Owned by Cartwright descendant Sandra Calpakis, the home has retained many original furnishings and family relics from past generations. Nearby is Matthew Cartwright's office mentioned in chapter one.

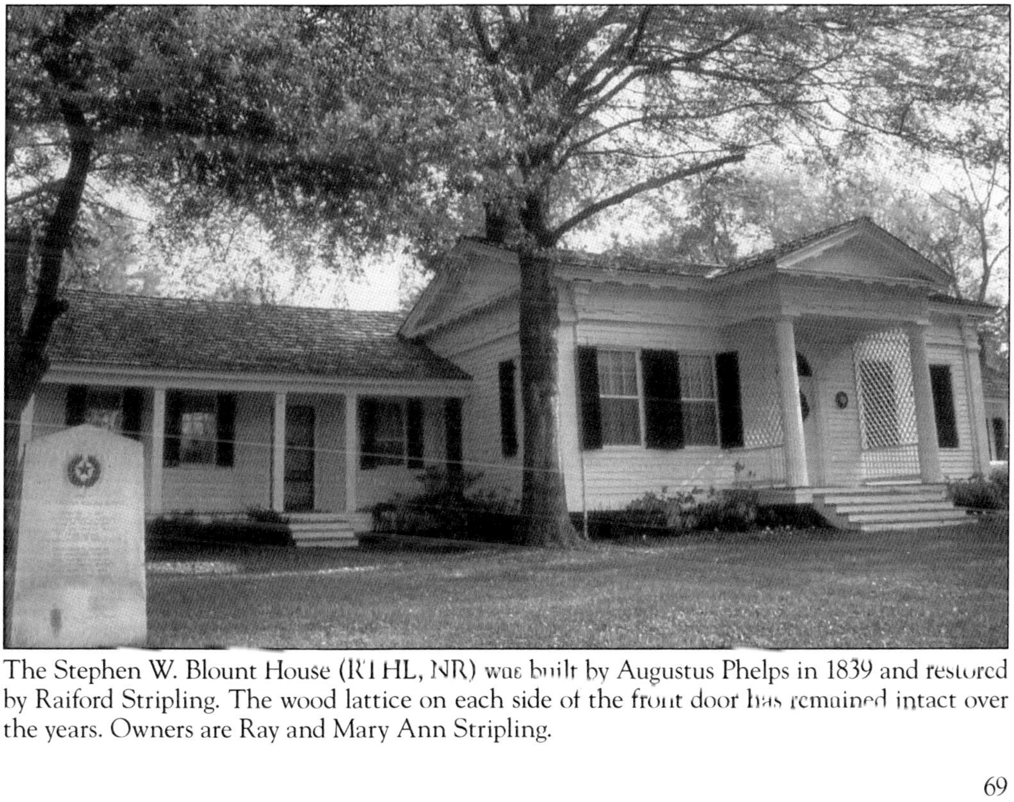

The Stephen W. Blount House (RTHL, NR) was built by Augustus Phelps in 1839 and restored by Raiford Stripling. The wood lattice on each side of the front door has remained intact over the years. Owners are Ray and Mary Ann Stripling.

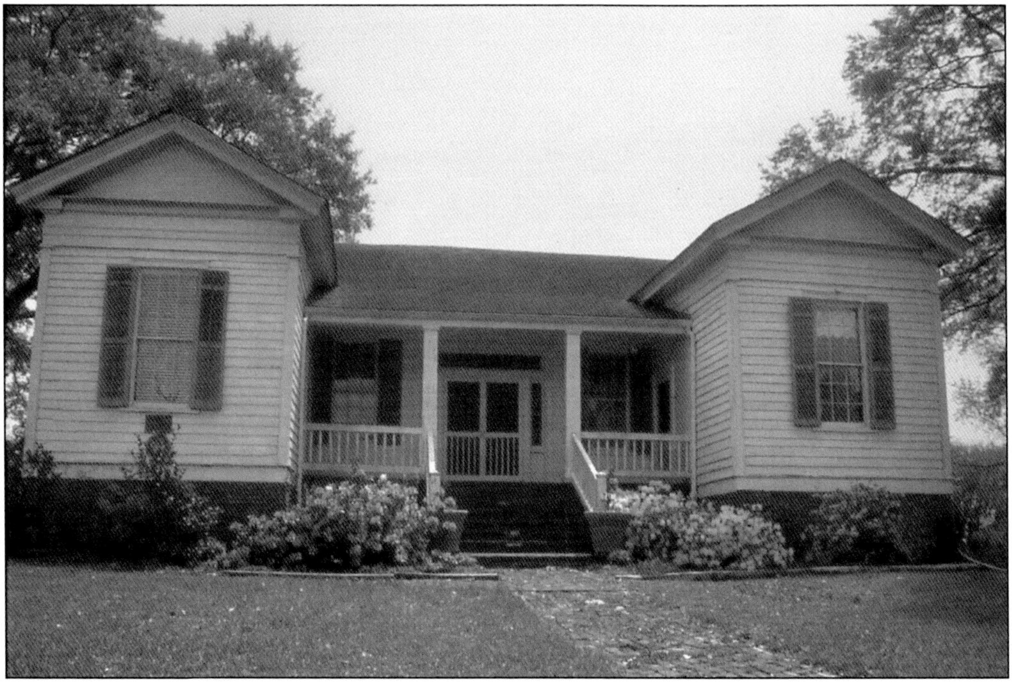

The Horn-Polk House (RTHL, NR) was built for Ransom Horn by his brothers W. H. and F. N. Horn in 1840. F. N. Horn purchased Augustus Phelps's tools after his untimely death and soon became a master craftsman in his own right. The owner is James Williams.

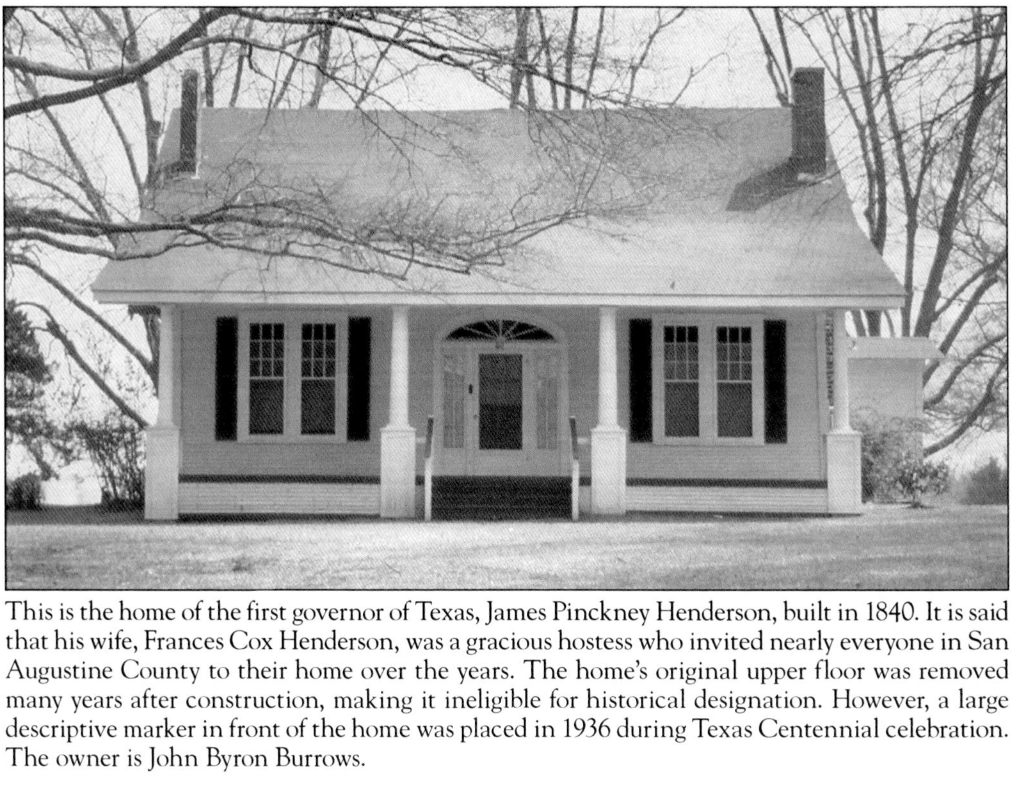

This is the home of the first governor of Texas, James Pinckney Henderson, built in 1840. It is said that his wife, Frances Cox Henderson, was a gracious hostess who invited nearly everyone in San Augustine County to their home over the years. The home's original upper floor was removed many years after construction, making it ineligible for historical designation. However, a large descriptive marker in front of the home was placed in 1936 during Texas Centennial celebration. The owner is John Byron Burrows.

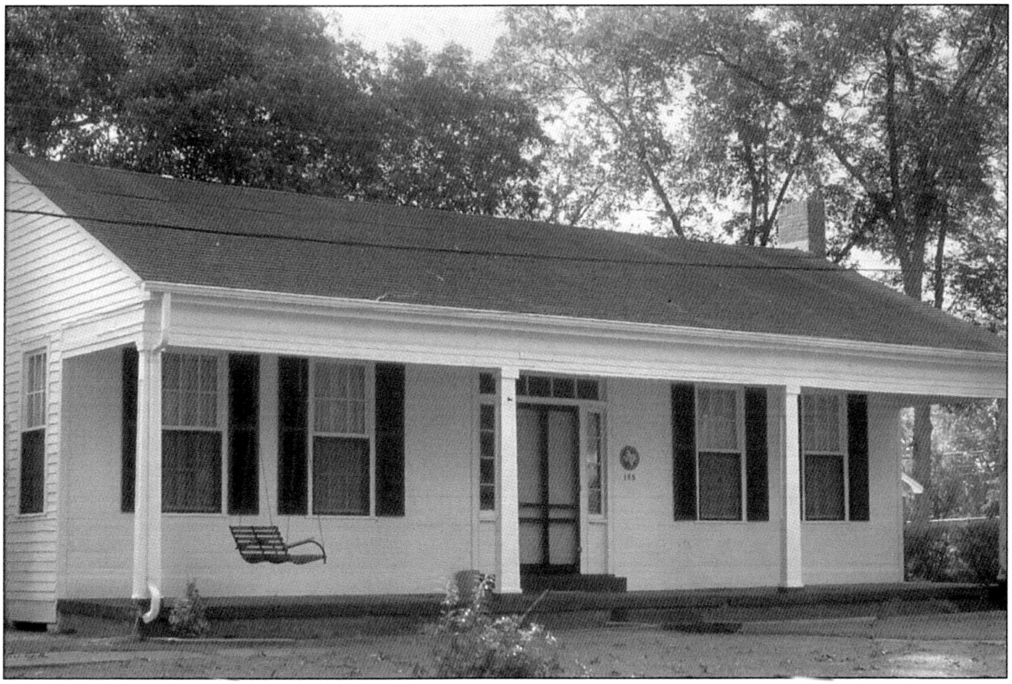

The Lafayette "Pet" Sharp Home (RTHL) was built in 1856. Historical information concerning the house indicates that it was likely built by the Horn brothers, mentioned earlier in this chapter. The owner is Gaar Bennett.

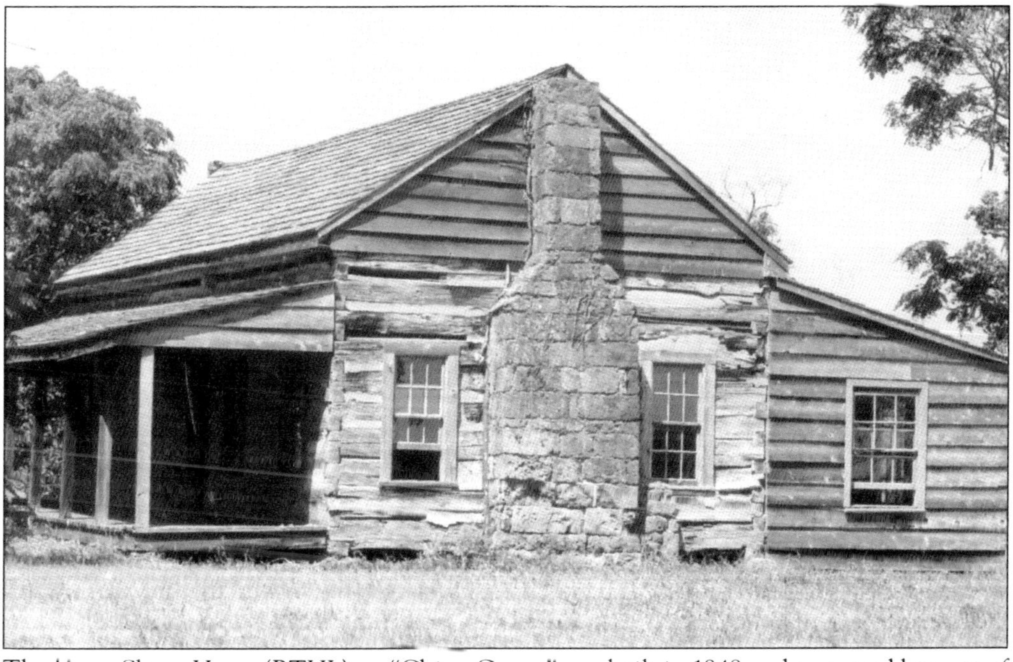

The Davis-Sharp Home (RTHL), or "China Grove," was built in 1848 and so named because of the large chinaberry trees surrounding the house in earlier times. It is owned by San Augustine County Historical Society, a gift from Jerry King. China Grove is the ancestral home of Sen. Kay Bailey Hutchison.

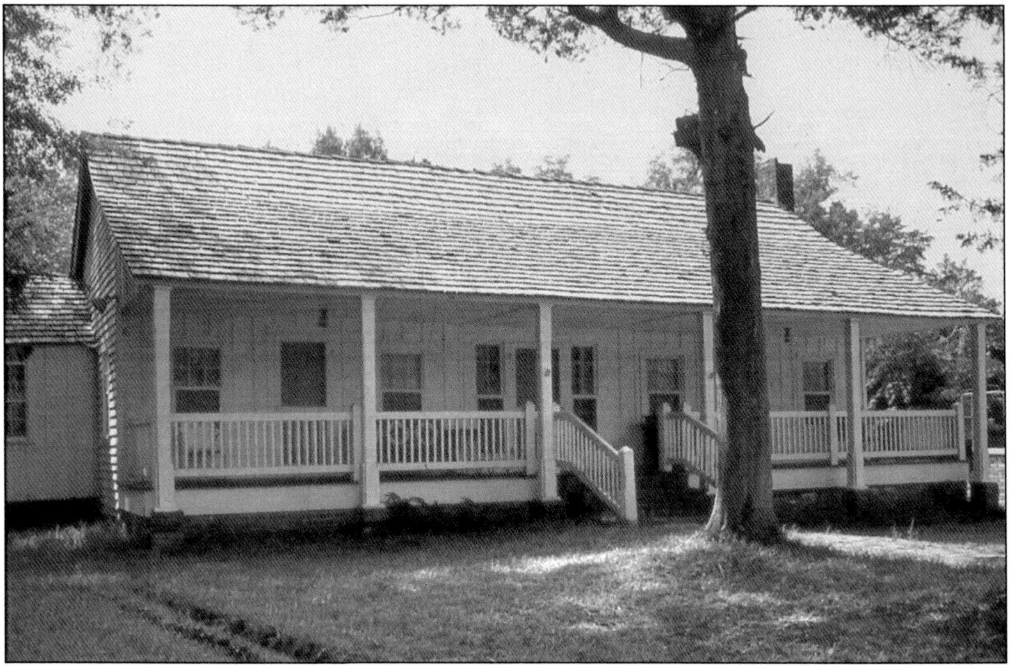

The Thomas Sebastian Cabot Wade Home (RTHL), "Hospitality House," was built in 1862. Family descendant and owner, Nelsyn Wade, hosts the Wade Reunion there each May.

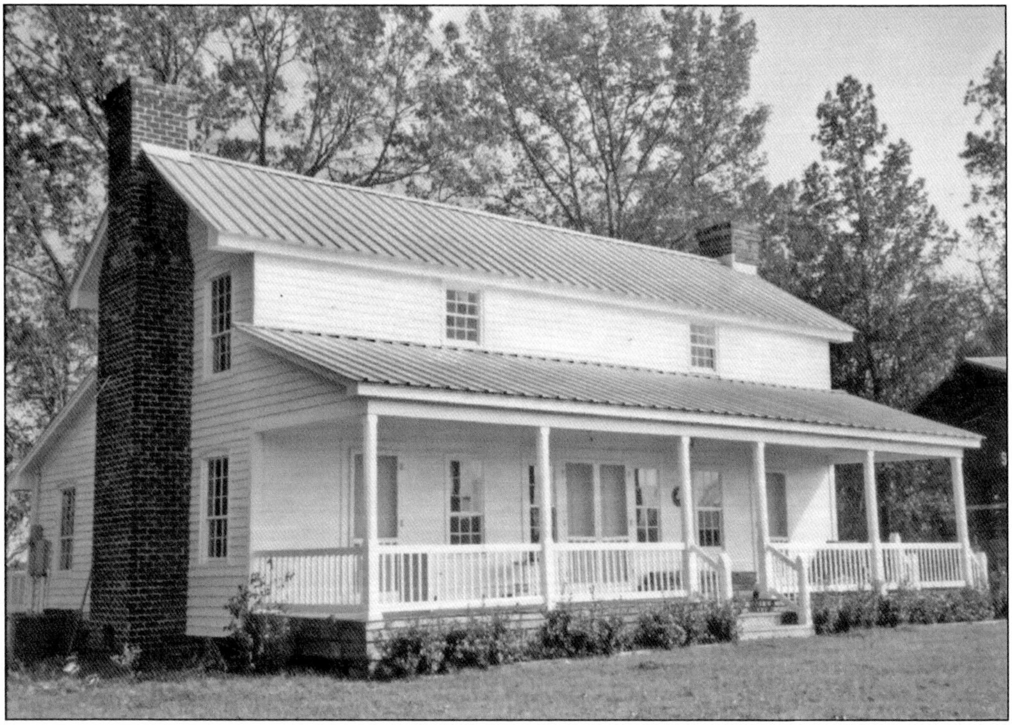

The Norwood-LeGrand House (RTHL) was built in 1870. To save this home, it was moved to the Mitchell farm where it has been fully restored. Close by is the restored depot as a railroad museum, mentioned earlier. The owner is Lucy Mitchell.

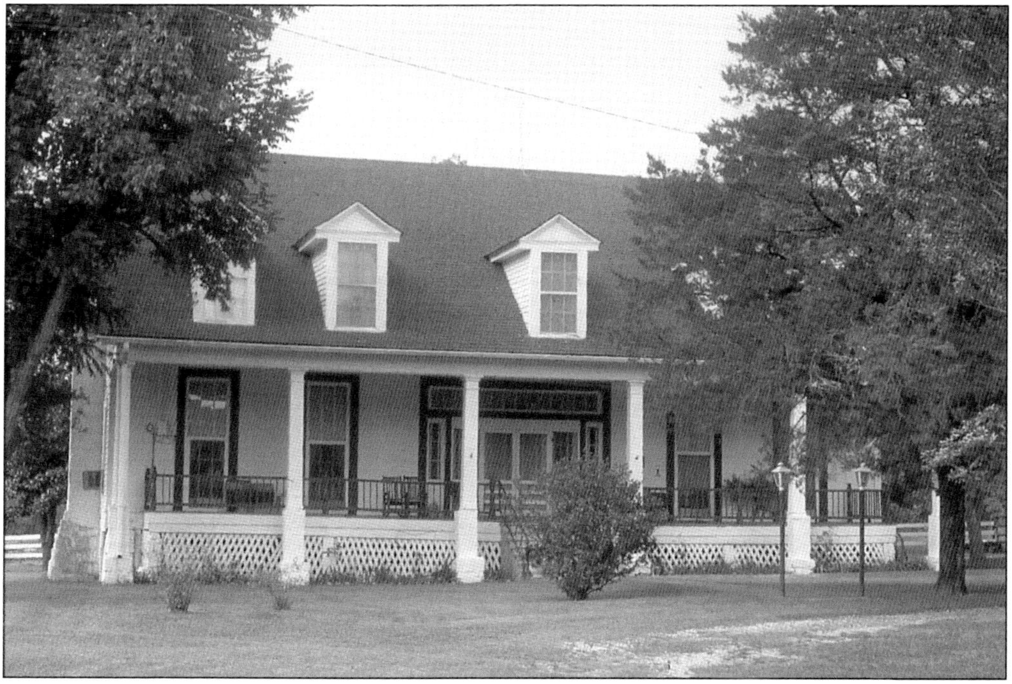

The William Garrett Plantation Home (RTHL, NR) was built in 1863 and has remained in the family for decades. Family-member Charlotte Dorsey Tull-Lott is the owner.

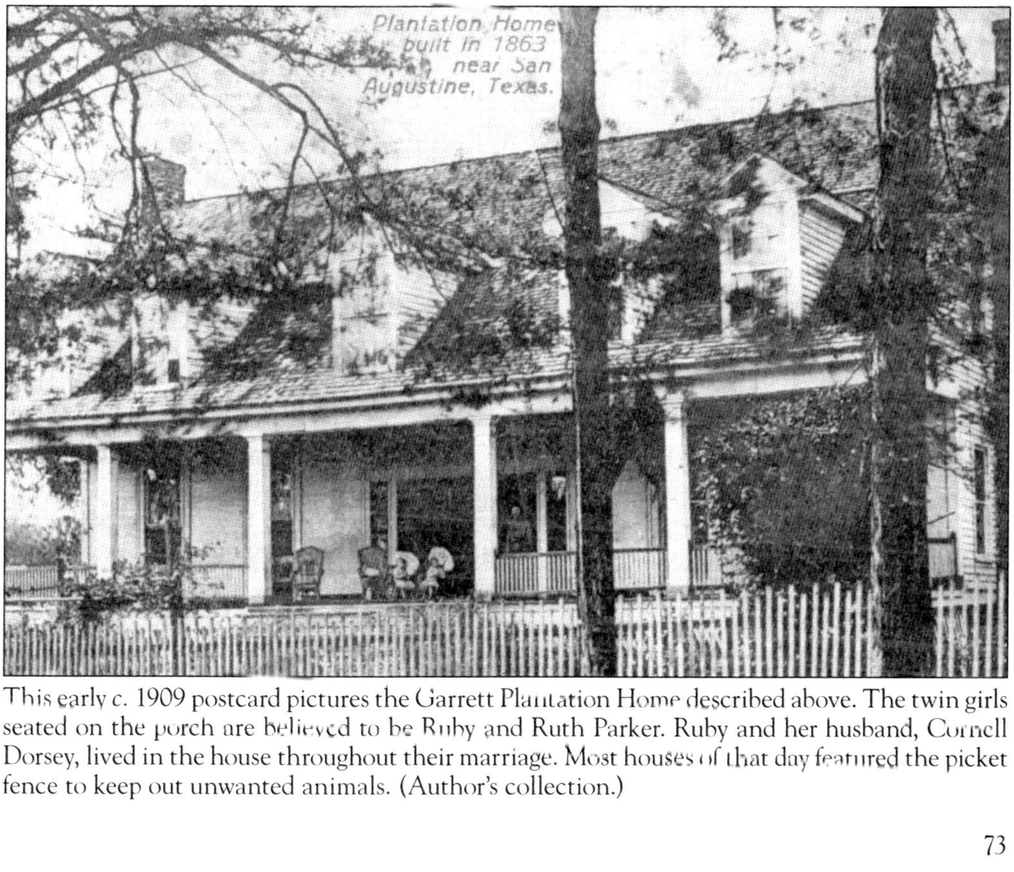

This early c. 1909 postcard pictures the Garrett Plantation Home described above. The twin girls seated on the porch are believed to be Ruby and Ruth Parker. Ruby and her husband, Cornell Dorsey, lived in the house throughout their marriage. Most houses of that day featured the picket fence to keep out unwanted animals. (Author's collection.)

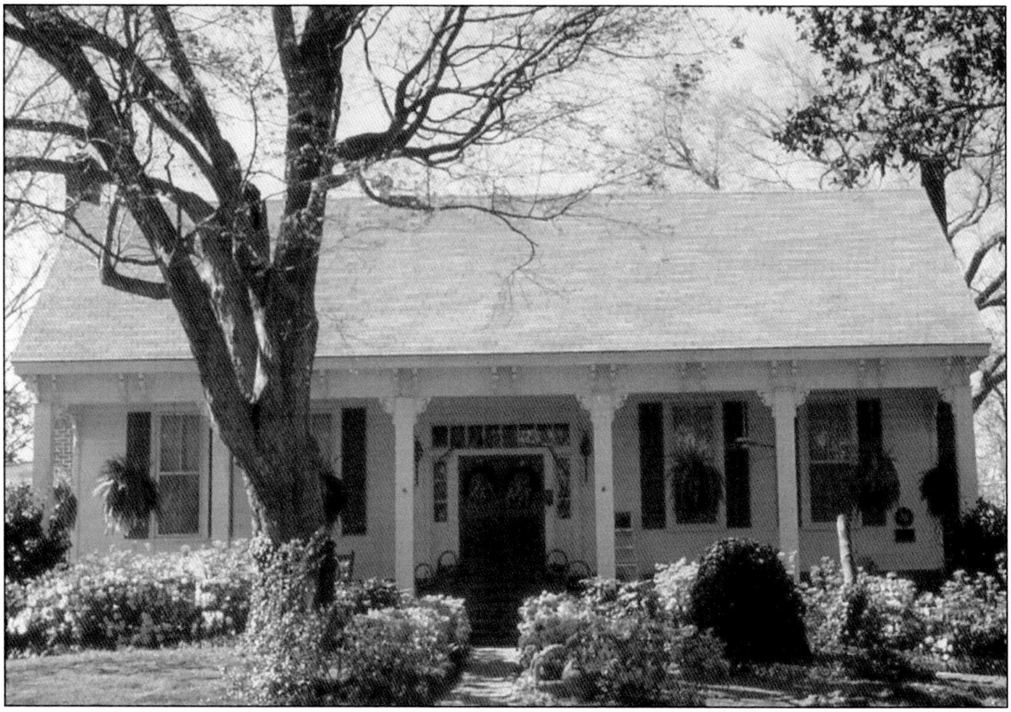

The Leonard-Leonidas Cartwright-Sharp Home (RTHL) was constructed in 1872. An addition to the main house was constructed in 1878. Owners are Dr. C. R. and Mary Jean Haley.

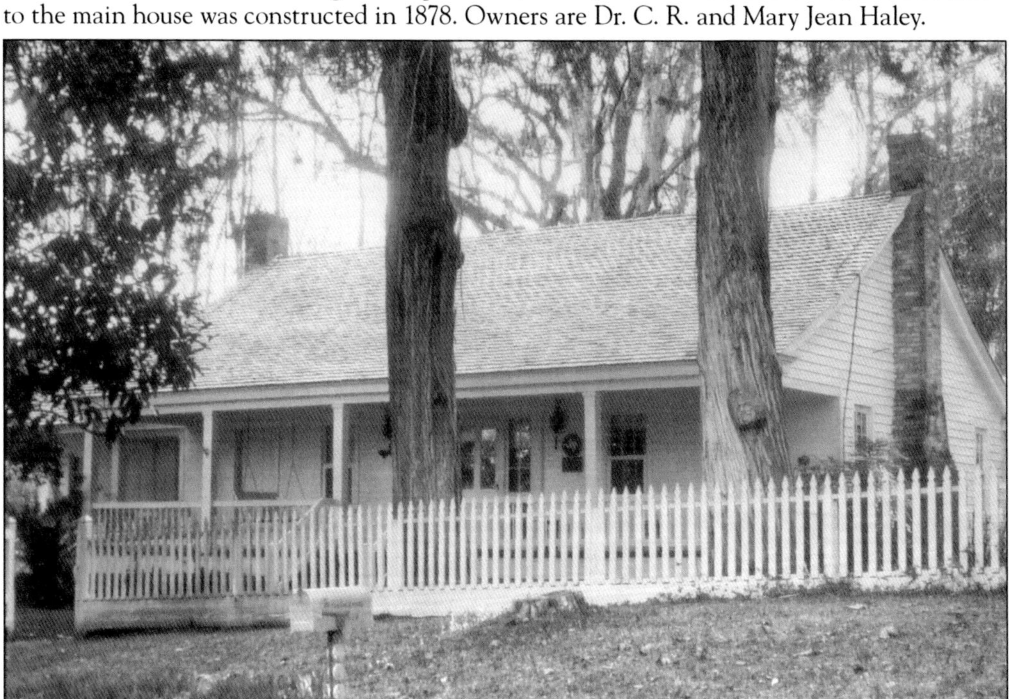

The Jacob Herring House (RTHL) was built in 1875 and restored by architects Raiford and Ray R. Stripling. Named "Straddlefork Farm" by ambassador to Australia Edward Clark and his wife, Anne, it is currently owned by Ann Ramsey.

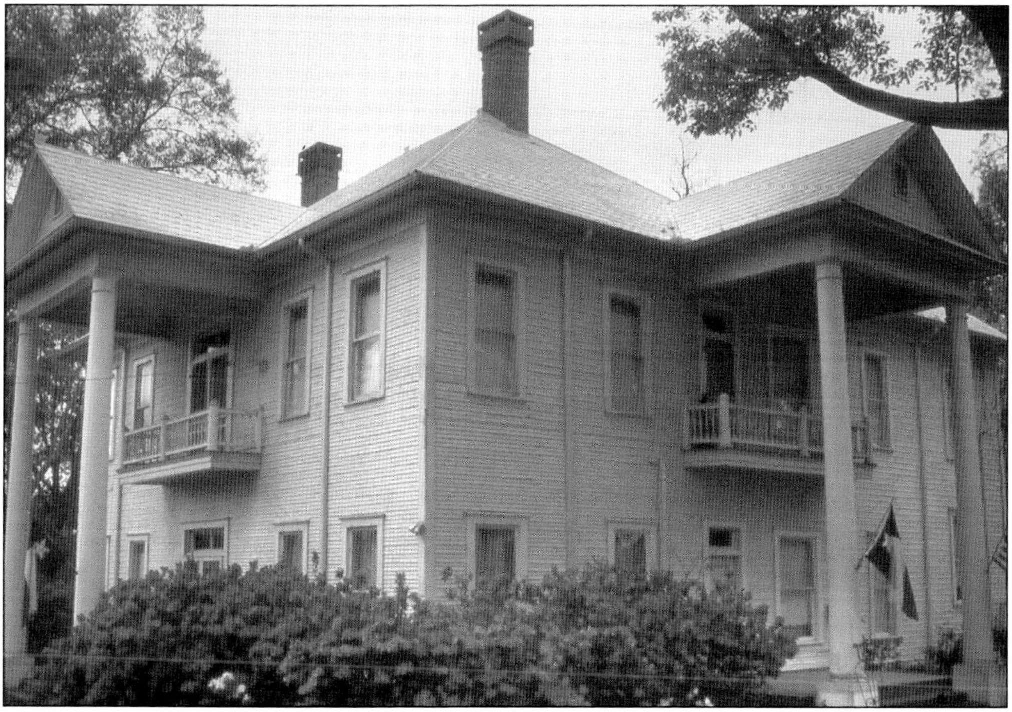

The John Matthew Cartwright Home was built in 1902. Today it is "The Columns," a popular bed-and-breakfast in San Augustine. Owners are Earl and Verna Chumley.

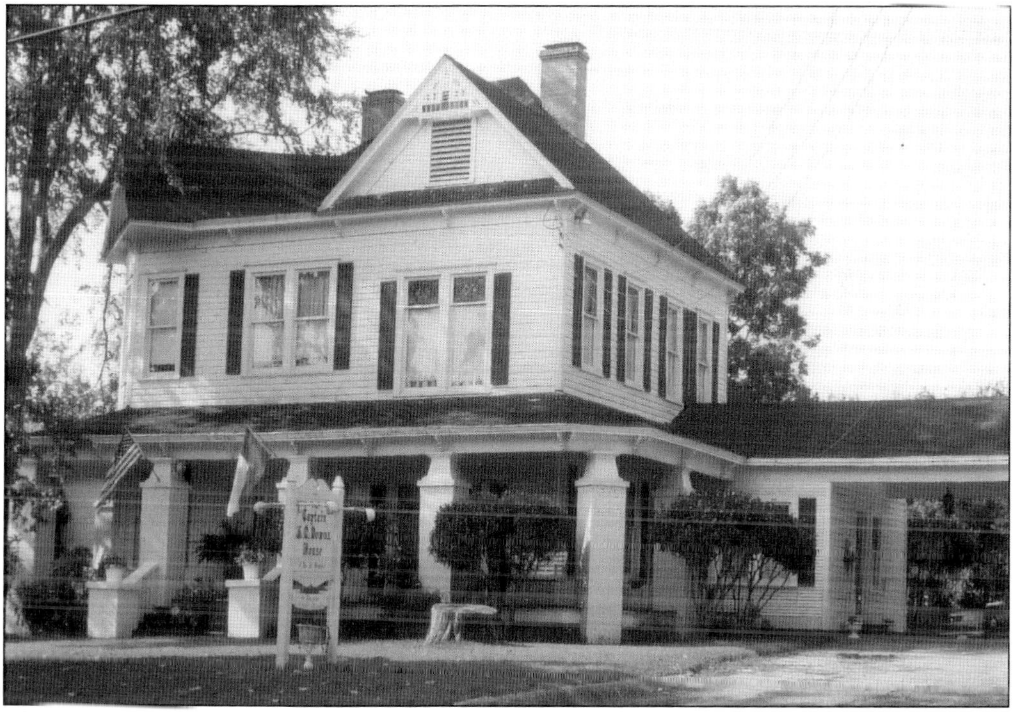

The Capt. E. D. Downs House was built in 1902. It is owned by Dorothy Fussell, who operates the home as a small hotel.

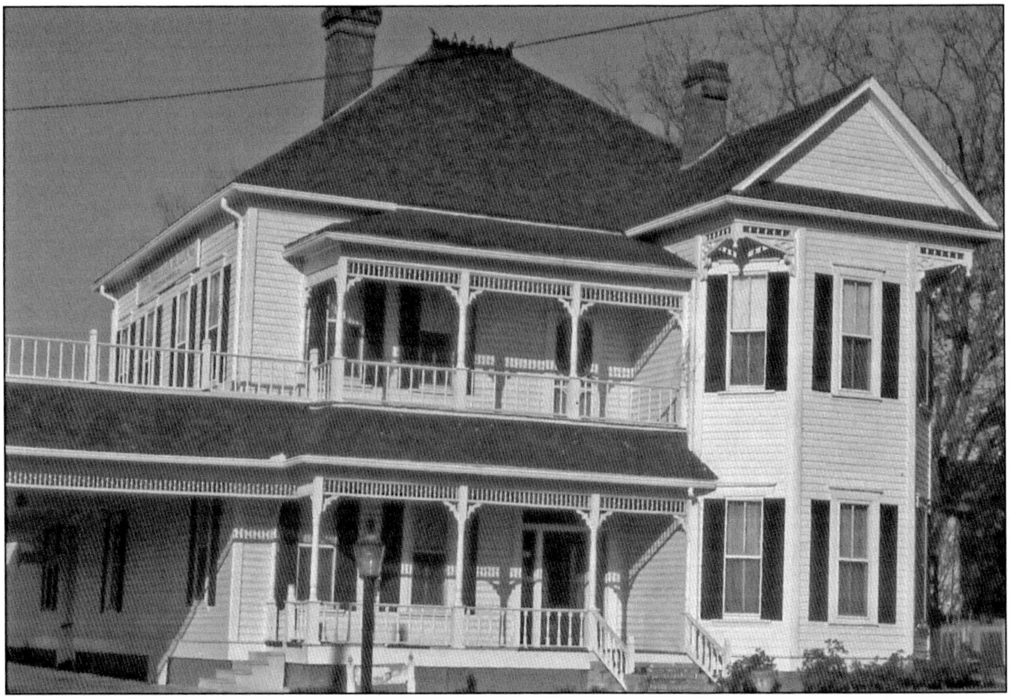

The Ben Whitton Home, constructed in 1902, is owned by attorney Bill Weems. A. E. (Jake) Whitton Surveyors have offices in this building.

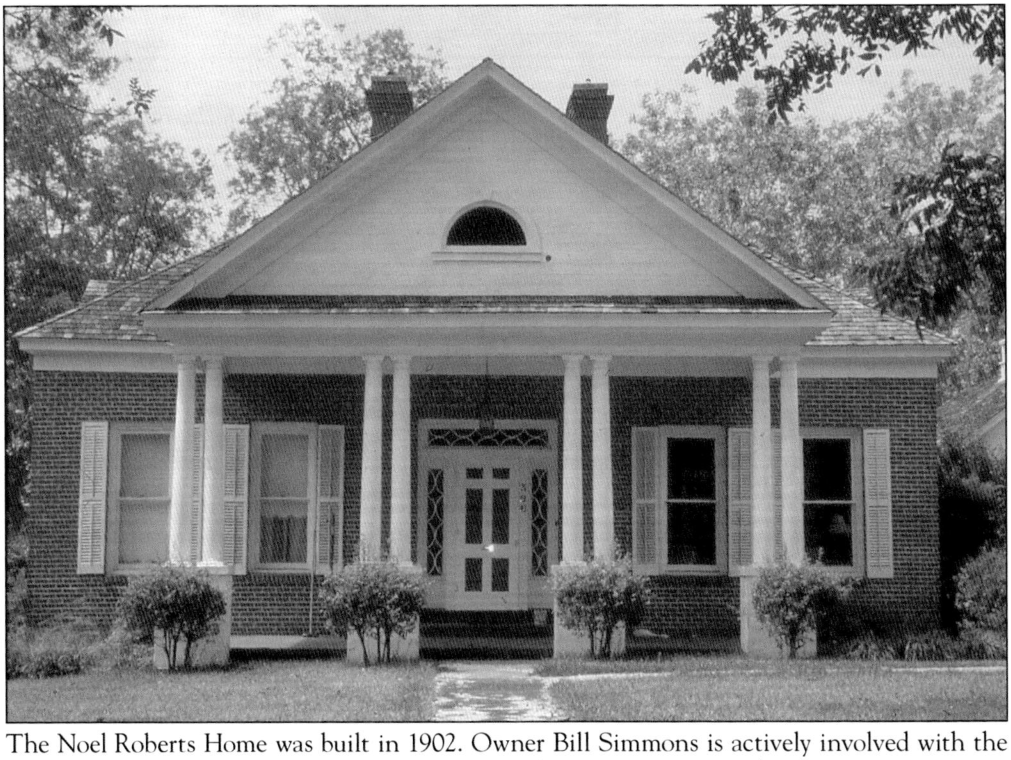

The Noel Roberts Home was built in 1902. Owner Bill Simmons is actively involved with the City of San Augustine's Mission Dolores Travel Information Center and Museum.

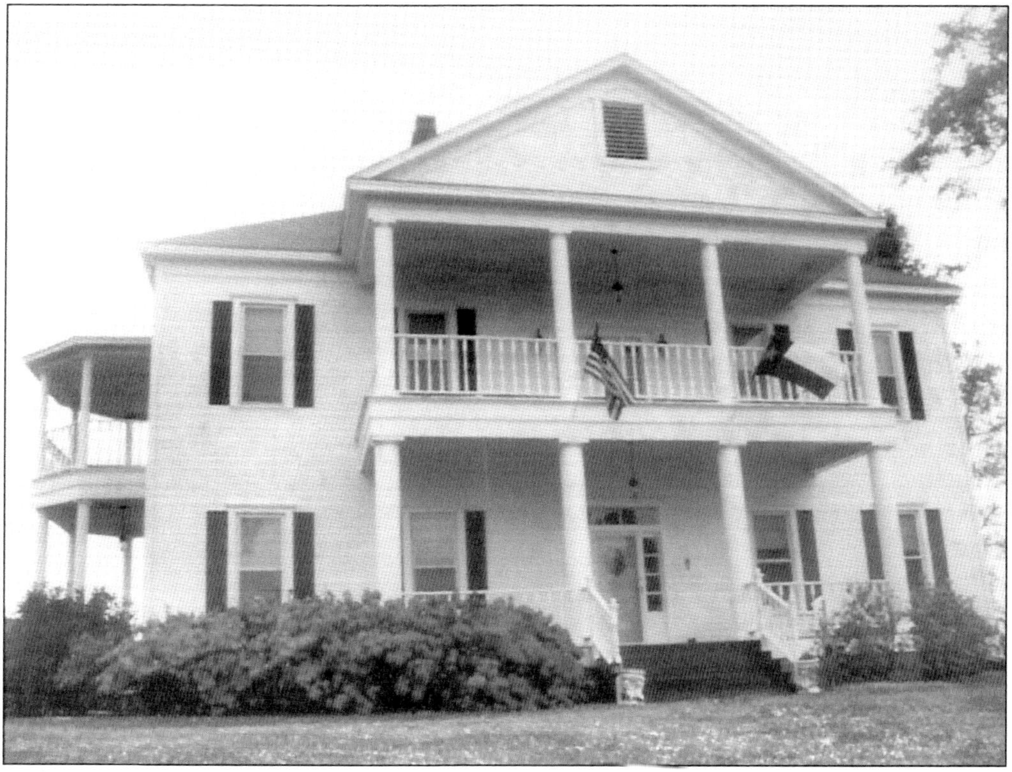

Built in 1903 atop a hill on Liberty Street is the James J. Bewley home. Original owner Bewley sat on the second floor balcony with binoculars to stay abreast of happenings in downtown San Augustine. The home is owned by Richard and Kathie Haley.

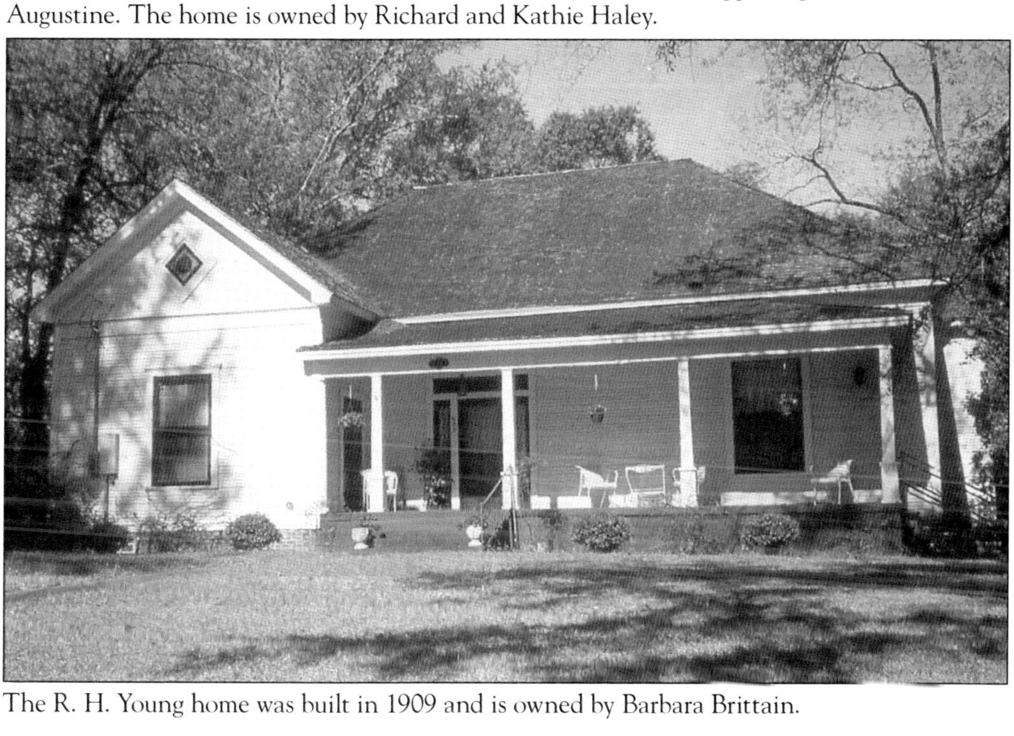

The R. H. Young home was built in 1909 and is owned by Barbara Brittain.

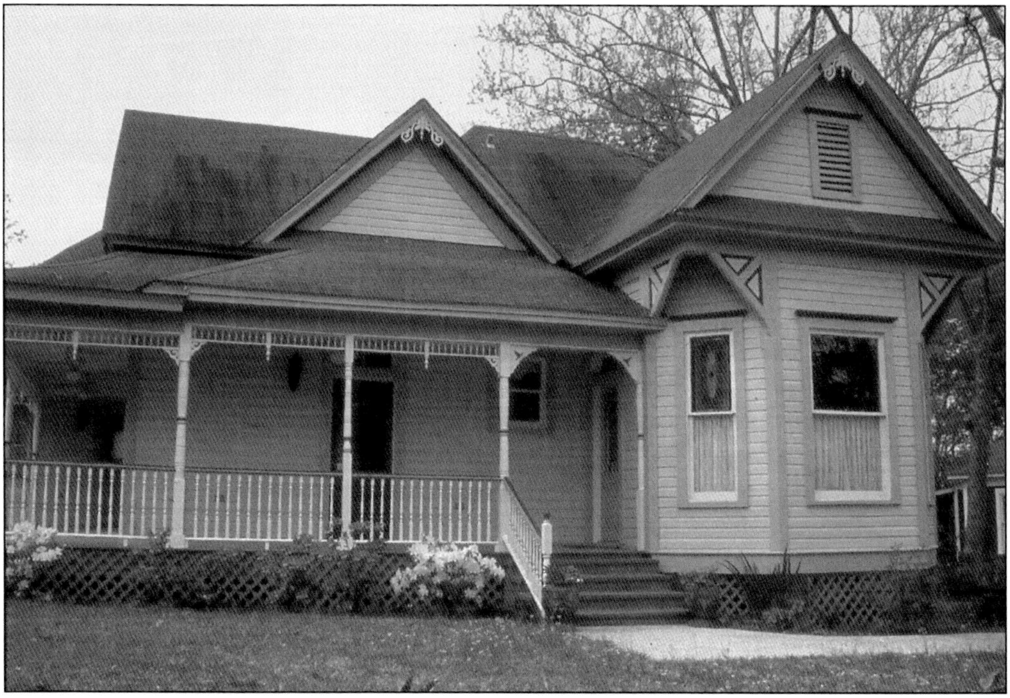

San Augustine Garden Club's headquarters home, "The Pink Lady," was constructed in 1909. It was originally owned by Jessie Crouch Smith. Located just a stone's throw from San Augustine Public Library, the Garden Club offers after-hours programming for English as a Second Language classes two evenings each week.

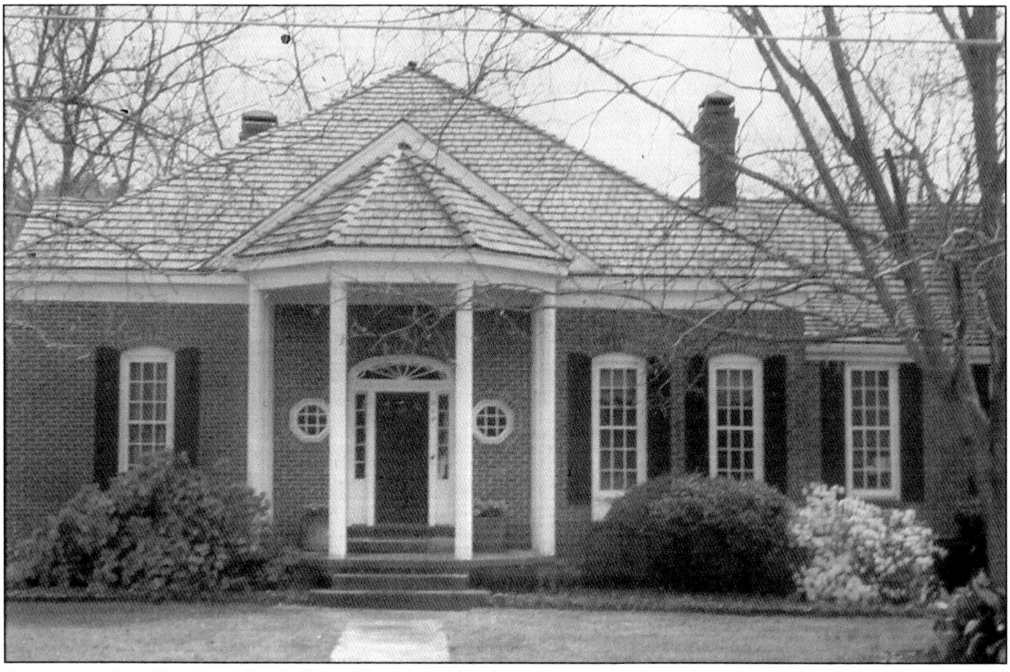

District judge Charles Mitchell and his wife, Barbara, own the Matthew Wood Home, constructed in 1910.

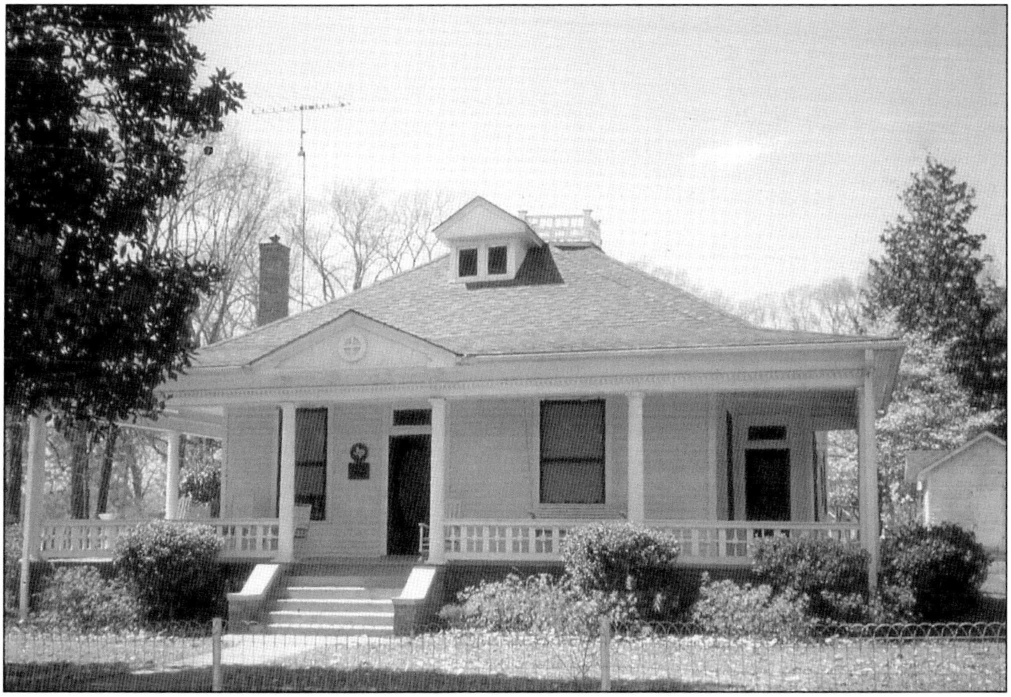

The Bland-Fisher Home (RTHL), built in 1912, was the boyhood home of federal judge Joe J. Fisher. The owners are Judge Fisher's son John Fisher and his wife, Jan.

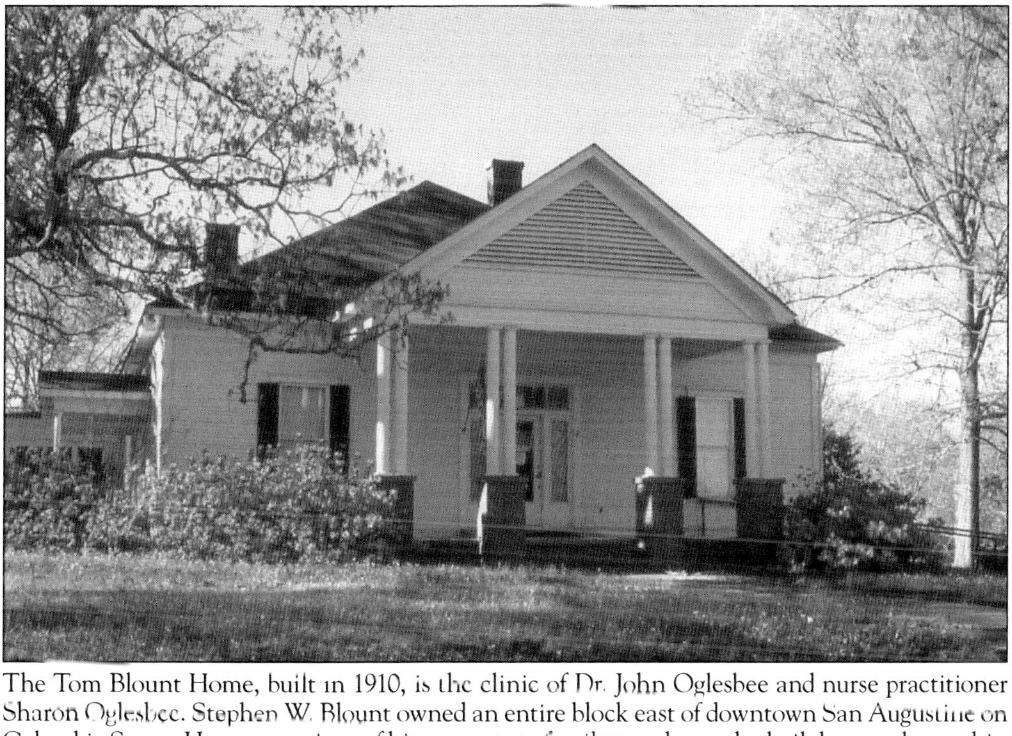

The Tom Blount Home, built in 1910, is the clinic of Dr. John Oglesbee and nurse practitioner Sharon Oglesbee. Stephen W. Blount owned an entire block east of downtown San Augustine on Columbia Street. He gave portions of his property to family members, who built homes close to his. The home pictured is one of three built by relatives of Colonel Blount in "The Blount Block."

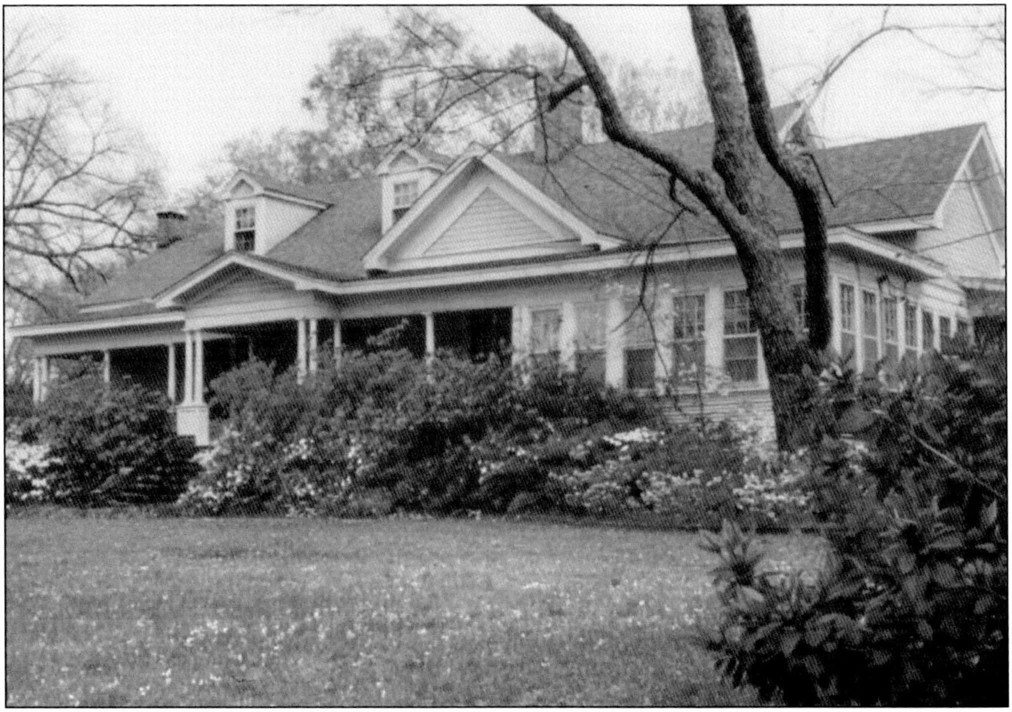

The 1910 Frank Blount Home in "The Blount Block" is owned by Cherry Mathews Burnett.

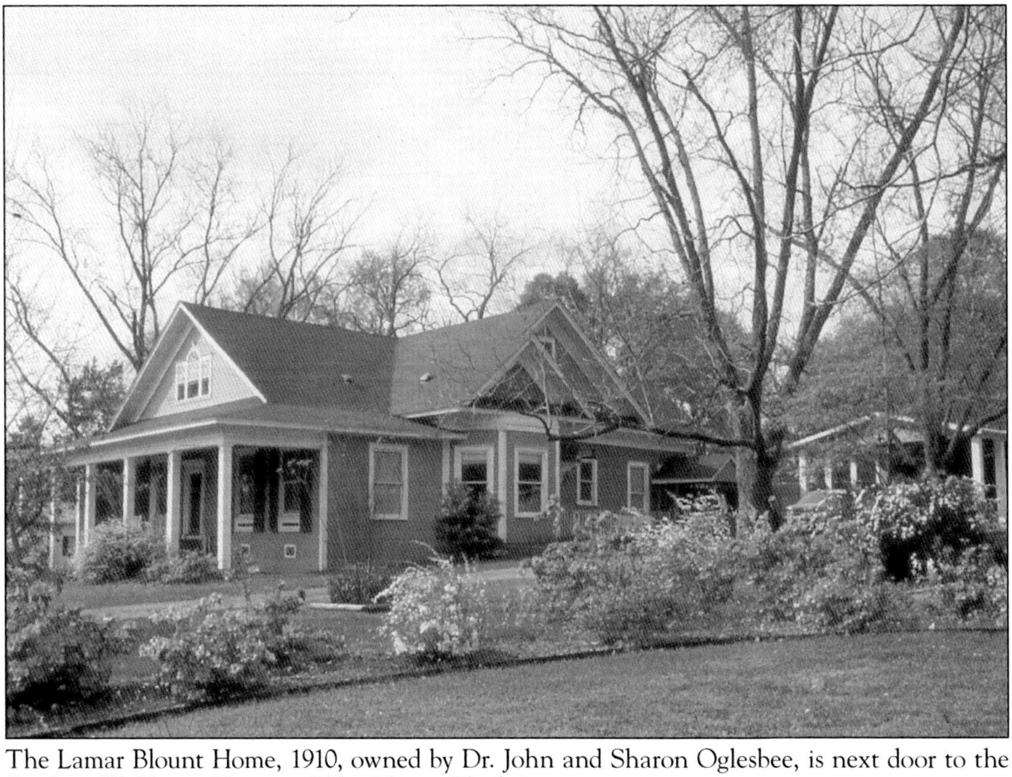

The Lamar Blount Home, 1910, owned by Dr. John and Sharon Oglesbee, is next door to the Stephen W. Blount Home in "The Blount Block."

Five

The Times They Were A'Changing

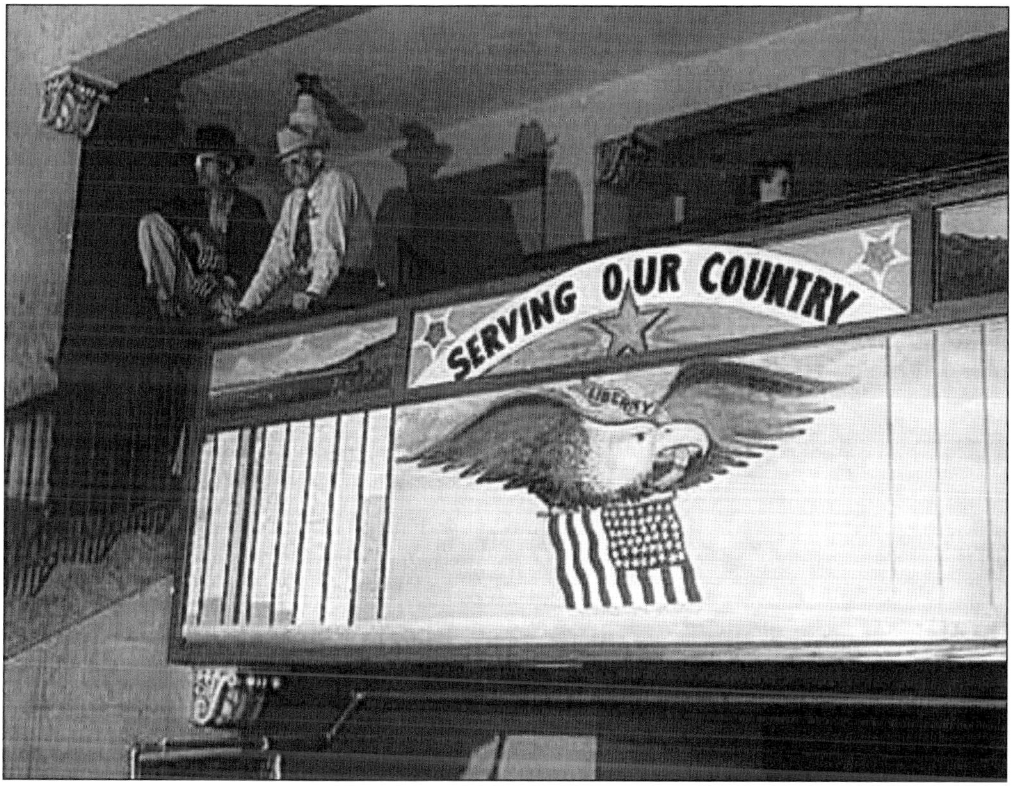

John Vachon, a photographer for the U.S. Office of War Information, visited San Augustine in the spring of 1943. One responsibility of OWI was to review and approve the format and informational content of government posters. Pictured is Sheriff John Halbert leaning over the second floor railing inside the San Augustine County Courthouse. (Photograph by John Vachon, OWI, 1943, Library of Congress.)

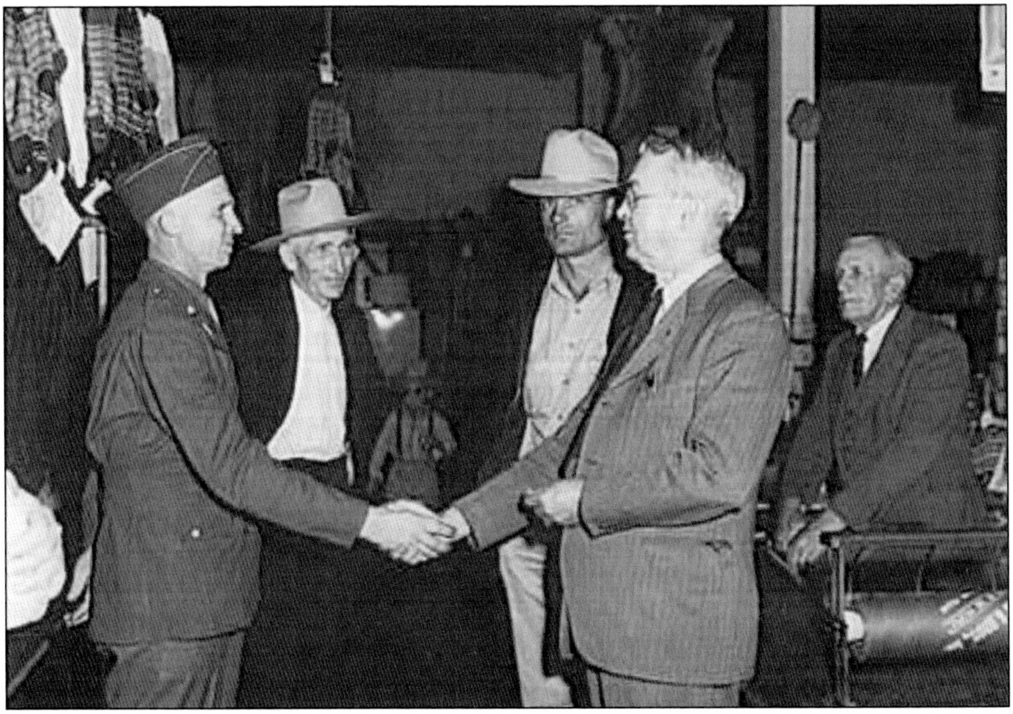

W. P. Wood, in the A. J. Wood and Brothers dry goods store, greets a soldier on leave while Jim Ingram (right) looks on. (Photograph by John Vachon, OWI, 1943, Library of Congress.)

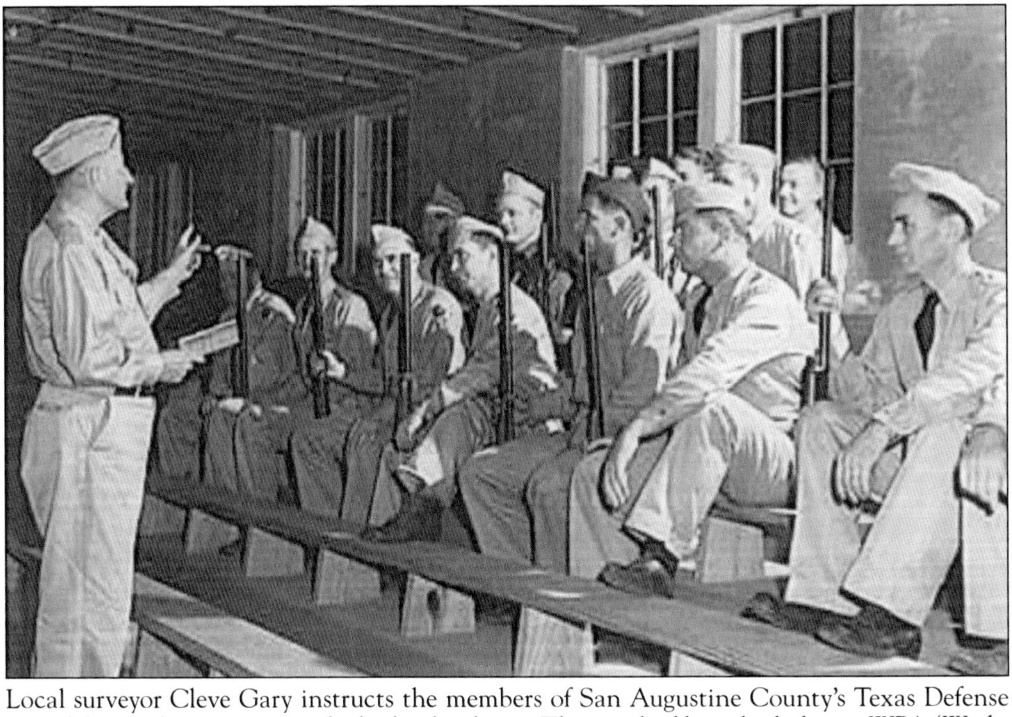

Local surveyor Cleve Gary instructs the members of San Augustine County's Texas Defense Guard during their practice in the high school gym. The gym had been built during WPA (Works Progress Administration) days. (Photograph by John Vachon, OWI, 1943, Library of Congress.)

Soldiers on leave converse on the courthouse square. The statue is of first Texas governor James Pinckney Henderson, erected in 1937 as a part of the 1936 Texas Centennial celebration. (Photograph by John Vachon, OWI, 1943, Library of Congress.)

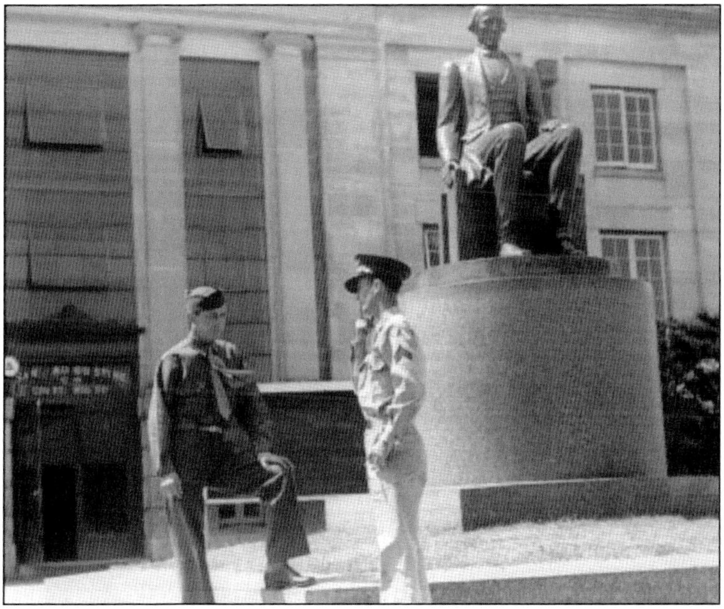

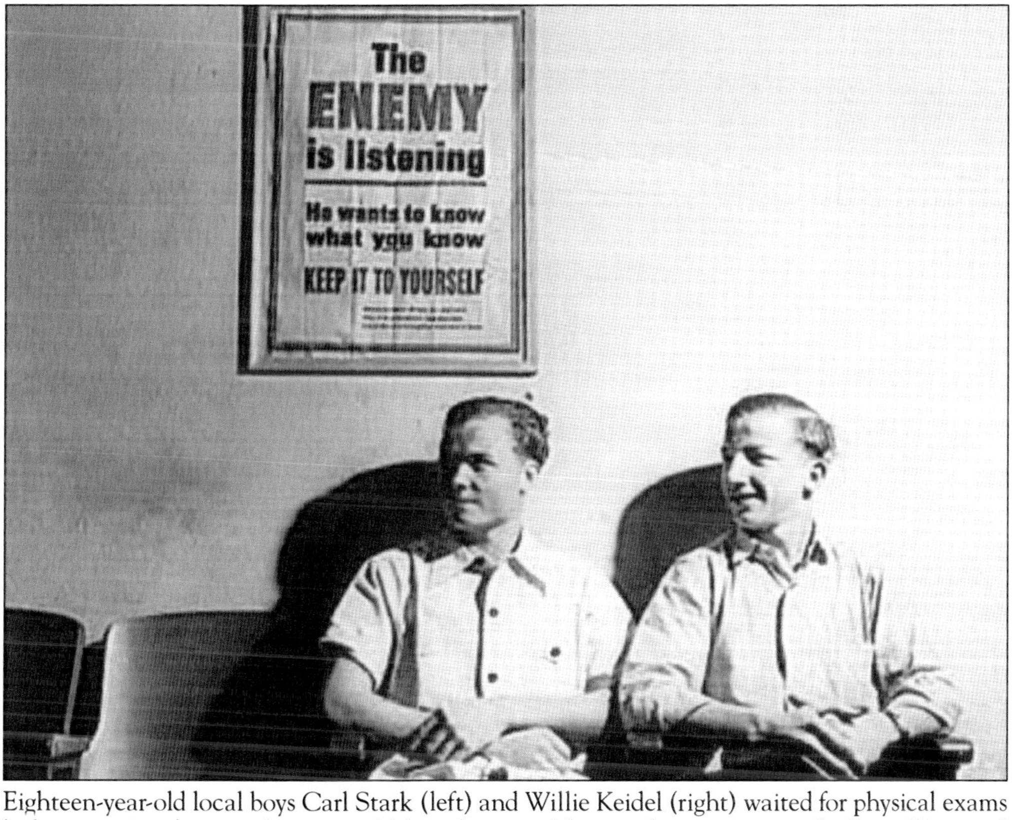

Eighteen-year-old local boys Carl Stark (left) and Willie Keidel (right) waited for physical exams before entering the armed services. Although most of the people appearing in the Russell Lee and John Vachon images from 1939 and 1943 were not identified by the photographers, it is fortunate that a number of still-living San Augustinians recognize many of them. (Photograph by John Vachon, OWI, 1943, Library of Congress.)

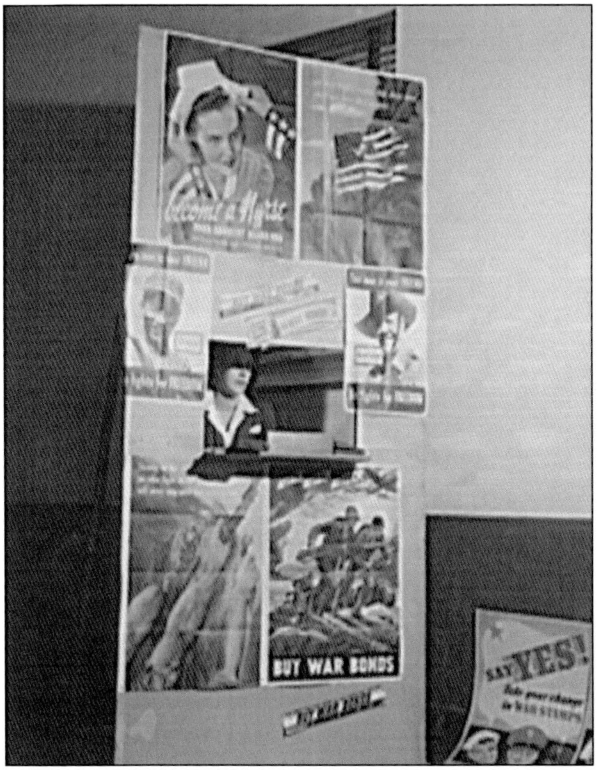

This patriotic booth was set up inside a local bank to sell war bonds and stamps with the caption "Take Your Change in War Stamps." San Augustine County citizens were frugal and diligent in their support of the war effort. Conserving was of prime importance. The saying came into vogue, "Use it up, wear it out, make it do, or do without." People planted victory gardens and places small signs on the dashboards of their cars that read, "Is this trip really necessary?" (Photograph by John Vachon, OWI, 1943, Library of Congress.)

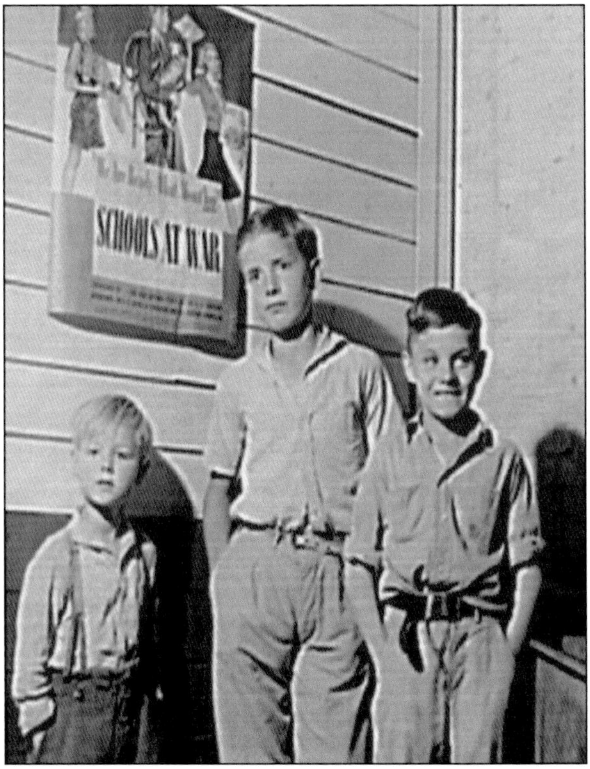

Rural school boys pose with the timely message of a war poster in the background. During World War II, the small rural schools operated throughout the county. Consolidation of the rural-area schools into San Augustine Independent School District and Broaddus Independent School District occurred mostly during the years 1947 to 1958, when transportation was less of an issue. (Photograph by John Vachon, OWI, 1943, Library of Congress.)

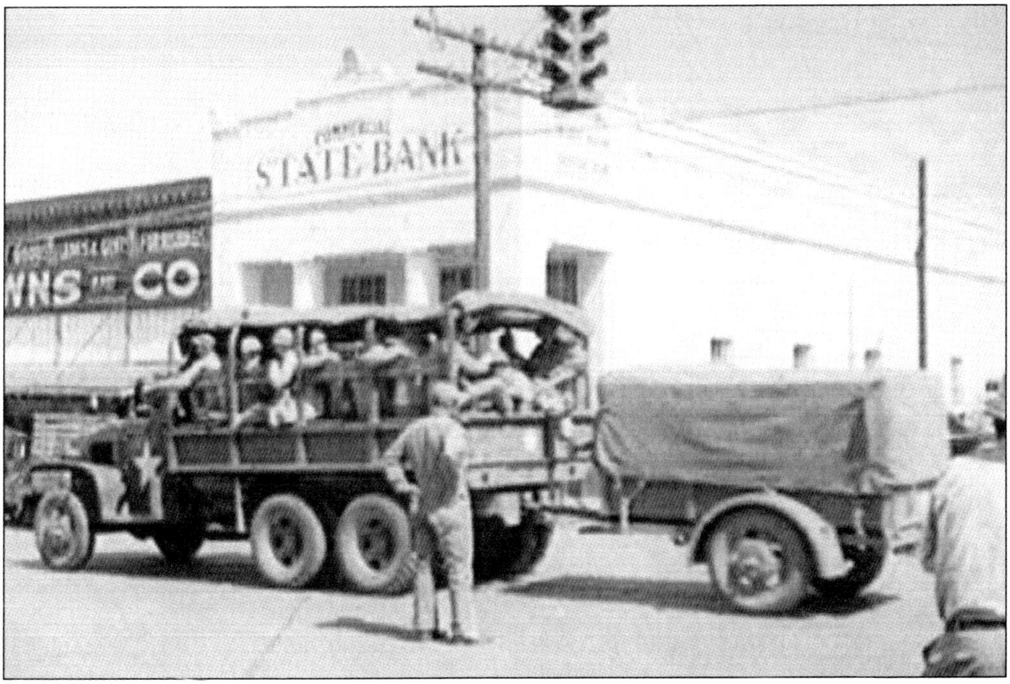

Army maneuvers along El Camino Real through downtown San Augustine were a frequent occurrence during the World War II years. (Photograph by John Vachon, OWI, 1943, Library of Congress.)

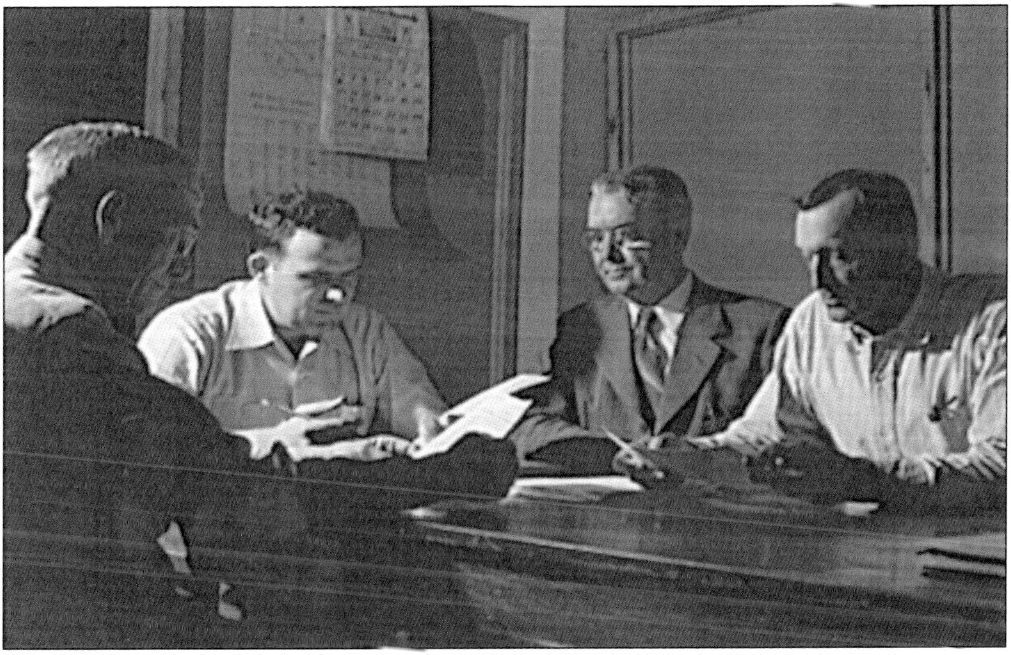

Meetings of the San Augustine County Rationing Board were a regular occurrence in 1943. Members in attendance were, from left to right, retired rural mail carrier Mr. Long, commercial bank president Thomas Curl, merchant W. P. Wood, and AAA (Agricultural Adjustment Administration) supervisor Mr. Brown. (Photograph by John Vachon, OWI, Library of Congress.)

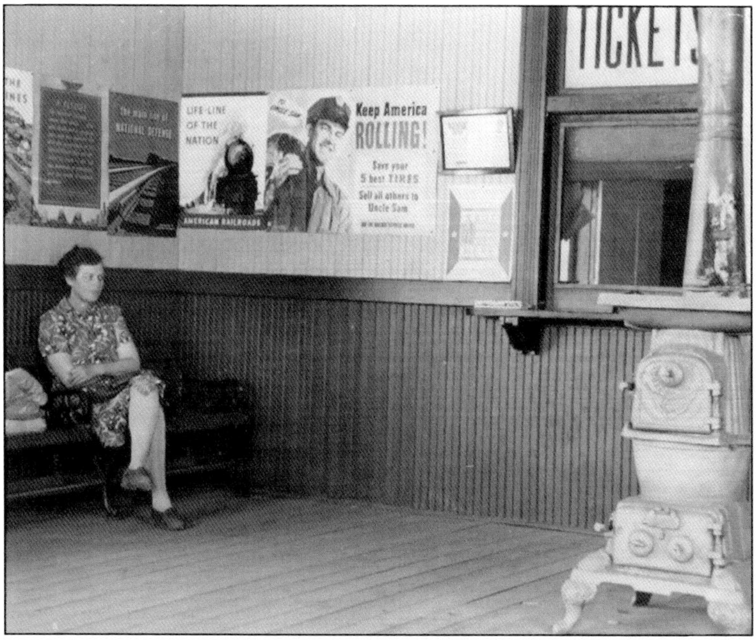

A woman believed to be Maureen Neeley waits patiently in the Santa Fe Depot in 1943, surrounded on all sides by war-related posters. Neeley, a resident of Jasper, often traveled by train to visit relatives in the San Augustine-Geneva area. Her children usually remained for longer visits while she returned home alone. (Photograph by John Vachon, OWI, Library of Congress.)

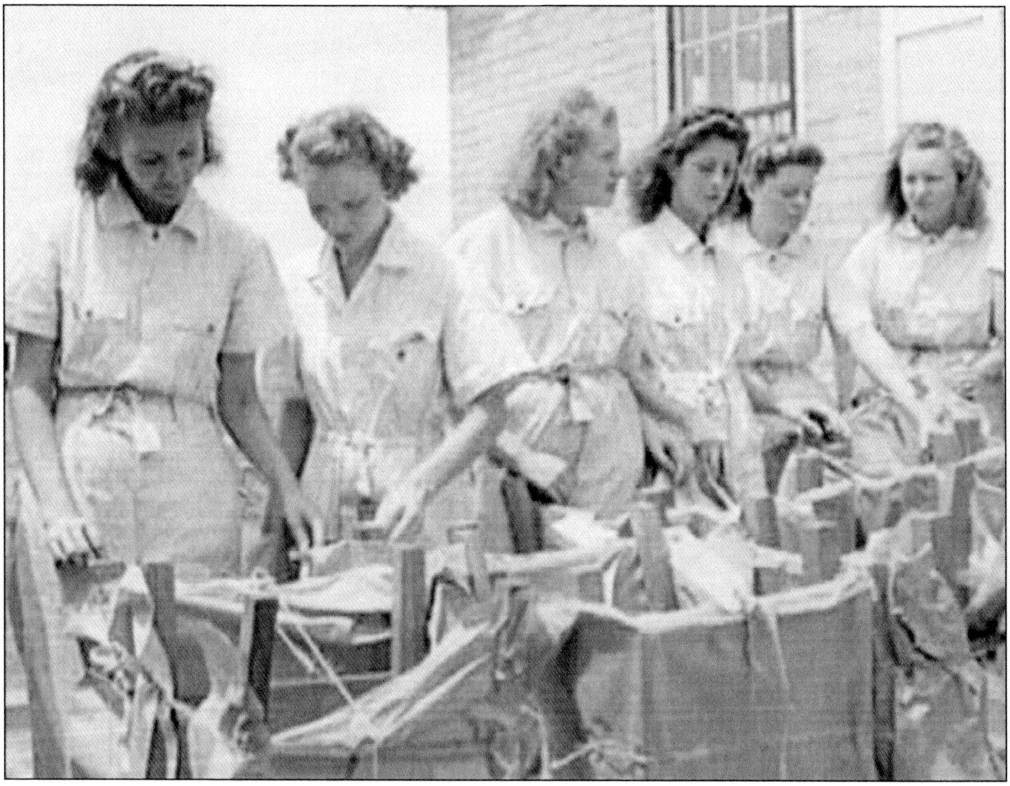

San Augustine County girls in the National Youth Administration's War Work Shops constructed wooden chairs for the war effort. These chairs were wrapped for shipping and then loaded onto trucks for transporting via Red Ball Freight Lines. (Photograph by John Vachon, OWI, 1943, Library of Congress.)

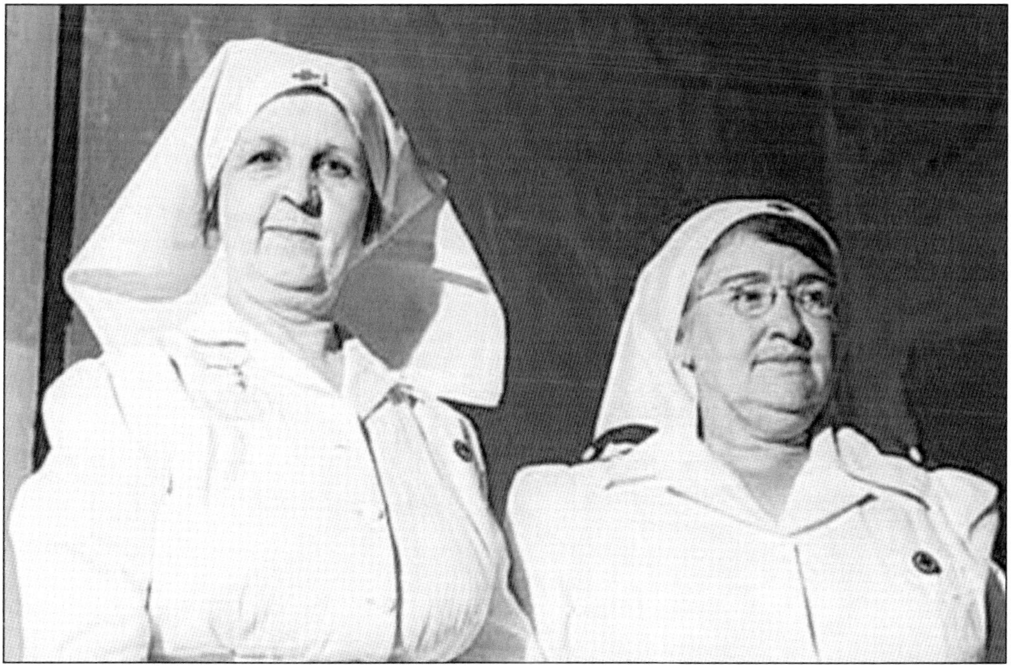

Florence Thomas (left) and Kate Rushing were cochairs of the San Augustine County women's group who made surgical bandages for the Red Cross. (Photograph by John Vachon, OWI, 1943, Library of Congress.)

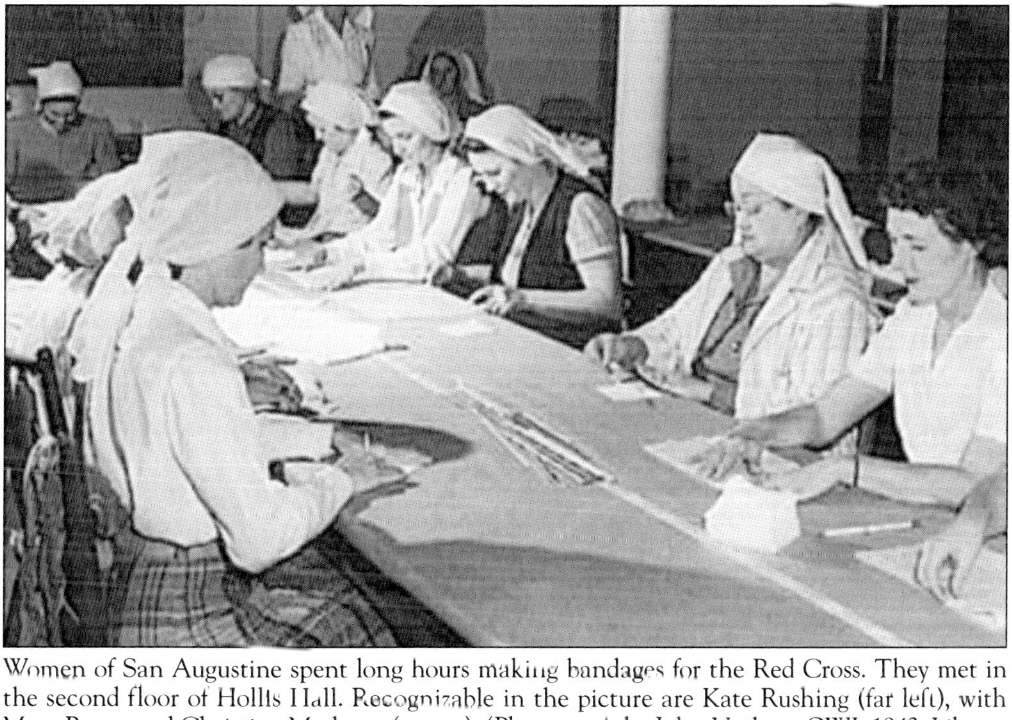

Women of San Augustine spent long hours making bandages for the Red Cross. They met in the second floor of Hollis Hall. Recognizable in the picture are Kate Rushing (far left), with Mary Bryan and Christine Mathews (center). (Photograph by John Vachon, OWI, 1943, Library of Congress.)

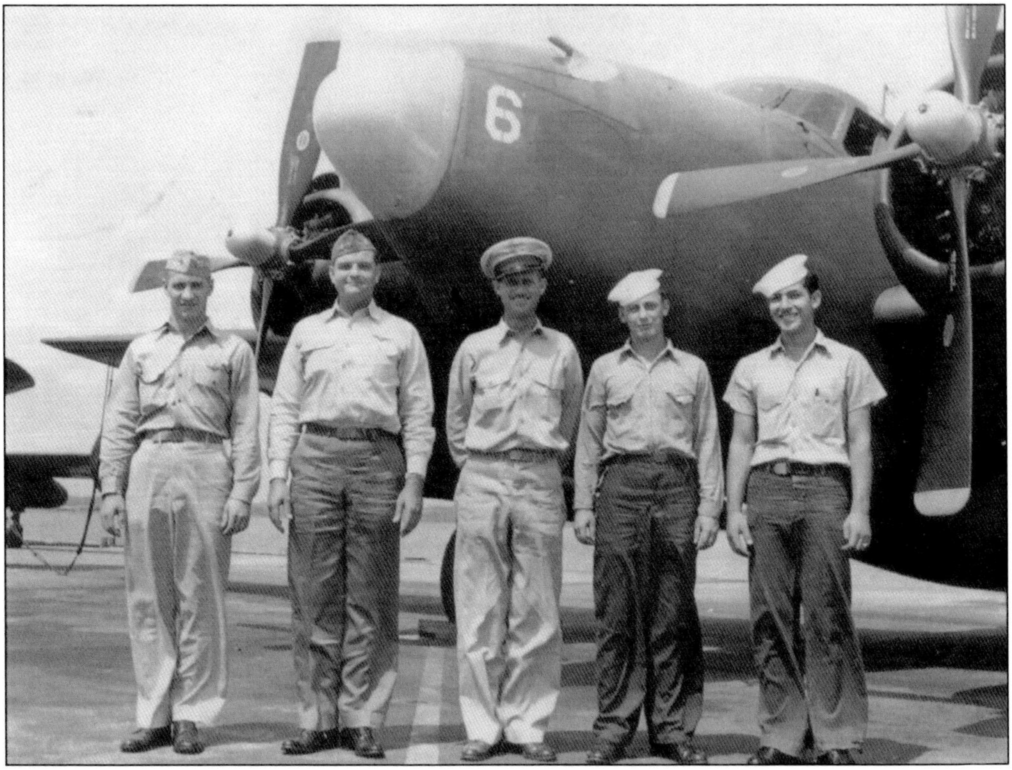

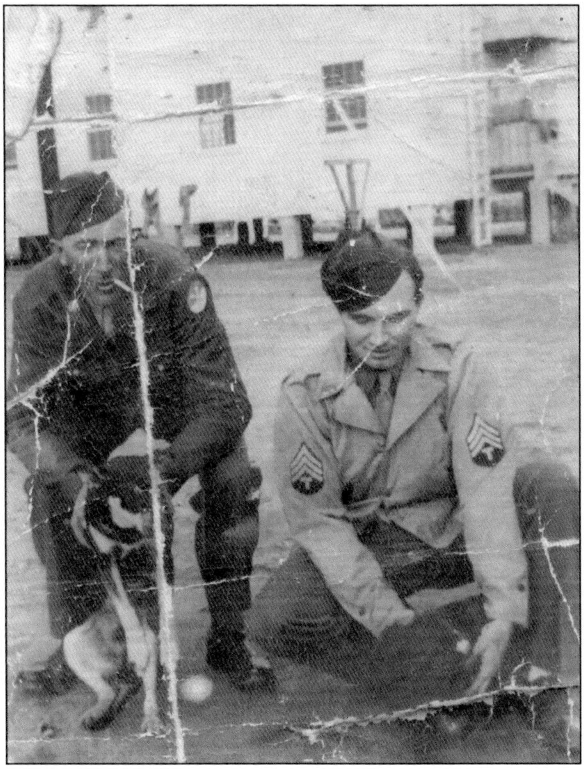

Navy pilot Val Sharp (left) is pictured with his crew in front of their Lockheed Harpoon PV-2. The navy primarily used this plane for antisubmarine patrol in both the Atlantic and Pacific Fleets. (Courtesy of Val Sharp.)

Clyde (Frog) Mathews, right, an army infantryman (foot soldier), traveled all the way across France during World War II. Frog often led the way as the infantry followed the mess truck, due to his extraordinary cooking ability. His homemade biscuits and gravy made him a favorite with the troops. After the war, he was in the road construction business with his brother Laurie (Boo) Mathews. In his spare time he still enjoyed cooking and became well known in San Augustine County for his excellent chili recipe. (Courtesy of Sharon Mathews Pollard.)

During his tenure in the U.S. Navy, Richard Murphy created a cartoon strip titled "Little Drip," which ran in the U.S. Navy newspaper *Hoist* in 1946. This photograph of Murphy was taken in San Diego, California. (Courtesy of Richard Murphy.)

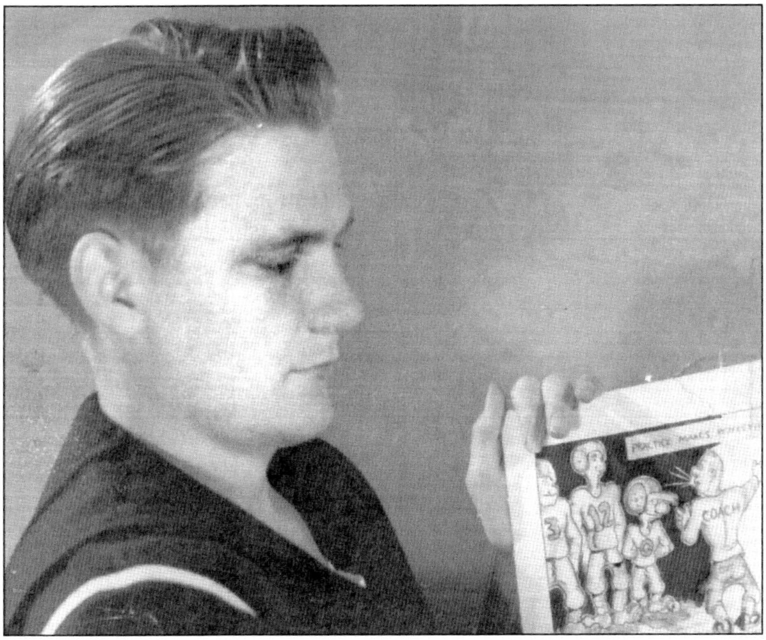

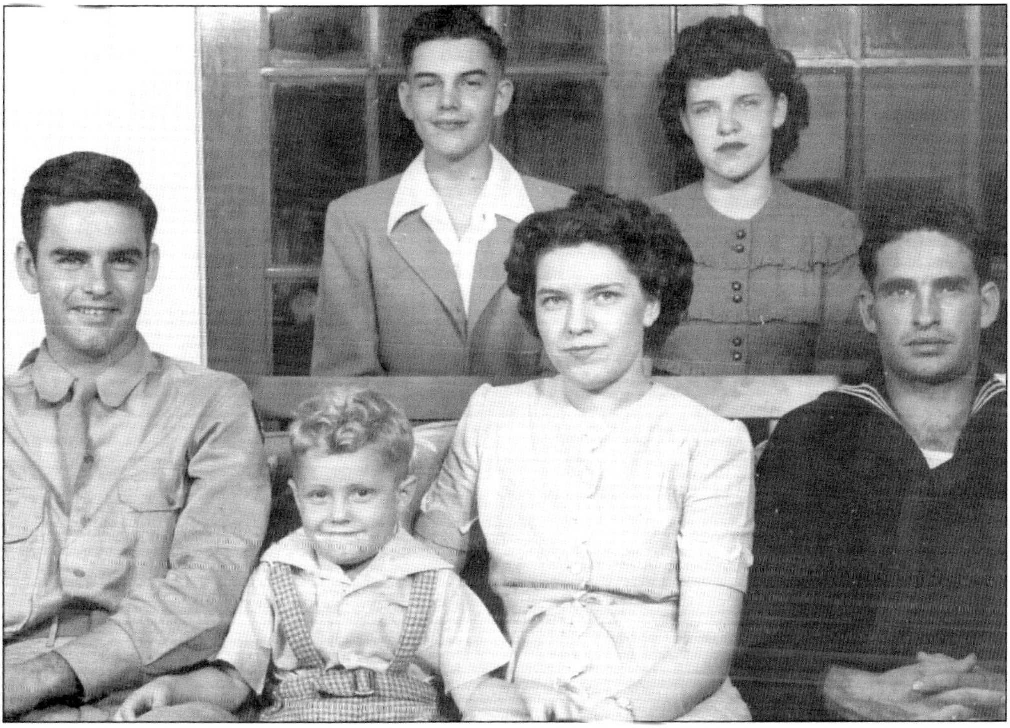

Members of the Epps family were together for this photograph taken in 1942. Pictured are, from left to right, (first row) Corkey Epps, Joe Bryan Bickley, Ruby Lillian Epps Bickley, and Wayne Epps; (second row) siblings R. E. Epps and Virginia Epps. (Courtesy of Joe Bryan and Nancy Bickley.)

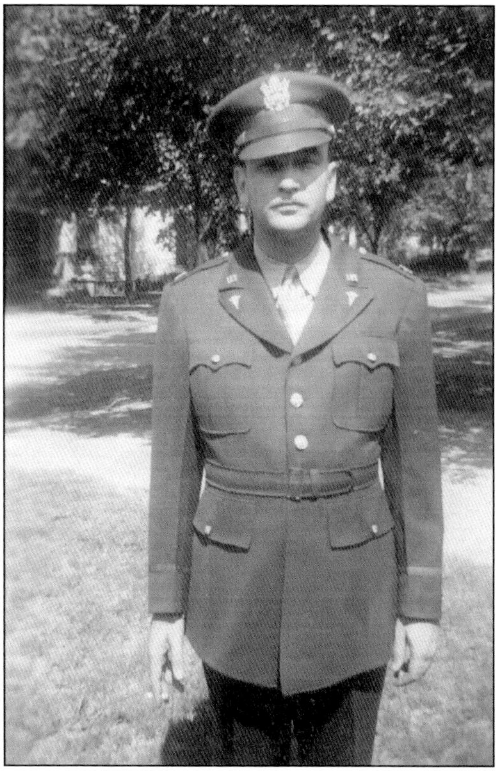

During World War II, San Augustine physician Dr. Ira F. Brake held the rank of major in the Army Medical Corps. He served first in North Africa, then in Italy. Later he transferred to the headquarters office of Gen. Mark Clark. Dr. Brake had begun his medical practice in San Augustine County in 1935 as a physician and surgeon. Over the years he delivered countless babies, many times in homes. After the war, he returned to San Augustine to resume his medical practice. There were no rural telephones in San Augustine County until years later, so oftentimes messages to the doctor were delivered "relay style." On one occasion the message was, "You'd best come on a mule . . . the creek's over the road, and the baby's coming." (Courtesy of Opal Ramsey.)

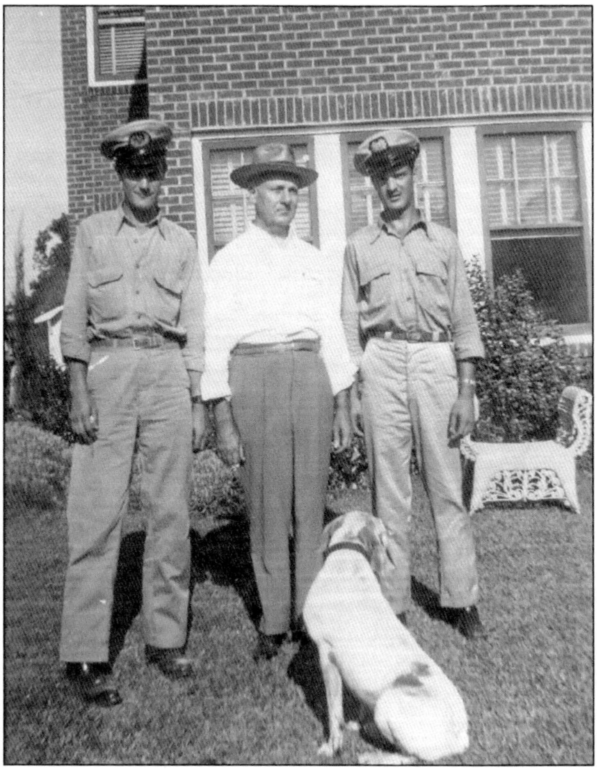

Ernest R. Sparks (center) is flanked by sons Leroy Sparks (left) and Hugh Sparks (right) during a furlough home in 1942. Ernest Sparks and his wife, Audra Ford, founded Home Life Association, a mutual insurance company, in 1936. Their seven children, Beeman, Marie, Frances, Hugh, Leroy, Betty Jean, and Claudine, worked in the family business during their early years. (Courtesy of Inez Sparks.)

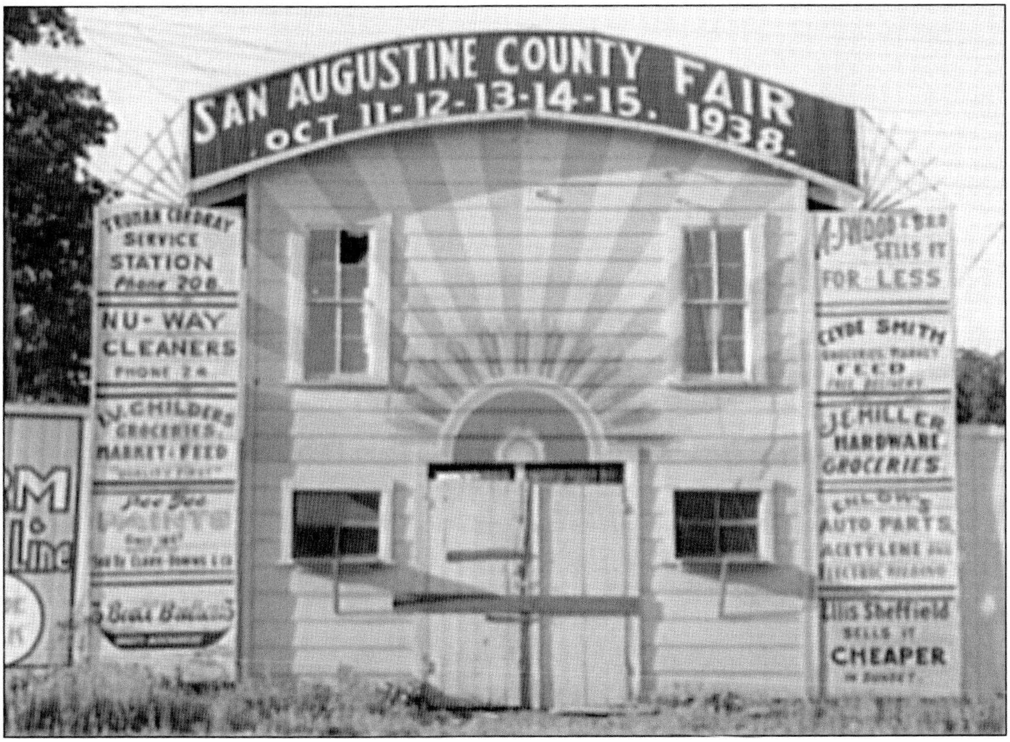

The large, several-acre site of the 1938 San Augustine County Fairgrounds was used for the prisoner of war camp at San Augustine during the years 1944–1945. Space constraints do not permit a long narrative describing events and persons at Camp San Augustine. Suffice it to say there are many heartwarming stories of friendships and lasting memories associated with that unique time in San Augustine County's history. (Photograph by Russell Lee, FSA, 1939, Library of Congress.)

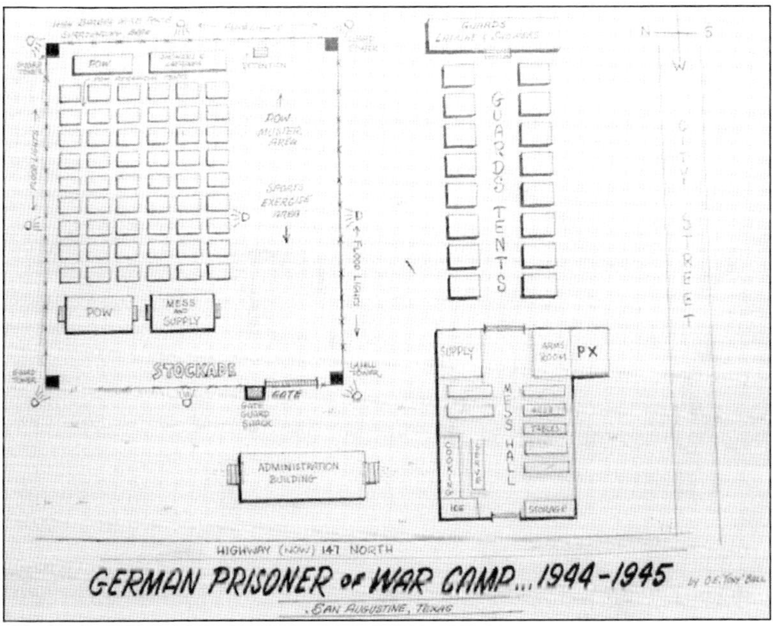

This layout of POW Camp San Augustine was taken from a drawing by supply sergeant O. E. (Tony) Ball. The prisoners were allowed to have cigarettes and beer. Supply sergeant Ball endeared himself to the POWs on one occasion when he brought a truckload of watermelons for their enjoyment. (Drawing courtesy of Tony Ball.)

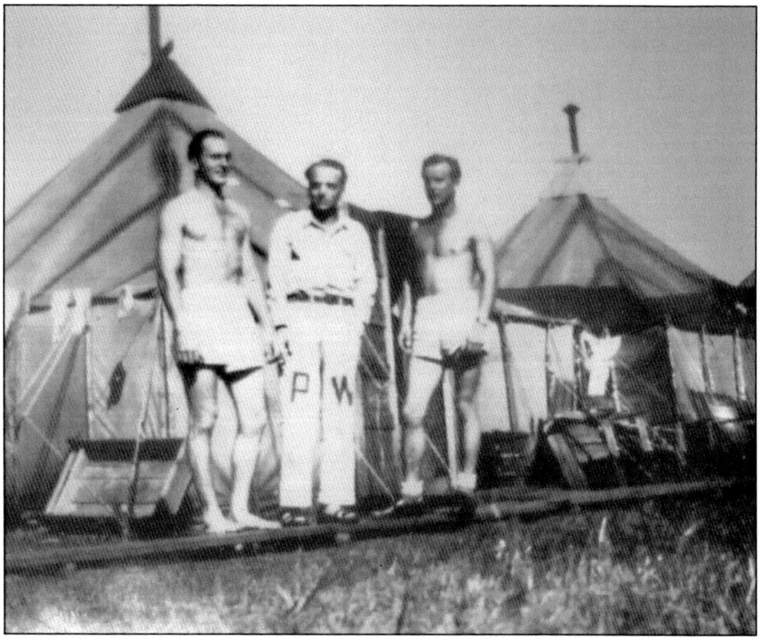

Three of the POWs (Rommel's troops) are shown in this photograph. Tents for their lodging are in the background. The Tannery family, owners of the Dorothy Mae Mattress Company, lived across the street from the POW camp and took the photographs shown in this chapter. (Courtesy of Dorothy Mae Tannery Wilkerson.)

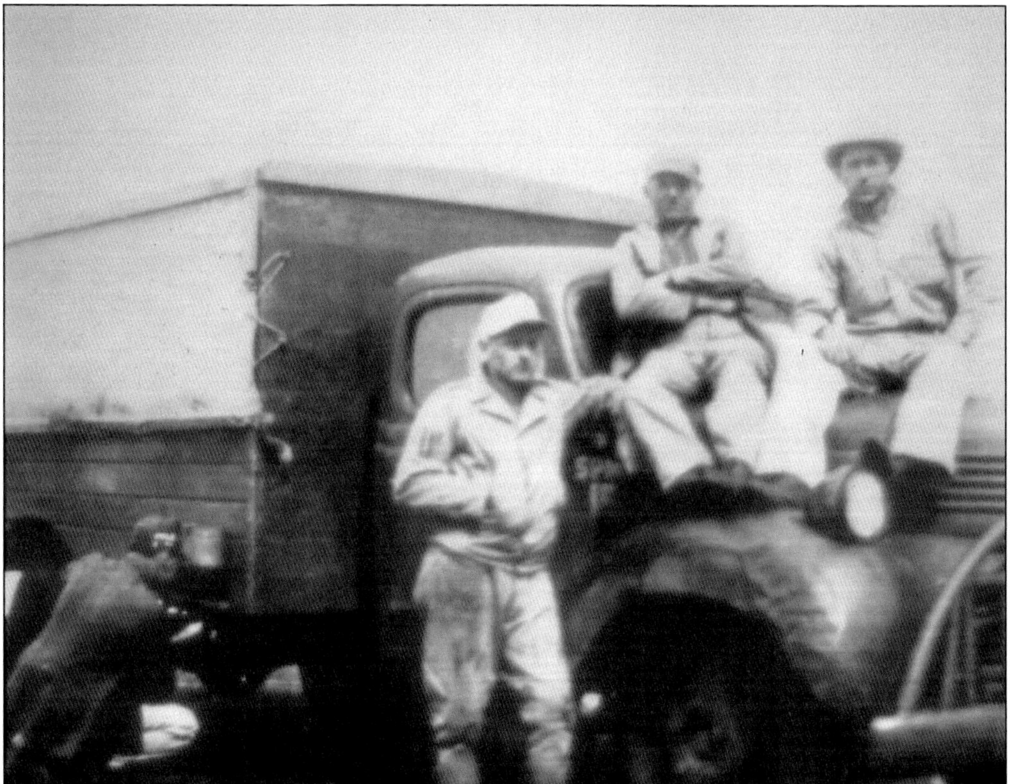

Pictured are three local men who served as guards/supervisors of the POWs during the harvesting of timber in the East Texas forests. (Courtesy of Dorothy Mae Tannery Wilkerson.)

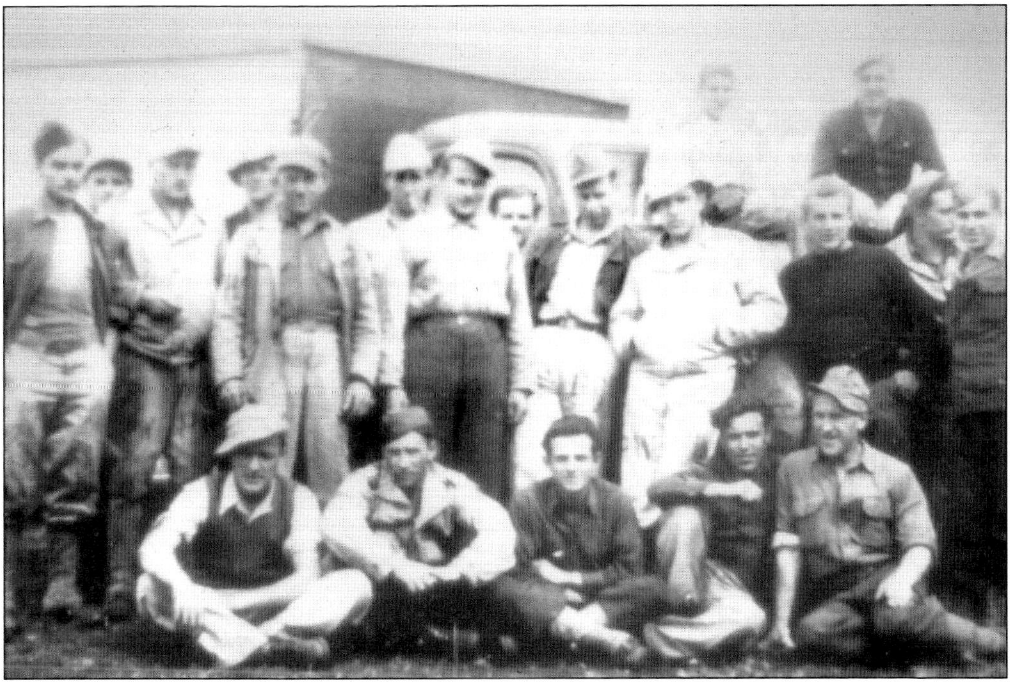

Military personnel, guards, and a few prisoners at POW Camp San Augustine gathered for this photograph. Tony Ball is seated at the far right. (Courtesy of Dorothy Mae Tannery Wilkerson.)

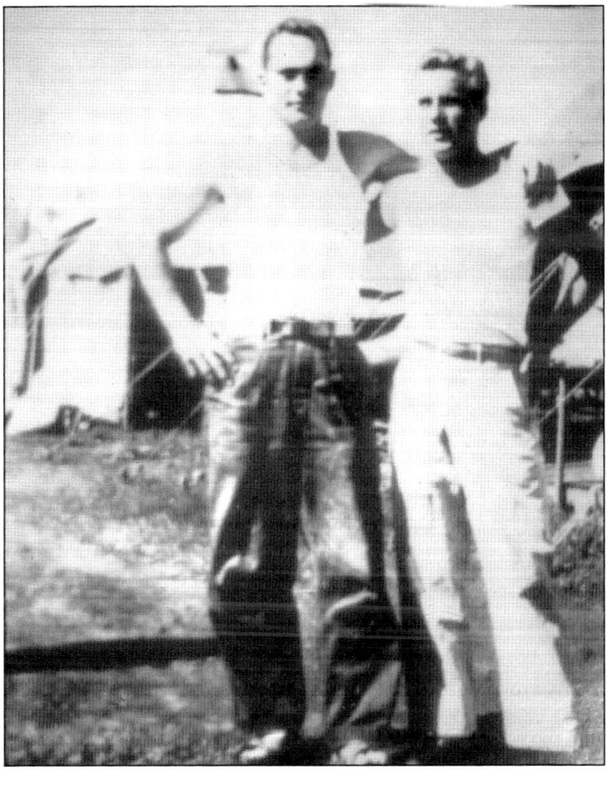

This photograph of two POW friends at Camp San Augustine reflects the noncombative demeanor generally felt by the prisoners. They were well treated and rarely attempted to escape. Tannery, when questioned as to whether his family felt afraid living so close to the camp, replied, "No, we're not afraid. If the POWs do escape, they are certainly going farther than our house." (Courtesy of Dorothy Mae Tannery Wilkerson.)

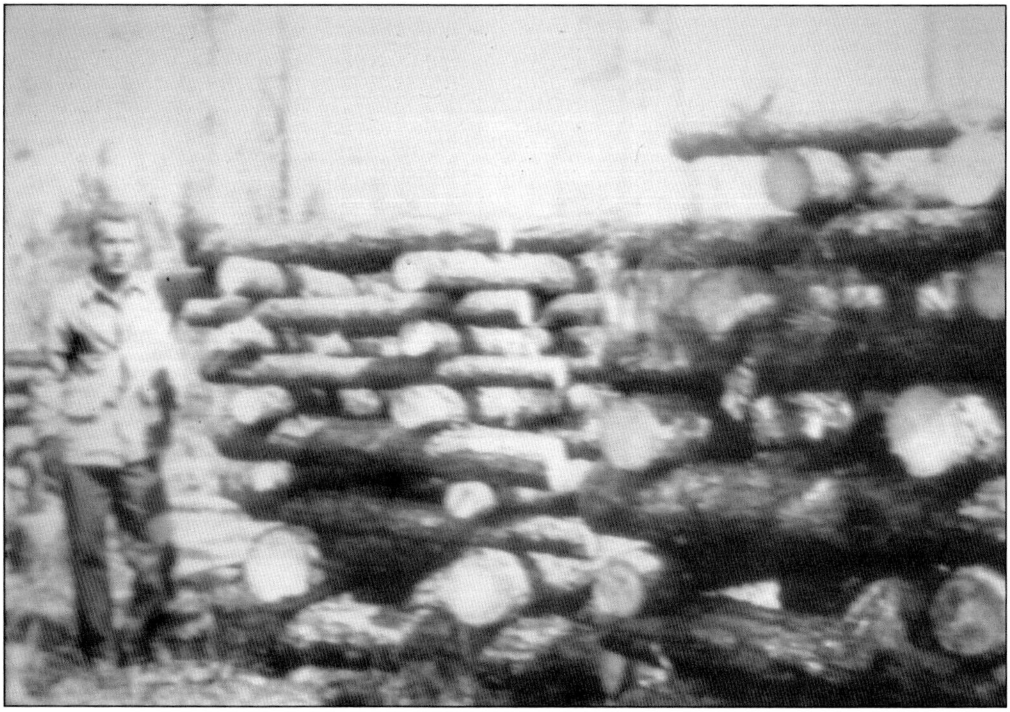

Pulpwood harvested by the POWs was stacked in this fashion. (Courtesy of Dorothy Mae Tannery Wilkerson.)

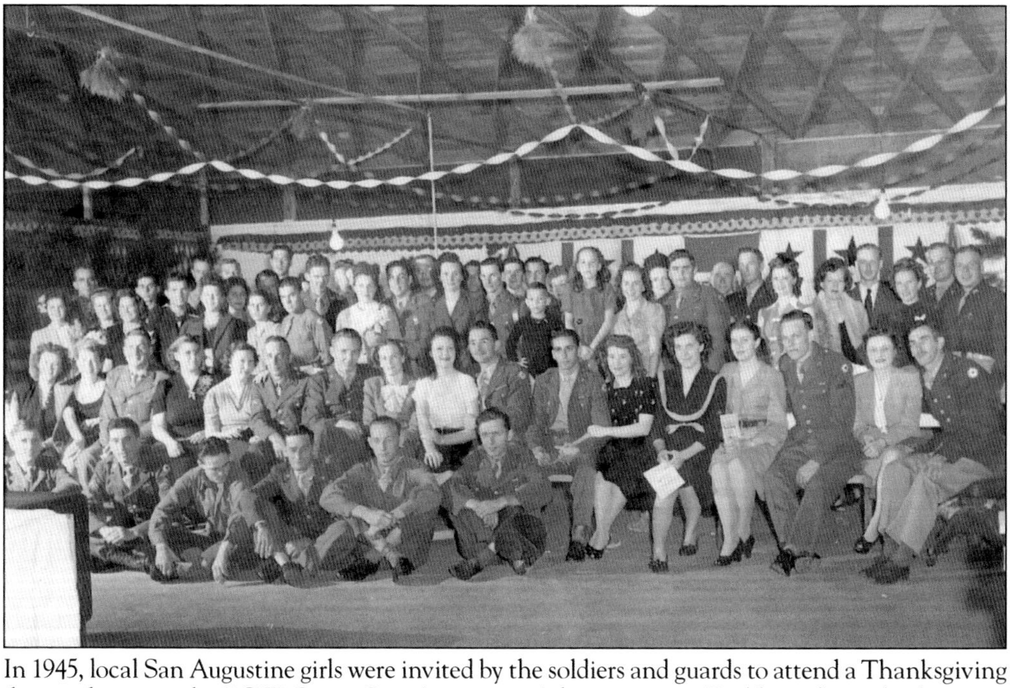

In 1945, local San Augustine girls were invited by the soldiers and guards to attend a Thanksgiving dinner dance in the POW Camp San Augustine Administration Building, formerly the main building of the San Augustine County Fairgrounds. The POWs assisted with cooking and serving the meal. (Courtesy of Dorothy Mae Tannery Wilkerson.)

Six

Our Folks and Their Worthy Pursuits

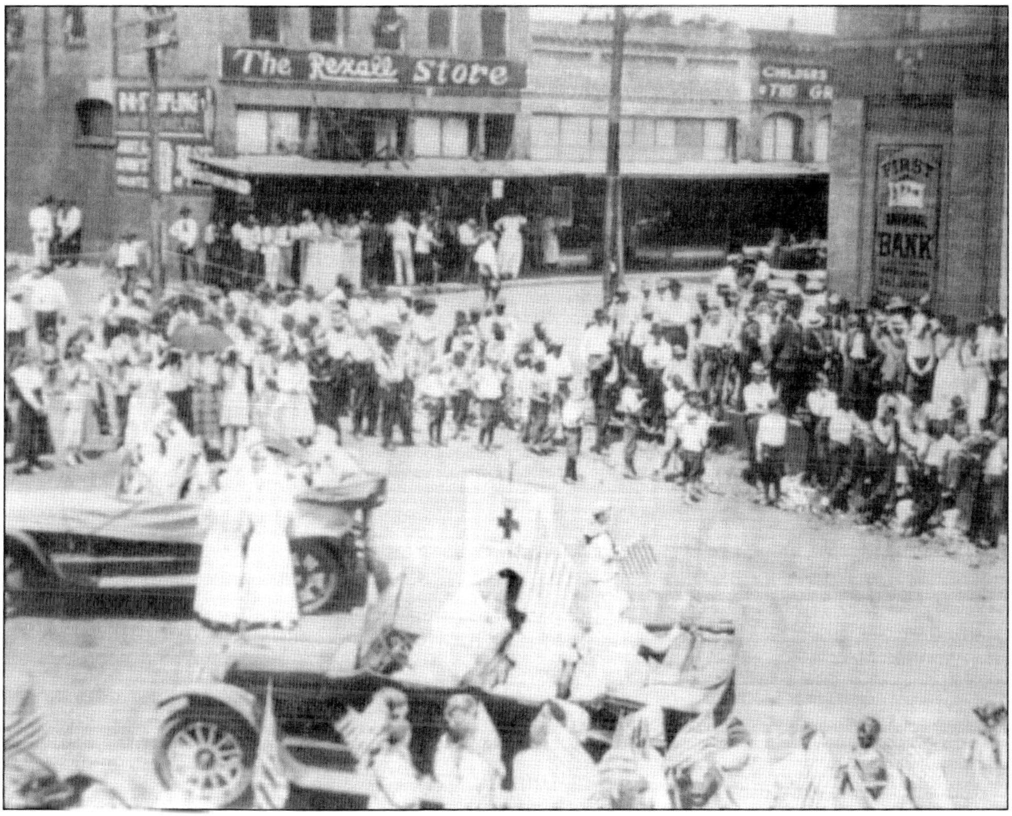

The 1917 Fourth of July parade brought out the usual large crowds to downtown San Augustine to join in the flag-waving festivities. (Author's collection.)

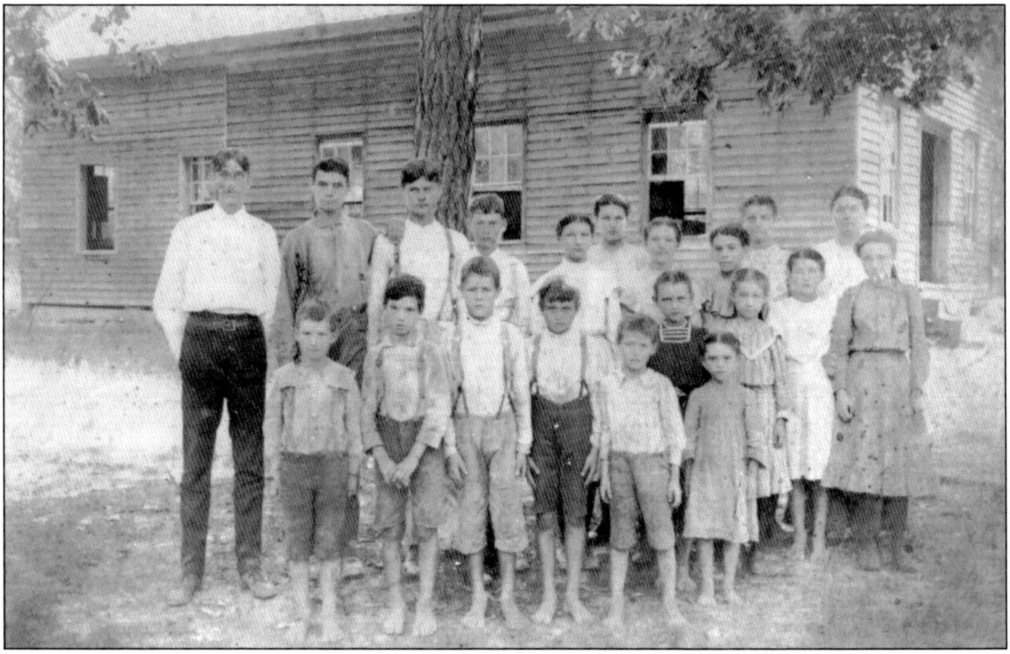

The old Liberty Hill schoolhouse was the setting for this photograph around 1902. The Liberty Hill Baptist Church now occupies this site. Identified in the picture are Olivia Bodine and Janie Bodine in the back row, both teachers at the school. (Courtesy of Al Broden.)

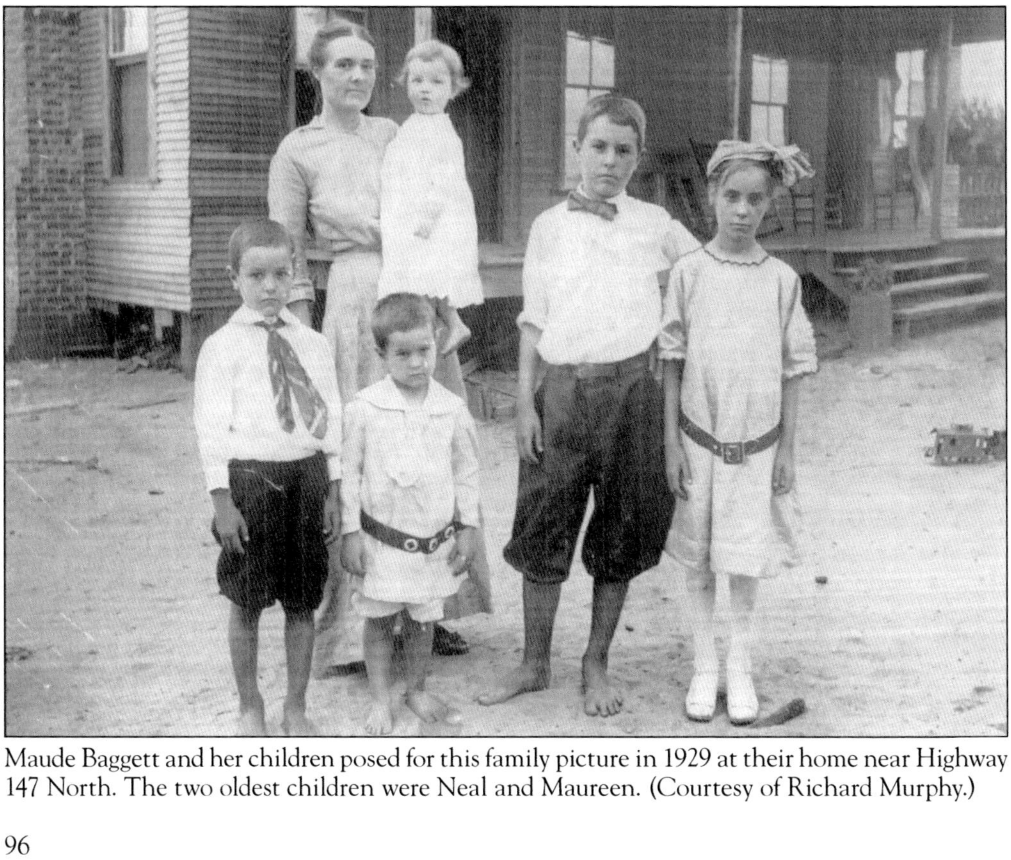

Maude Baggett and her children posed for this family picture in 1929 at their home near Highway 147 North. The two oldest children were Neal and Maureen. (Courtesy of Richard Murphy.)

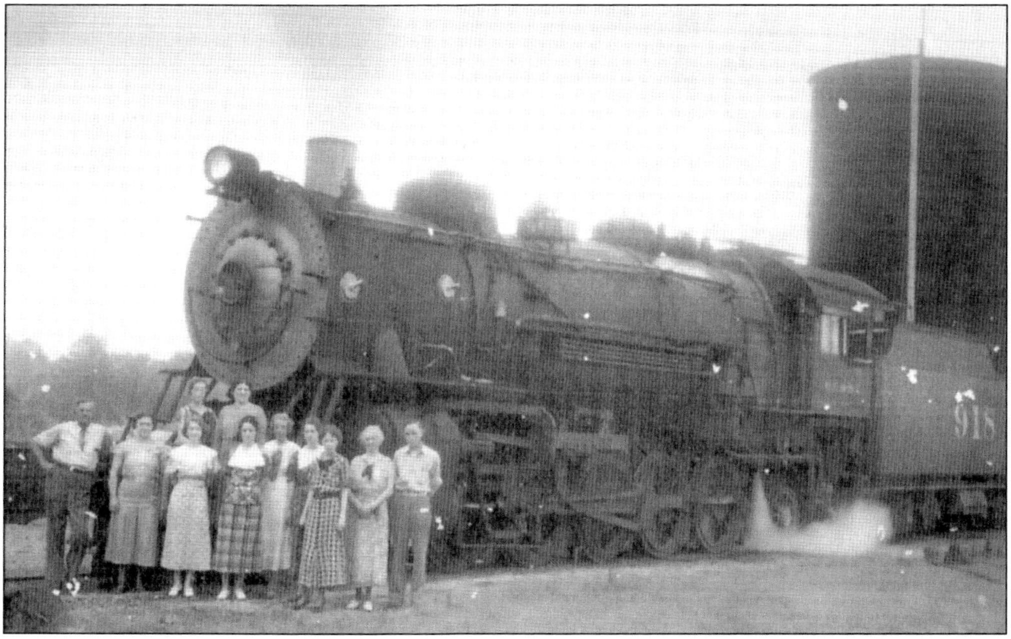

These folks gathered in front of the Gulf, Colorado, and Santa Fe engine for this picture taken in 1925. Recognizable in the group are Atheniar Wade, Lucille Whitehurst, and Exa Clark. (Courtesy of Nelsyn Wade.)

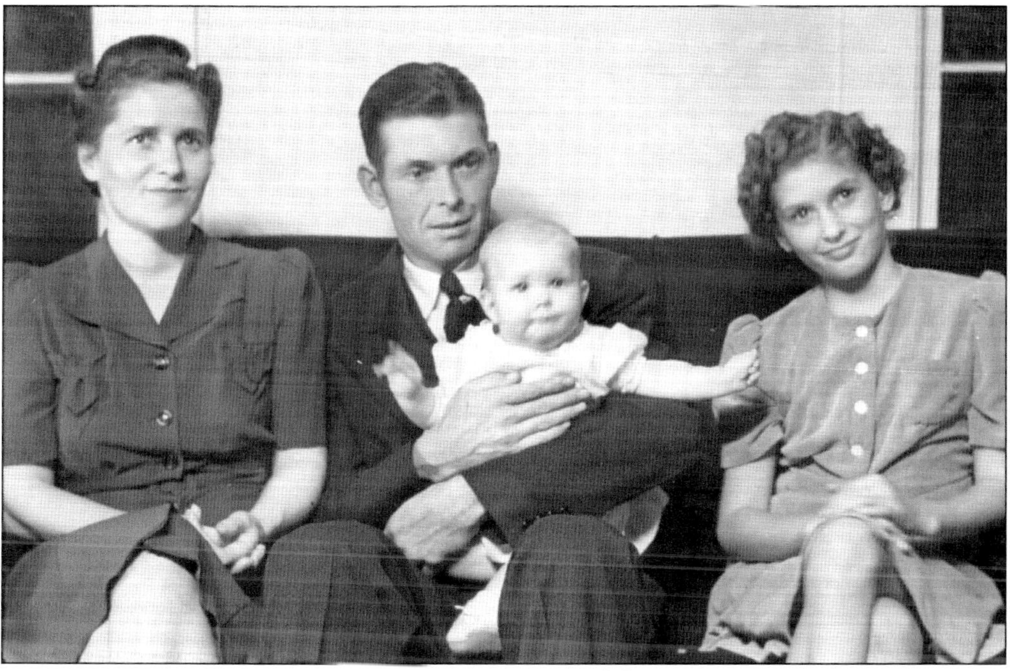

U.S. Forest Service ranger John Johnson holds daughter Johnida, flanked by his wife, Harlowe, and daughter Evva Dene. Johnson was actively involved with the Civilian Conservation Corps in San Augustine in 1933. Harlowe Johnson's career as a teacher spanned several generations, including serving as principal of San Augustine Elementary School. The elementary school gym is named in her honor. (Courtesy of James Williams.)

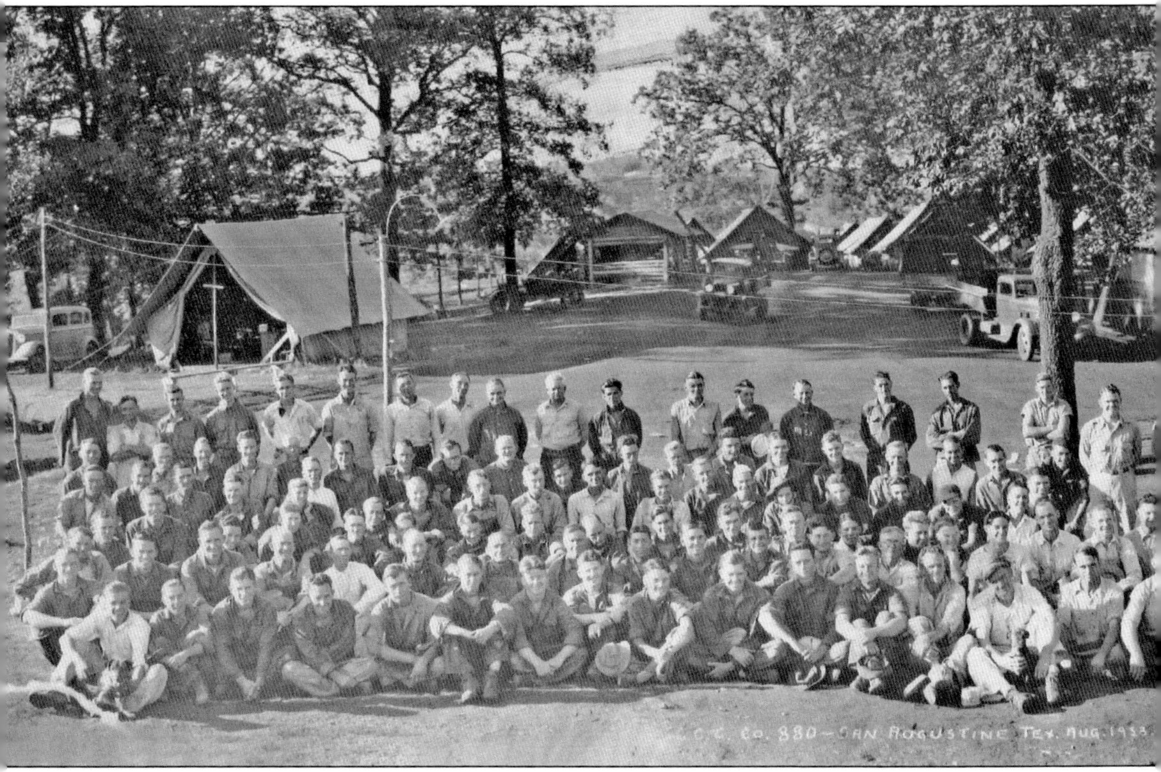

The Civilian Conservation Corps (CCC) was designed to provide employment for young men without jobs, typically ages 18 to 22, in the aftermath of the Great Depression. San Augustine County's CCC Camp enrollees are pictured above in 1933. The men were required to serve a minimum of six months, work a 40-hour week, and receive wages of $30 per month, of which $25

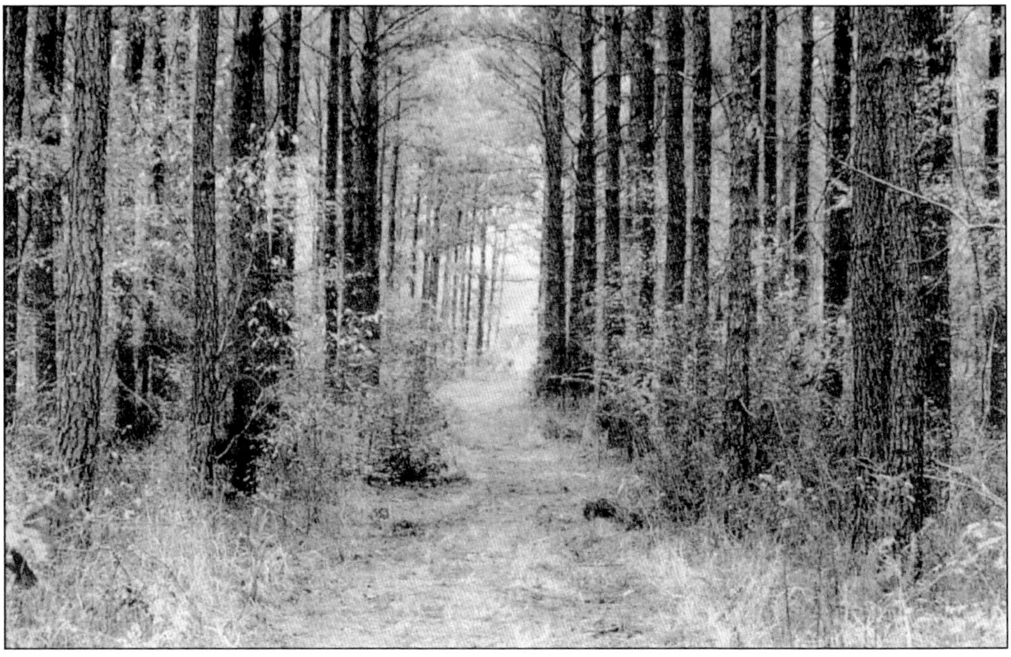

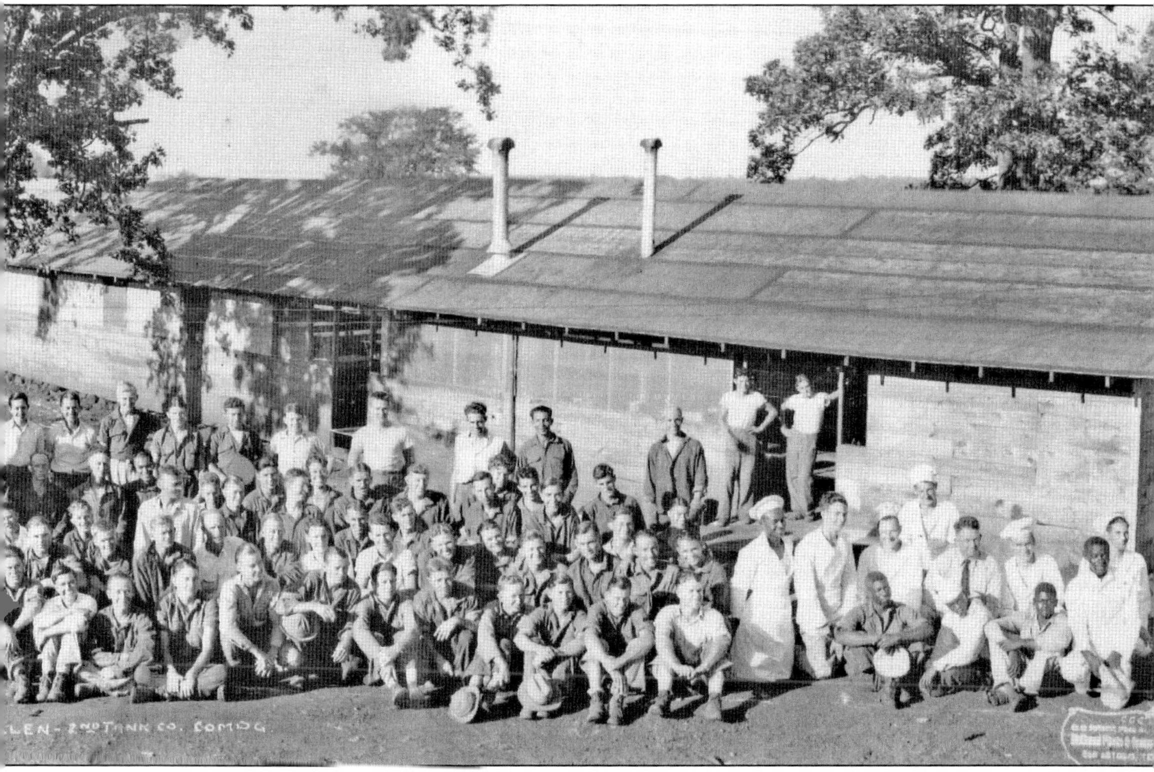

was sent directly to family dependents. U.S. Forest Service ranger John Johnson of San Augustine worked closely with this program. Seen in the images below, the forests and waterways of East Texas provided ample work space and training opportunities for the young men employed by the CCC. (Above, courtesy of R. D. Griffin; below, photographs by the author.)

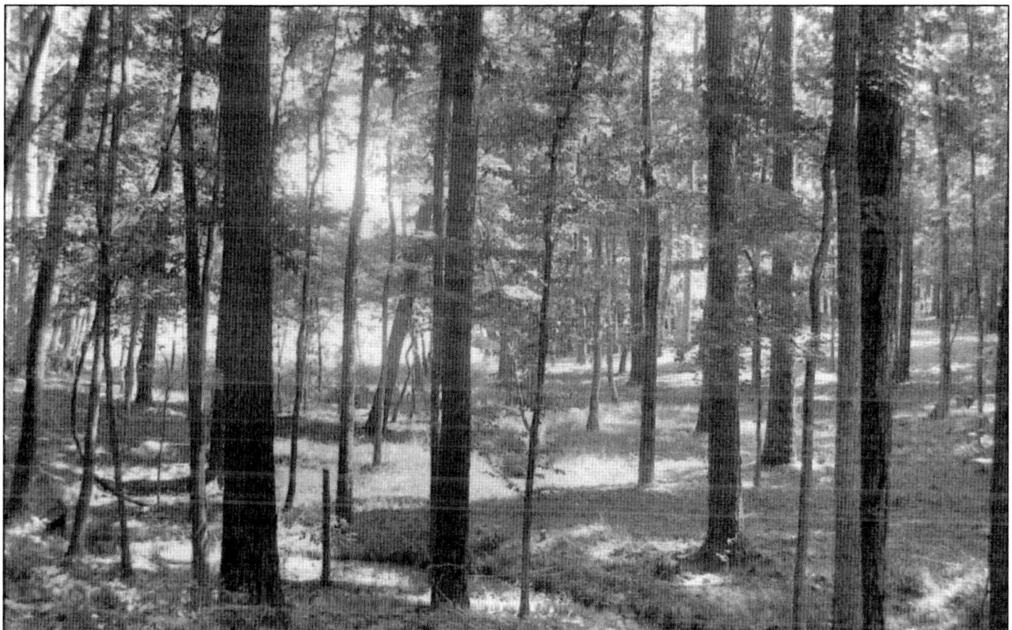

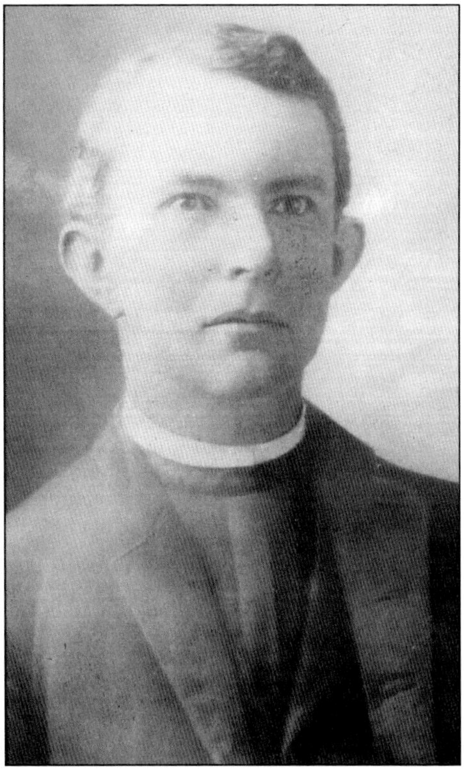

The Reverend Dr. George Louis Crocket received his education in San Augustine's public schools and at the University of the South in Sewanee, Tennessee. This photograph was taken soon after his graduation from Sewanee. Crocket was a meticulous historian whose book, *Two Centuries in East Texas*, has provided a wealth of historical information on every facet of life in San Augustine County through the 1930s. (Courtesy of Christ Episcopal Church; photograph by author.)

In November 1911, the Reverend Dr. George L. Crocket organized Boy Scout Troop No. 1 in Texas in San Augustine. This picture was taken on January 29, 1928, in Nacogdoches, Texas. Dr. Crocket is pictured (second row, second from left) in this group of area Boy Scouts. San Augustinian Charles McMillan, age 12, is also pictured (second row, right). In later years, McMillan established his law practice in San Augustine and served as county attorney. The event pictured was in honor of visiting chief Scout executive James E. West, of Washington, D.C. (Courtesy of James Williams and Jerry Payne.)

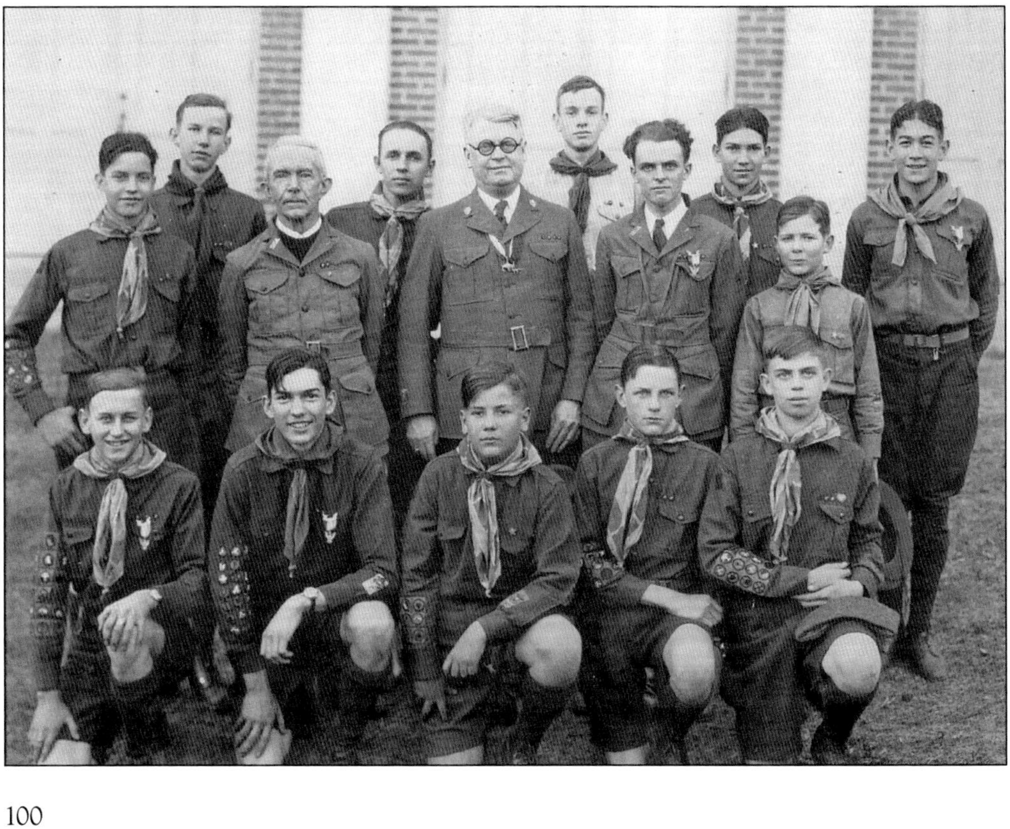

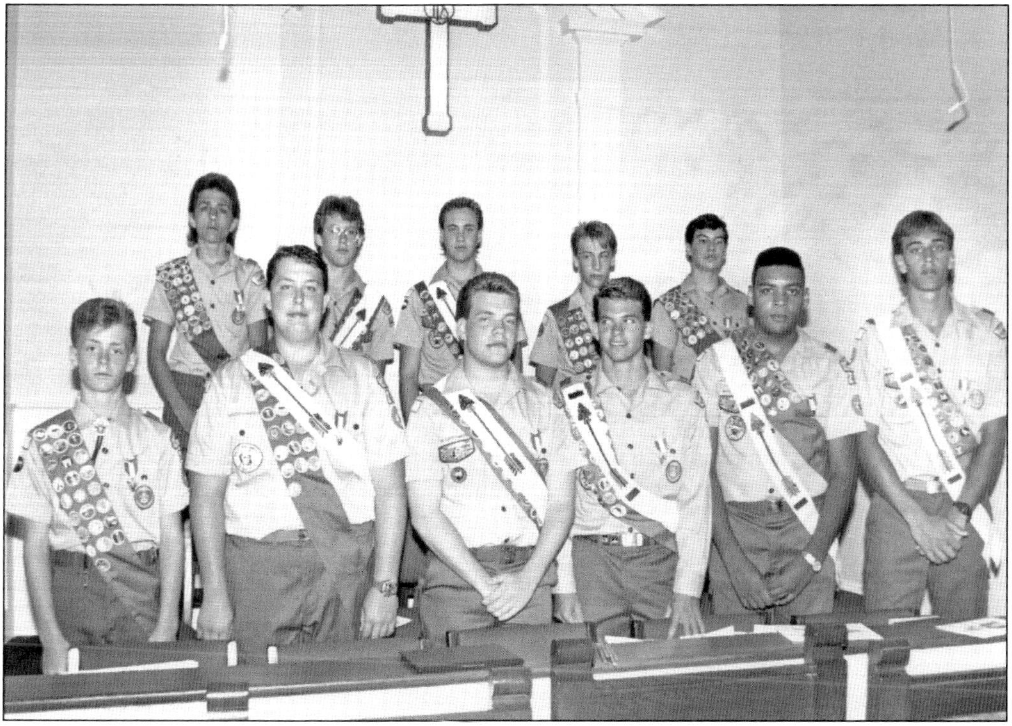

Because of the foresight and diligence of Dr. Crocket and the scoutmasters who followed him, scouting has continued over the ensuing years in San Augustine County. In June 1989, eleven scouts received scouting's highest honor, the Eagle Award. This was the largest number of recipients at one time in the local troop's history. Scouts honored were, from left to right, (first row) John Raymond Johnson, John Fussell, Jason Ellis, Scott Castle, Dexter Richards, and Forrest Oglesbee; (second row) William Hoverson, Cade Downs, Charles Goodwin, Eric Goodwin, and Greg Sherman. (Courtesy of *San Augustine Tribune*.)

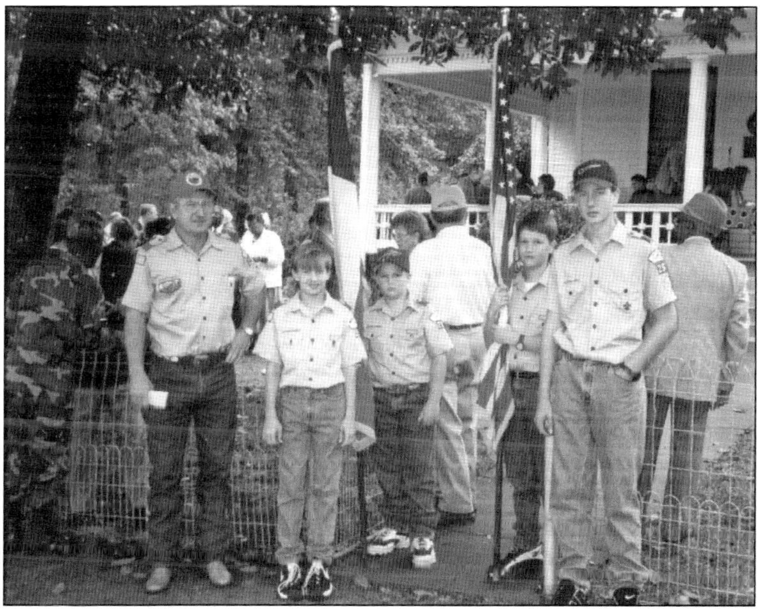

A group of scouts with scoutmaster John Mathews assisted with a patriotic ceremony at the historic Fisher-Bland Home in the mid-1990s. (Photograph by the author.)

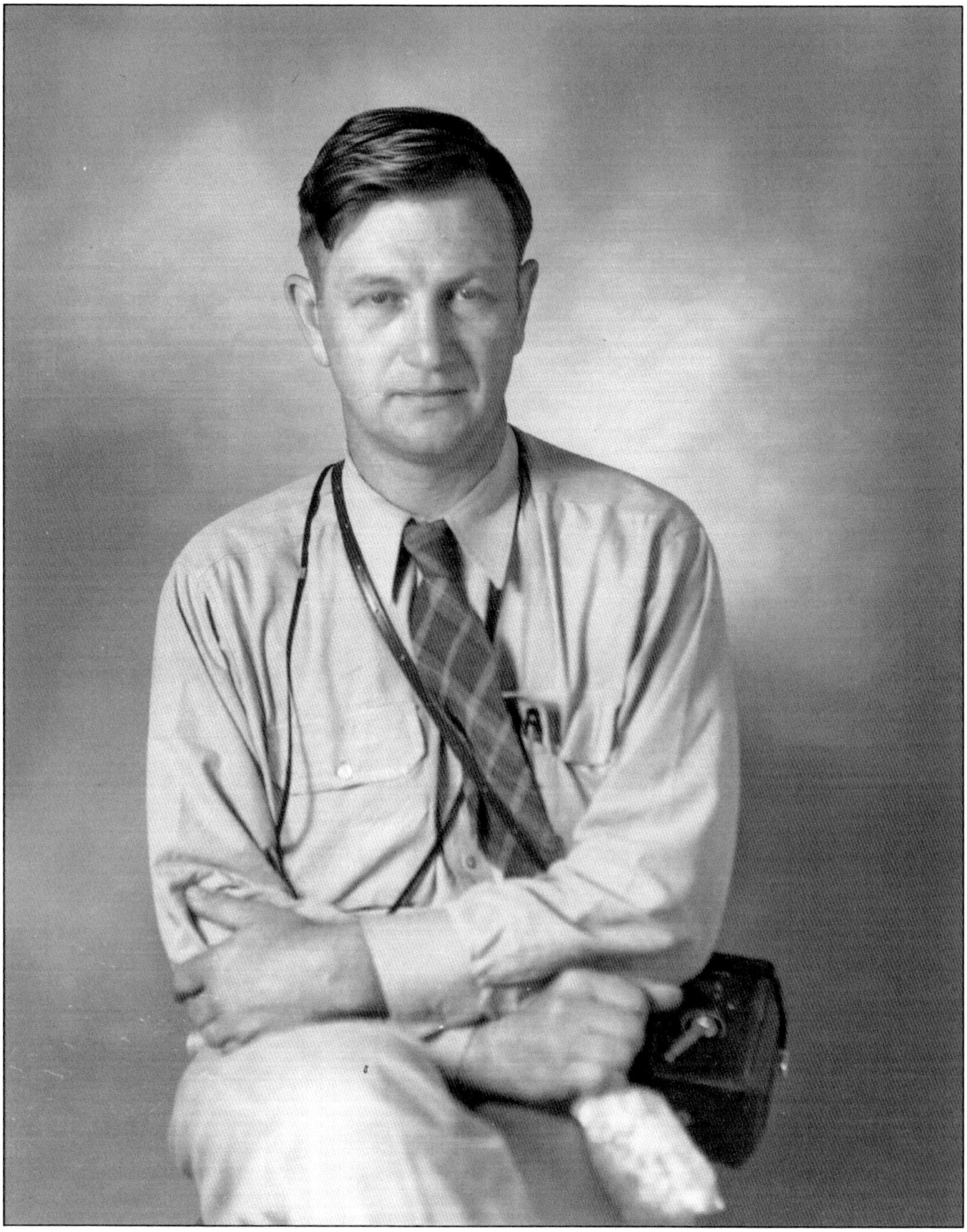

In 1939, U.S. Farm Security Administration photographer Russell Lee was instructed to make a documentary of small town rural life after the Depression. He and his wife, Jean, came to San Augustine, where they stayed at the Hotel Hampton. After Lee's death, Richard Murphy had occasion to visit with Jean, who said, "When we came to San Augustine we stayed at a real nice hotel, and we loved the food there. Instead of moving on, we decided to stay for awhile. Russell took thousands of photos in San Augustine, with more than 300 now in the Library of Congress." (Courtesy of Richard Murphy.)

Mary Bryan, whose home-cooking skills were legendary, was the hospitable owner of Hotel Hampton. It is unusual for a small town such as San Augustine to receive such in-depth coverage as indicated by the photographic images from 1939 and again from 1943, when John Vachon of the Office of War Information came. Turns out that Lee and Vachon worked together in the same photography group for the U.S. government. Many San Augustinians are convinced that Lee encouraged Vachon to come to rural East Texas, specifically San Augustine, where he would be welcomed and fed like a king. (Courtesy of *San Augustine Tribune*.)

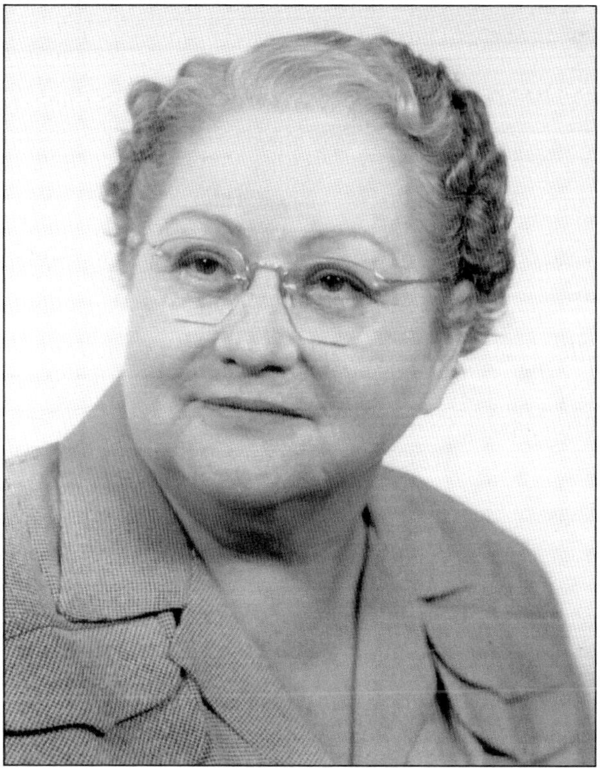

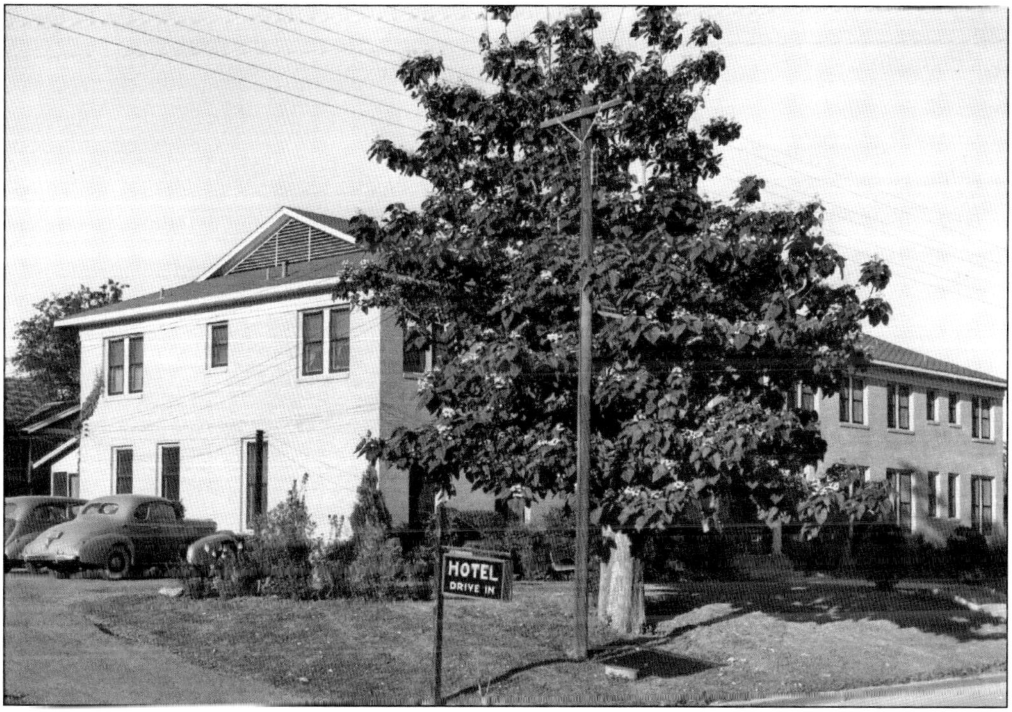

Russell Lee photographed the Hotel Hampton in the spring of 1939, when he and Jean, his wife, were in San Augustine. (Russell Lee, FSA, 1939, Library of Congress.)

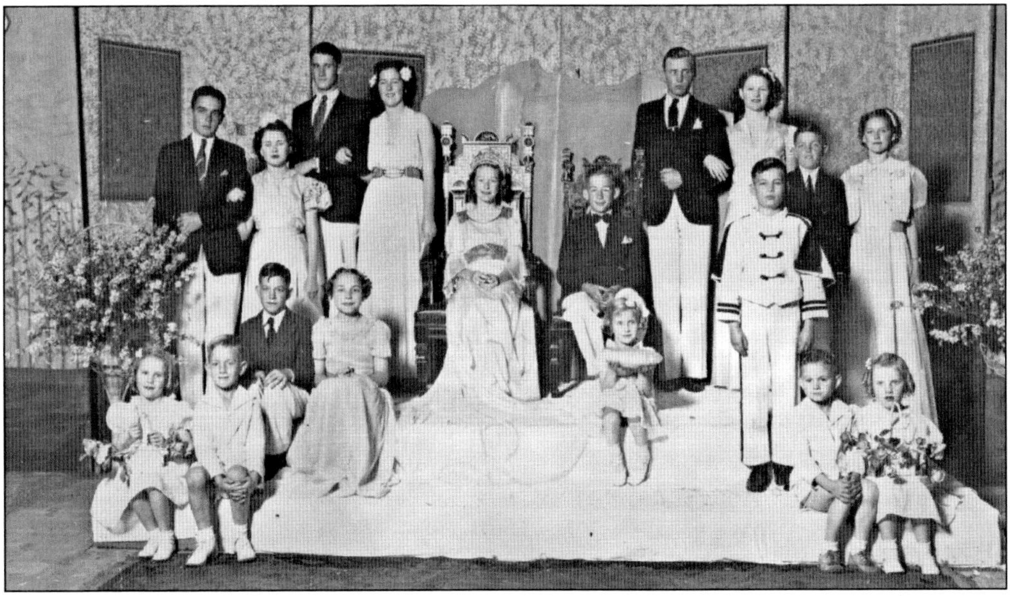

The San Augustine High School King and Queen Court was always an anticipated event. In 1938, participants included "Queen" Ann Hall and "King" Edward Thomson Jr. Pictured are, from left to right, (first row) McXie Whitton, John Harvey Butts, Bobby Perry, and Miriam Whitton; (second row) Kenneth Stephenson, Sue Caldwell, Sue Butts, and Curtis Haley or Arthur Smith Jr. (standing); (third row) Henry Sublett, Johnnie Taylor, Gene Bishop, and Wilma Berry; (fourth row) Hugh Sparks, Kathallen Cobb, Ann Hall, Edward Thomson Jr., Hollis Eppes, and Lois Butler. (Courtesy of Dr. C. R. Haley.)

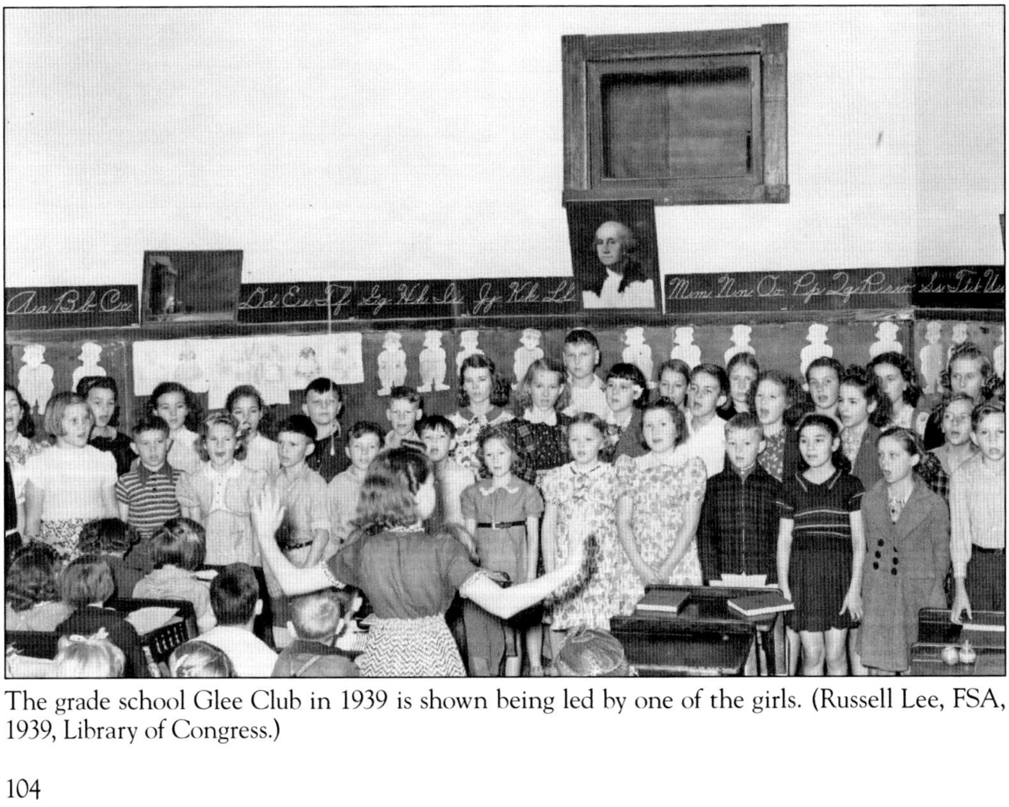

The grade school Glee Club in 1939 is shown being led by one of the girls. (Russell Lee, FSA, 1939, Library of Congress.)

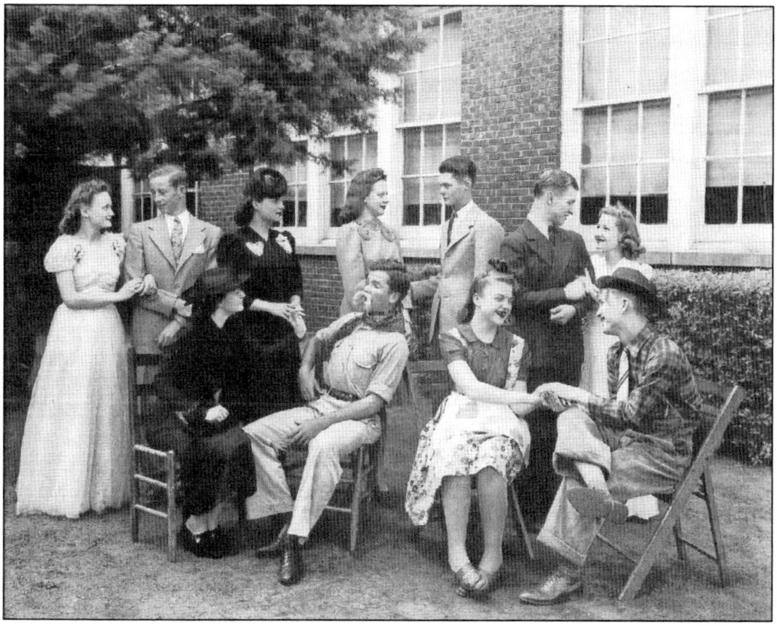

The senior class play of 1941 featured, from left to right, (first row) Anne Hall, Kenneth Skillern, Dorothy Nan Ingram, and Eugene Tannery; (second row) Juanell Smith, Edward Thomson Jr., Hattie Mills, Addie Lou Bogard, James Nichols, Val Sharp, and Johnnie Fay Hines. (Courtesy of Val Sharp.)

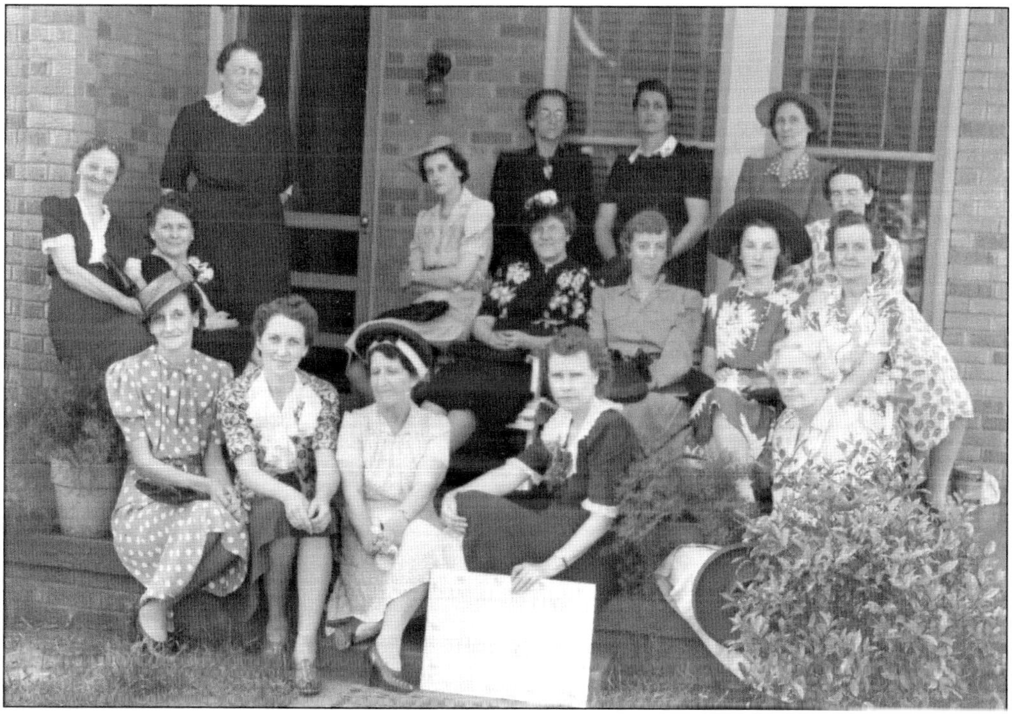

San Augustine Study Club's members are pictured in 1941. This forward-thinking group is considered the forerunner of two of today's influential women's organizations: San Augustine Garden Club and Women's Service League. Pictured are, from left to right, (first row, seated) Lena Jones, Bennie Youngblood, Alice Corts, Blanche Richey, and Mary Blount; (second row, seated) Florence Eddings, Avis Smith, Anna V. Cartwright, Atheniar Wade, Lucille Whitehurst, Frances Wood, Leila V. Rushing, and Anna Fay Wood; (third row, standing) Vera Hanks, Minnie Thomson, Mrs. M. M. Calloway, and Vera Nooner. (Courtesy of Martha Butts and Nelsyn Wade.)

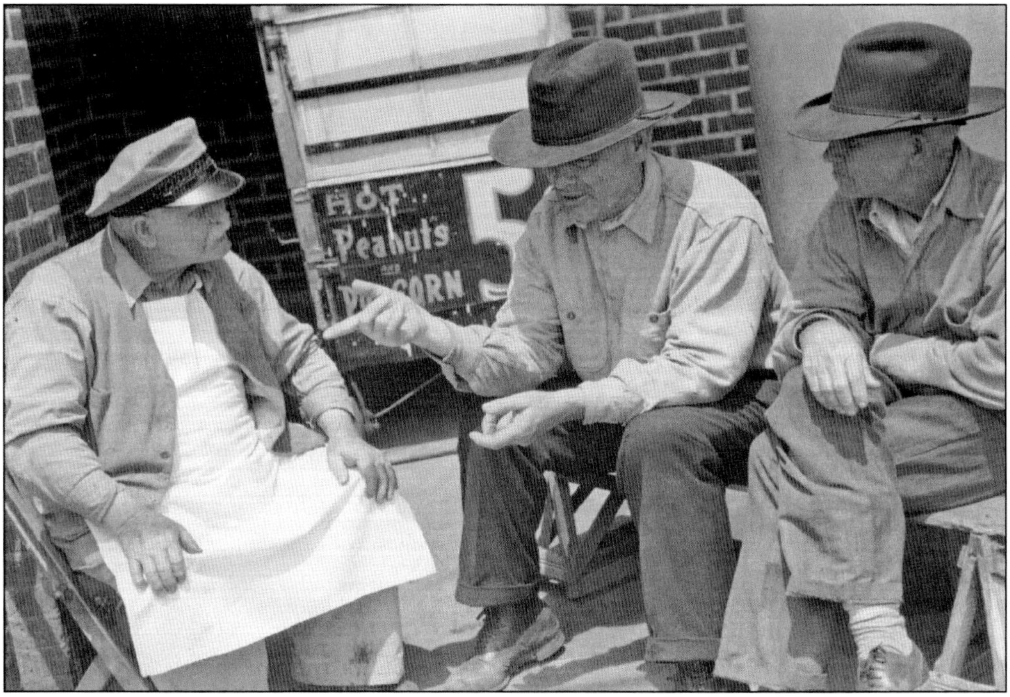

"Pop," or Joe McKechney (left), was the popcorn and peanut man in San Augustine. (John Vachon, 1943, OWI, Library of Congress.)

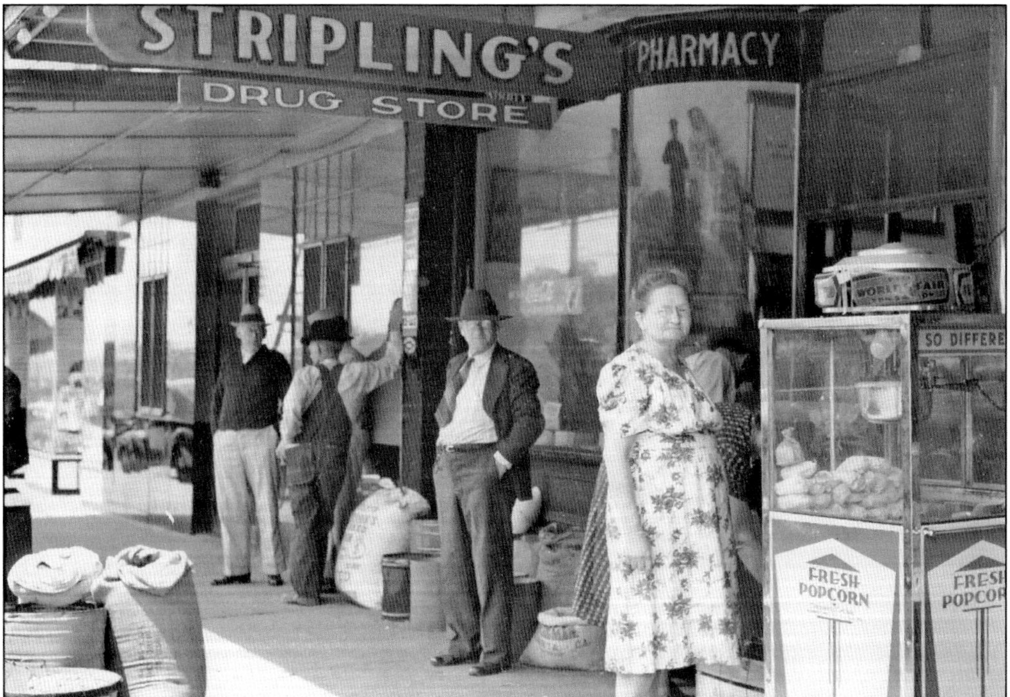

By 1943, downtown San Augustine had become more modern in appearance. Obviously San Augustinians were still enjoying popcorn. (Courtesy of Richard Murphy.)

Oscar Taylor posed in front of his country store in the 1930s. He loved history and enjoyed sitting for hours on the hookworm bench at his store visiting with friends Lee Whitton, the Reverend C. A. Tower, Dr. George Crocket, Lister Smith Sr., Holman Price, Ralph Sharp, Baxter Cartwright Sr., Willie Sharp, and W. K. (Bud) Knight. Out front stood two vintage gasoline pumps with see-through glass containers filled with bright orange fuel. Children liked to spend their allowances there for penny Baby Ruths and nickel soft drinks. They enjoyed petting Oscar's dog, a want-to-be-collie named Watch. Taylor's wife, Belle Johnson Taylor, was one of the last living real Daughters of the Republic of Texas. (Author's collection.)

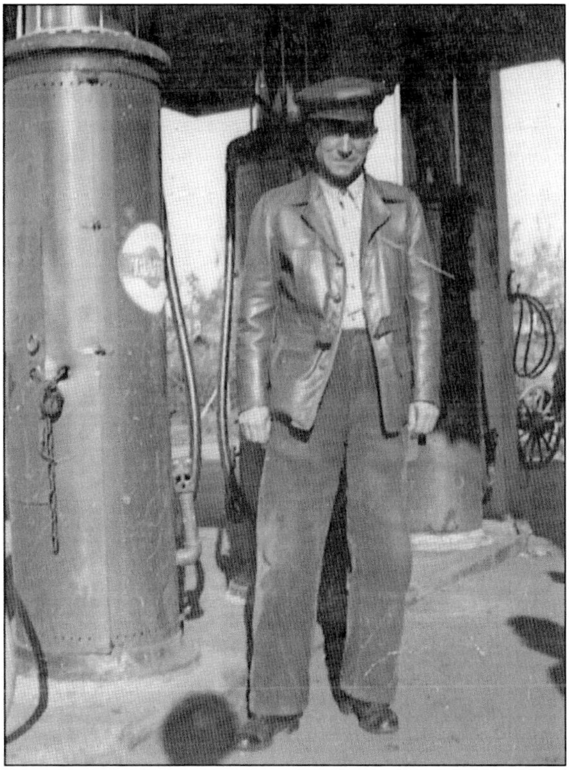

The Auction Barn in 1939 was bustling with activity on weekly auction day. (Russell Lee, FSA, Library of Congress.)

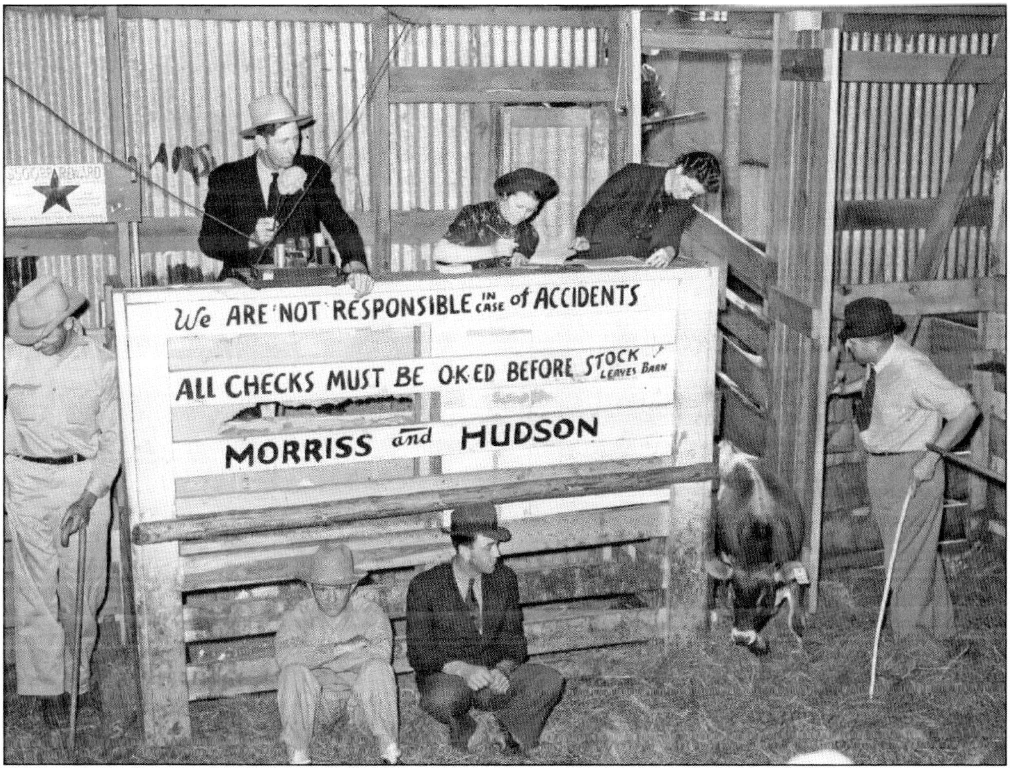

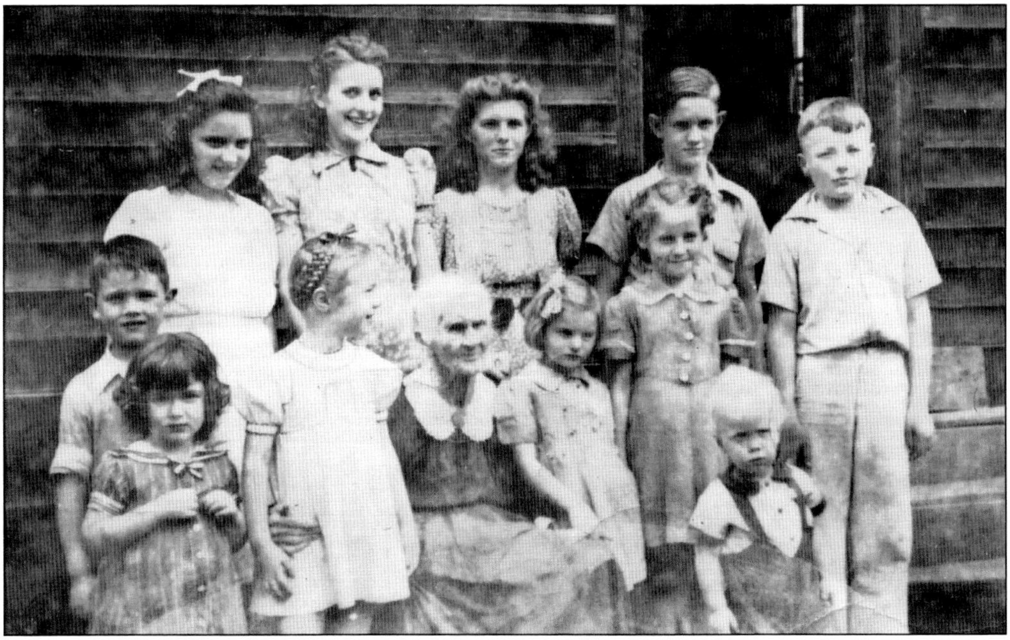

Family members gathered in 1941 with great-grandmother Knight. Pictured are, from left to right, (first row) Charlotte Anne Dorsey and Carl Francis Dyes; (second row) James Williams, Charlotte Ruth Washington, great-grandmother Knight, and two Martin children; (third row) Dorothy Knight, Agnes Williams, two more Martin children, and Jack Parker. (Courtesy of James Williams and Agnes Sparks.)

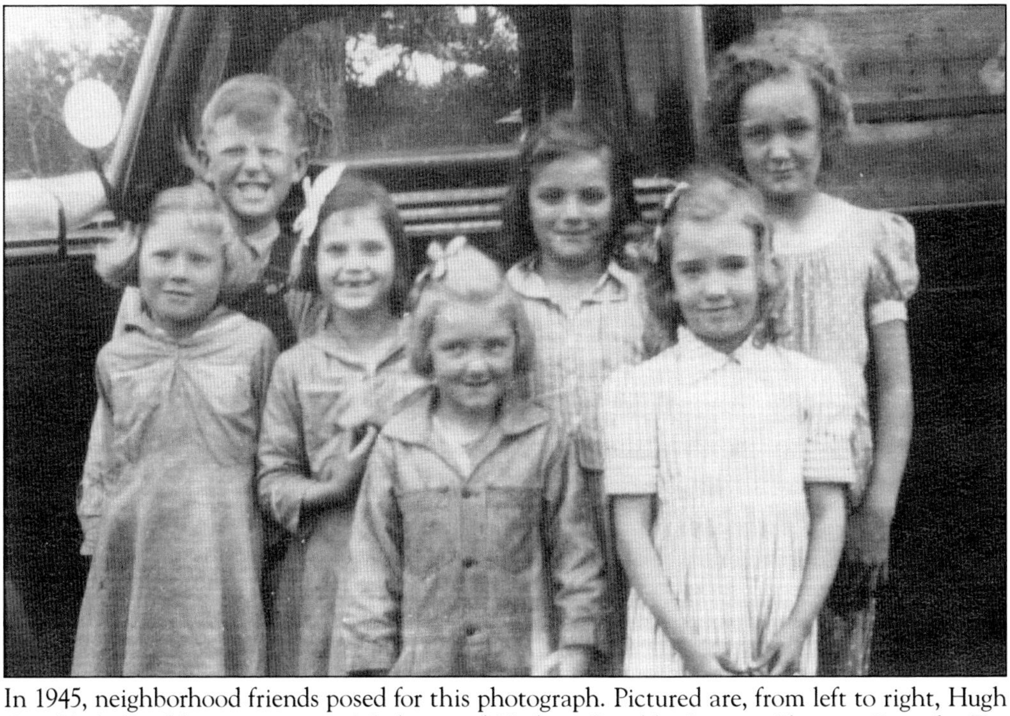

In 1945, neighborhood friends posed for this photograph. Pictured are, from left to right, Hugh Gamble behind his twin sisters Merline and Verline Gamble, Jimmie Skipper, Dorothy Fay Sharpton, Shirley Skipper, and Maxie Skipper. (Courtesy of Verline Gamble Stewart)

Native son Ben Ramsey was called a "living legend of wit and wisdom in Texas politics" by Dick Moreland of the *Dallas Morning News*. His political career began in 1932 as a state representative. Over a 45-year span, Ramsey was elected state senator, lieutenant governor, and finally chairman of the Railroad Commission. He retired in 1976, never having lost an election. (Courtesy of *San Augustine Tribune)*

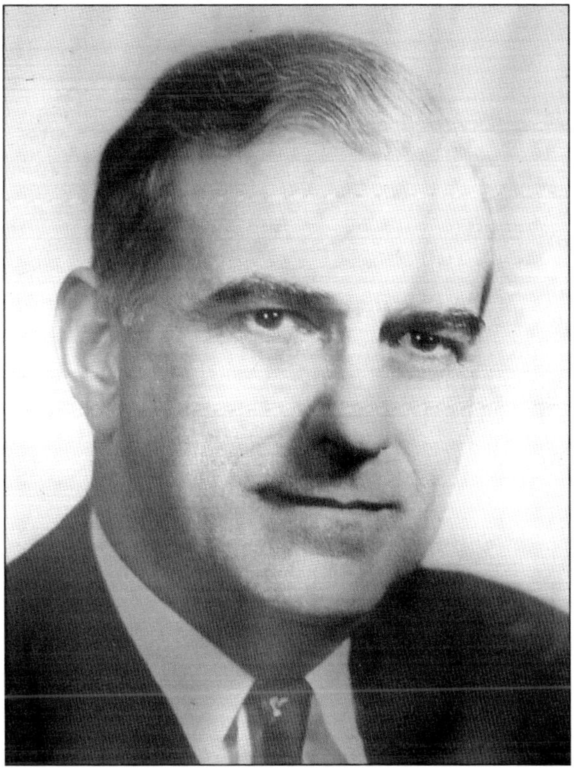

U.S. photographer John Vachon photographed the San Augustine City Council convened in regular session during his visit to East Texas in 1943. In attendance were, from left to right, city manager Troy Mitchell, J. W. Richey Sr., Herman Clark, Mayor A. E. Rushing, city attorney Smith Ramsey, R. V. Hall, and Clyde Smith. (John Vachon, OWI, 1943, Library of Congress.)

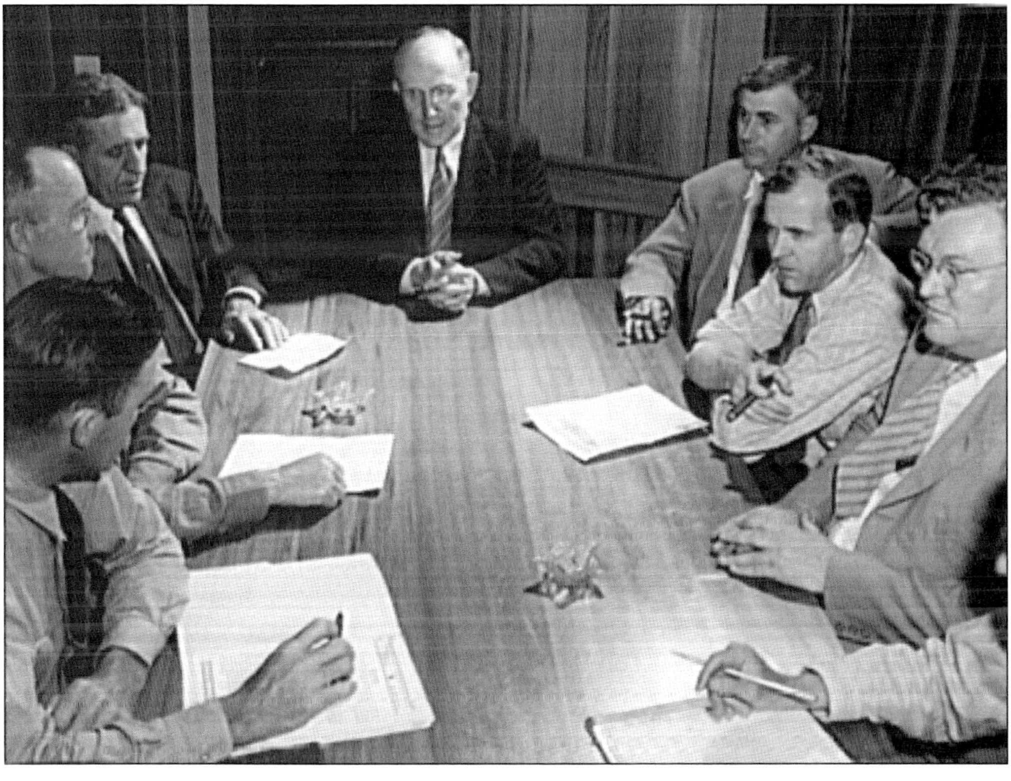

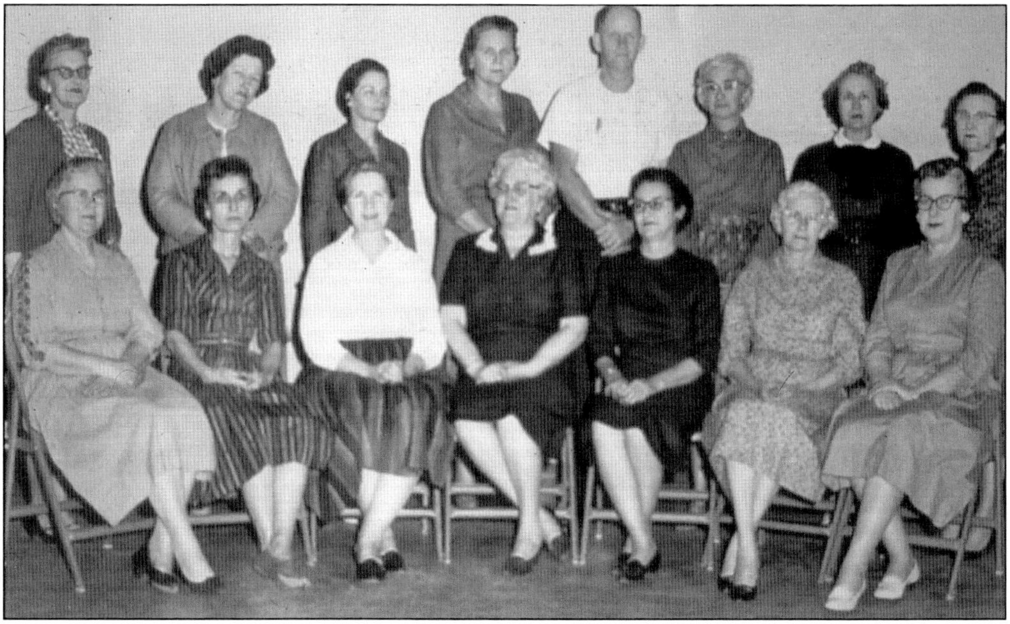

Teachers at San Augustine Elementary School in the mid-1940s included, from left to right, (first row) Ruby Dorsey, Georgia Mathews, Mrs. Baumgartner, Margaret Wade, Mary E. Saunders, principal Mary Blount, and Louise Smith; (second row) Mrs. Ed McPhail, Ruth Teel, Ida Mary Balch, Bennie Poss, Ed McPhail, Lurette Mitchell, Betsy Blount, and Mary Mathews. (Author's collection.)

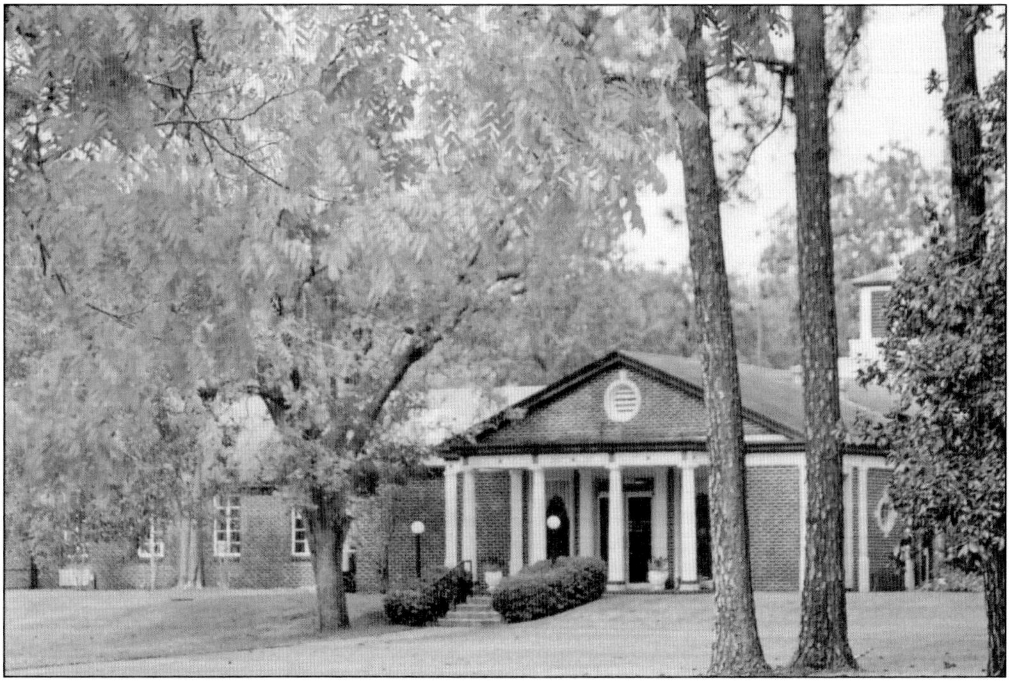

San Augustine's hospital was built in 1948 and has seen major additions and improvements since that time, many of which were implemented with the financial assistance of the T. L. L. Temple Foundation. The state-of-the-art hospital facility operates under the management of Lufkin-based Memorial Health System of East Texas. (Photograph by the author.)

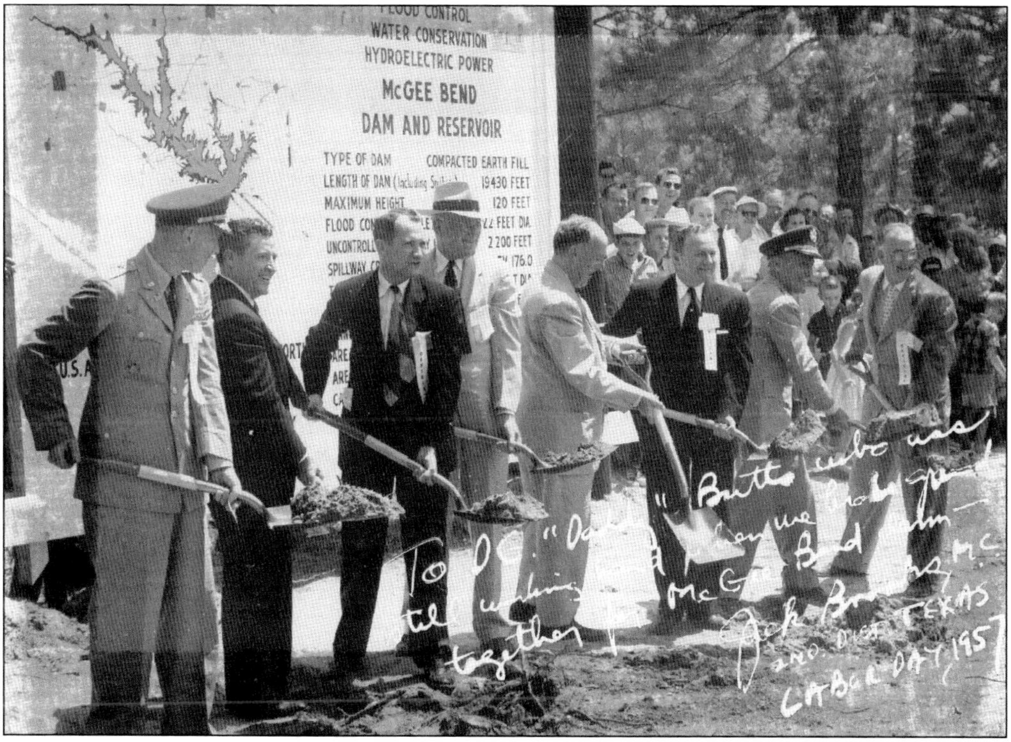

On Labor Day 1957, the groundbreaking ceremony was held for McGee Bend Dam and Reservoir. Representatives of the U.S. Army Corps of Engineers were on hand for the event. U.S. Rep. Jack Brooks of Beaumont and D. G. Butts of San Augustine (third and fourth from the left) were featured on the program. The 550-mile shoreline of the lake has made a significant economic impact on San Augustine County, particularly in the Broaddus area. The lake's name was later changed to Sam Rayburn Reservoir in memory of Speaker Sam Rayburn of the U.S. House of Representatives from Texas. (Courtesy of Martha Butts.)

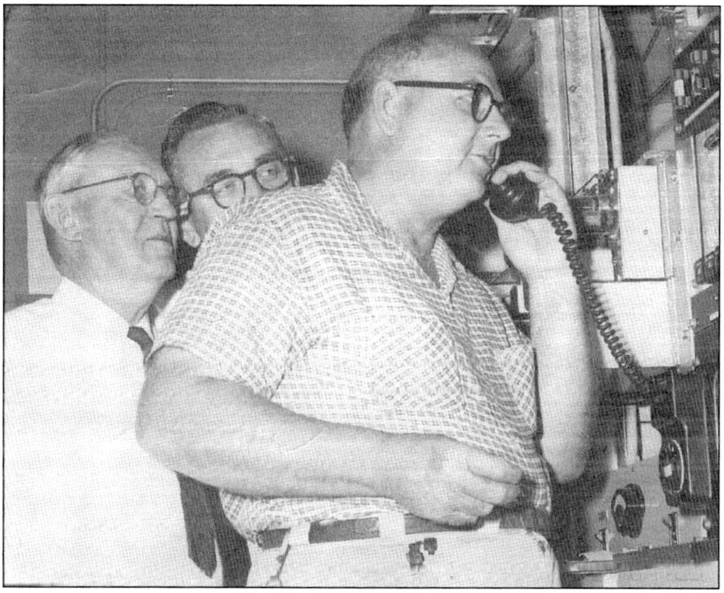

A landmark day in Broaddus was June 19, 1959, as mail carrier Roman D. Griffin tried out the new telephone dial system, while company officials W. G. Winters and J. B. Swink looked on. (Courtesy of R. D. Griffin.)

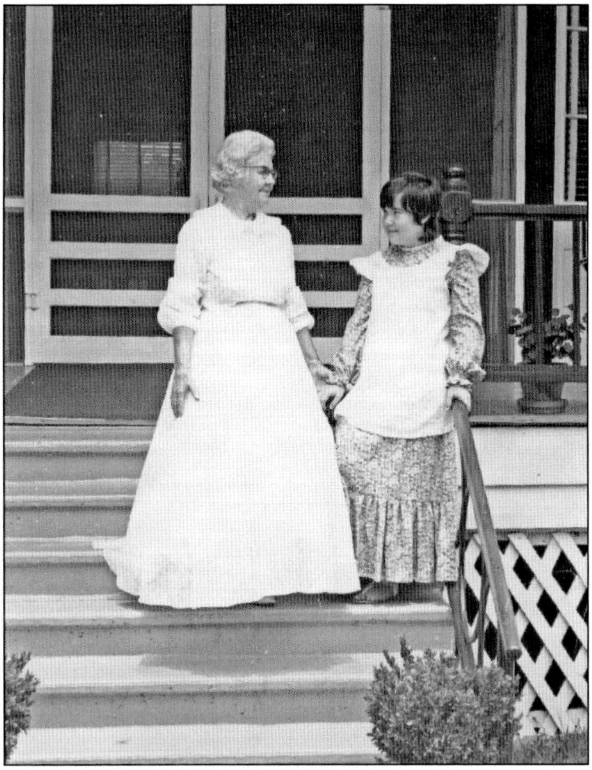

Ruby Dorsey stands on the steps of the William Garrett Plantation House with her granddaughter Jennifer Tull during the Daughters of the Republic of Texas Tour of Homes in 1965. (Courtesy of James Williams.)

In 1967, San Augustine County Historical Society was planning a pageant to commemorate 250 years since the founding of Mission Dolores. Committee members were, from left to right, (first row) Dr. C. R. Haley, Ruby Dorsey, and B. R. Mathews; (second row) Julia Wade, Cornell Dorsey, Wanda Roper, Steve Kardell, and Raiford Stripling. (Courtesy of *San Augustine Tribune*.)

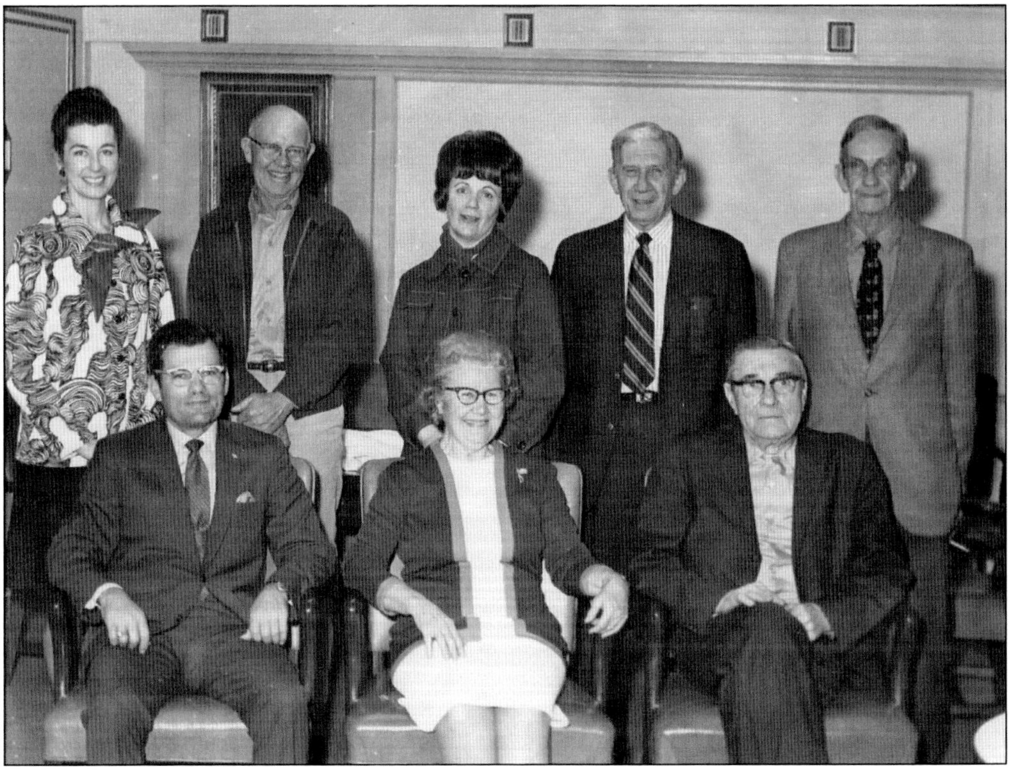

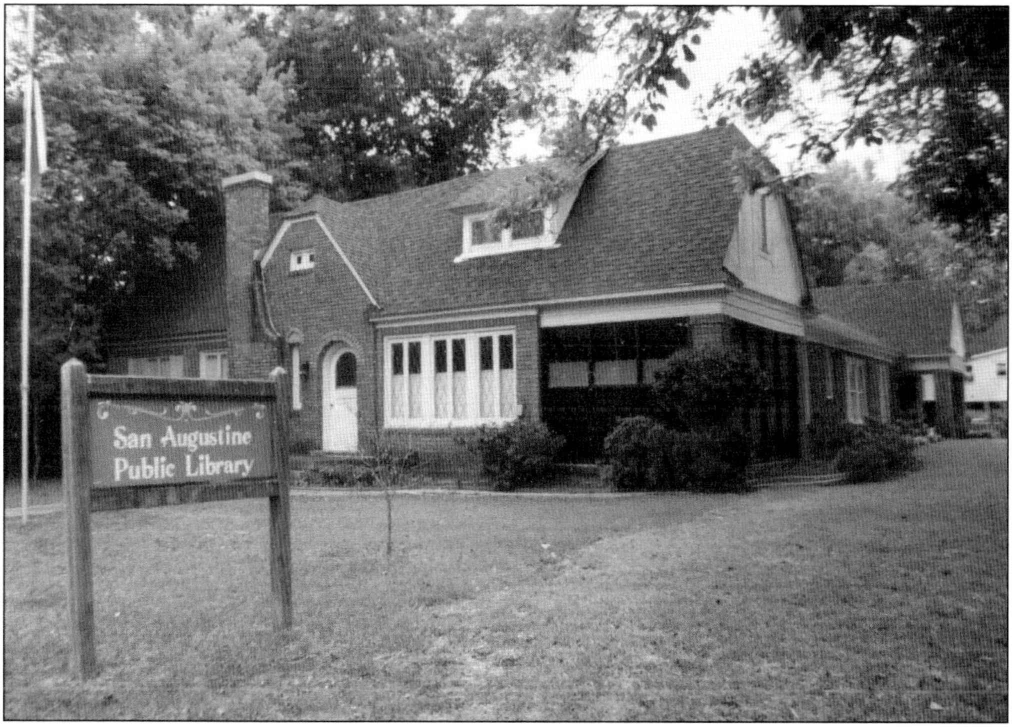

San Augustine Public Library opened its doors in 1971 with two boxes of books and a promise by the young women's organization, Women's Service League, that they would help promote a library of the first order in San Augustine County. Located in the former Iona Hotel in a convenient location on the corner of Columbia and Ayish Streets, the San Augustine Public Library has been a success story for the past 39 years. In 2001, the popular library underwent a doubling of space to better accommodate its many patrons. The history and genealogy sections are among the best in Texas. (Photograph by the author.)

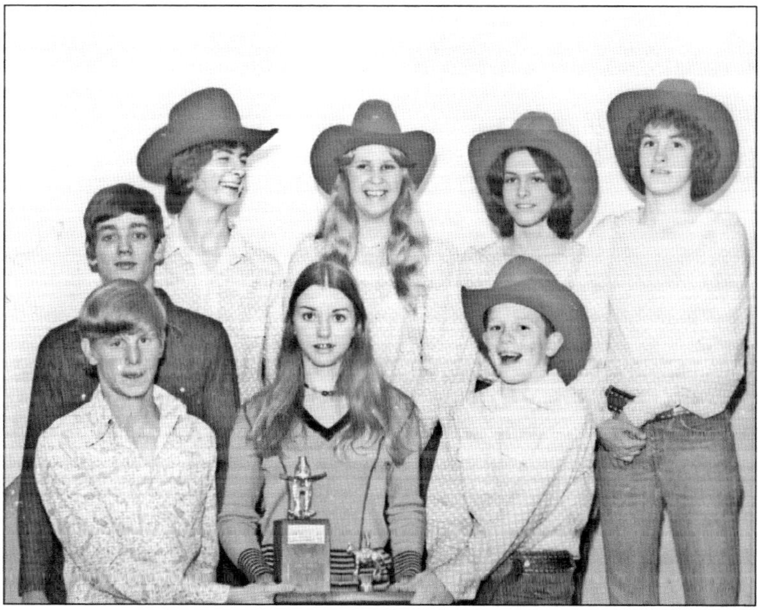

San Augustine's relay team members were grand prizewinners in Houston in 1970. Team members included, from left to right, (first row) Mike Bridges, Karen Davidson, and Keith Alford; (second row) David Davidson, Dale Birdwell, Patricia Hall, Sandra Birdwell and Charlotte Birdwell. (Courtesy of *San Augustine Tribune*.)

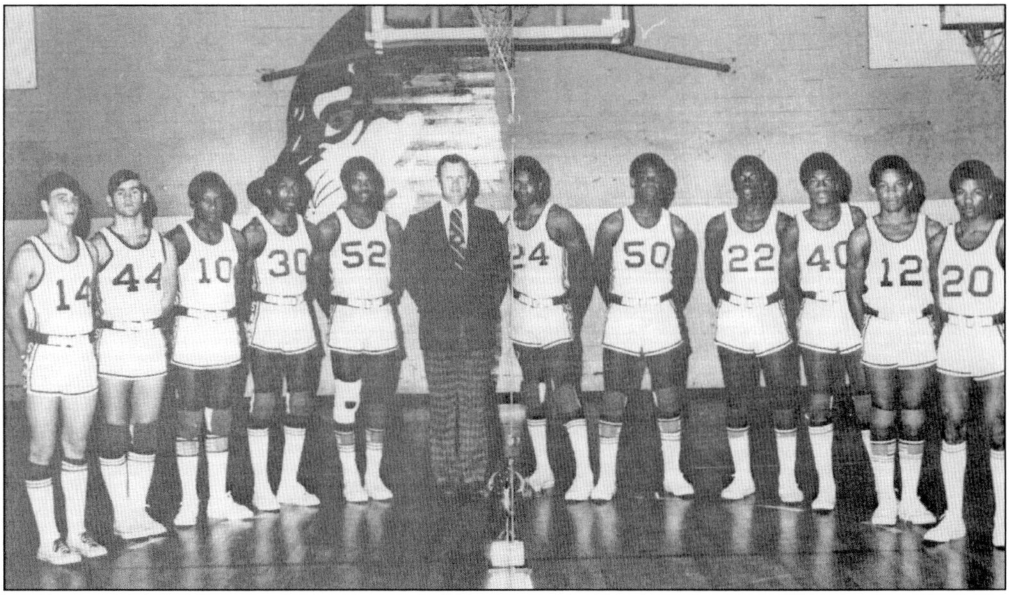

San Augustine High School basketball team won the state championship in 1973. Coach Henry Whittlesey is pictured with the team. Both coach Whittlesey and his wife, Mary, have long been connected with the San Augustine Independent School District (SAISD). Mary Whittlesey was a recipient of the Gilbert I. Low Teaching Excellence Scholarship in 2010, the year of the award's inception. (Courtesy of SAISD superintendent Walter Key.)

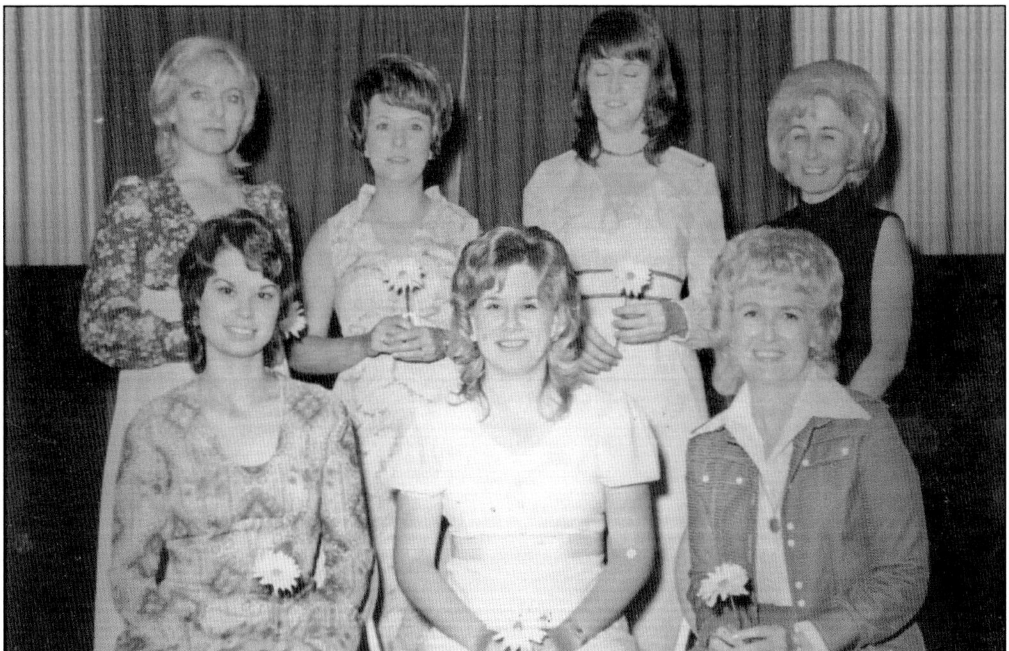

Officers for the Young Homemakers Club in 1973 were, from left to right, (first row) president Terry Wall, first vice president Charla Rogers, and second vice president Linda Jackson; (second row) third vice president Martha Ramey, secretary-treasurer Amelia Jeanes, reporter Glenda Fowler, and parliamentarian Louise Tompkins. (Courtesy *San Augustine Tribune.*)

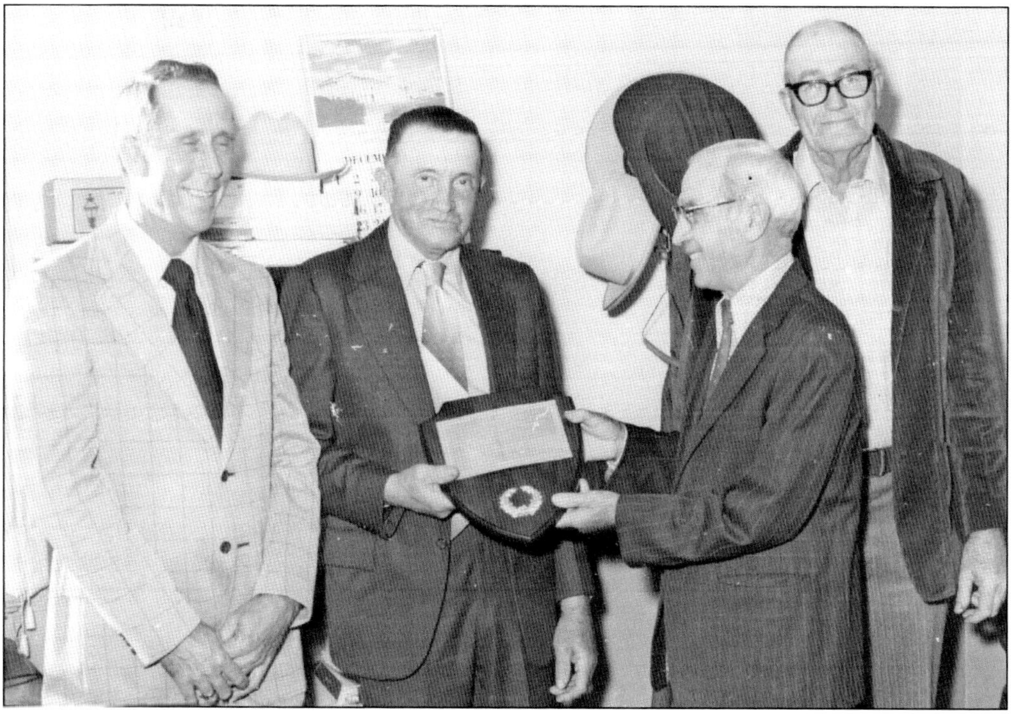

In 1974, county commissioner Bennie Sharpton, retiring after 20 years of service to San Augustine County, was presented a plaque by county judge Wyatt C. Teel. Commissioners T. J. Woods (left) and John Arnold were present during the presentation. (Courtesy of *San Augustine Tribune.*)

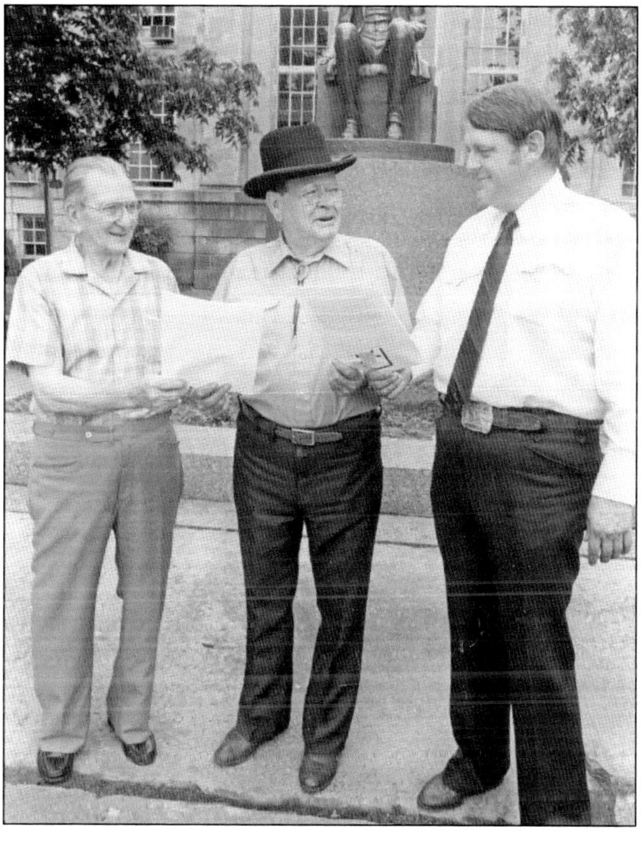

Sam Malone of the *San Augustine Rambler* (center) discussed future plans for the Texas sesquicentennial celebration with Mayor Walter Richey (left) and county judge Jack Nichols in 1985. (Courtesy of *San Augustine Tribune.*)

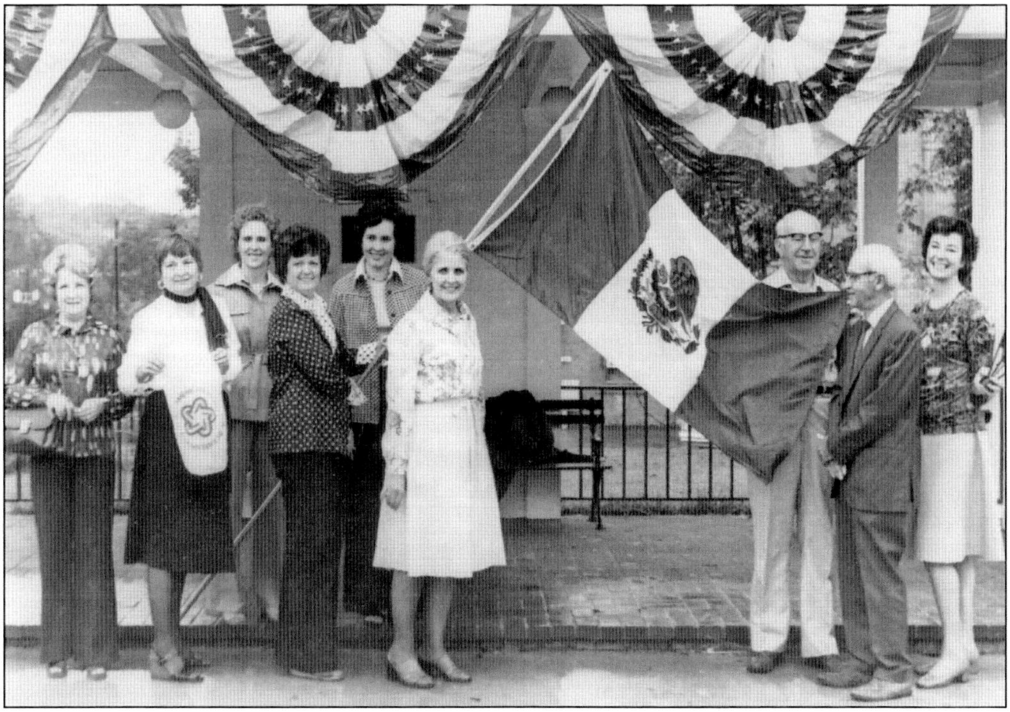

In 1976, San Augustine celebrated the bicentennial year of this nation. Members of the bicentennial committee presented the special flag designed for the observance to county judge Wyatt C. Teel at the Stripling Pavilion on the courthouse square. Pictured are, from left to right, Carolyn Ladner, Polly Crisp, Mary Jean Haley, Wanda Roper, Betty Oglesbee, Agnes Sparks, B. J. Butts, Judge Teel, and Julia Wade. (Courtesy of *San Augustine Tribune*.)

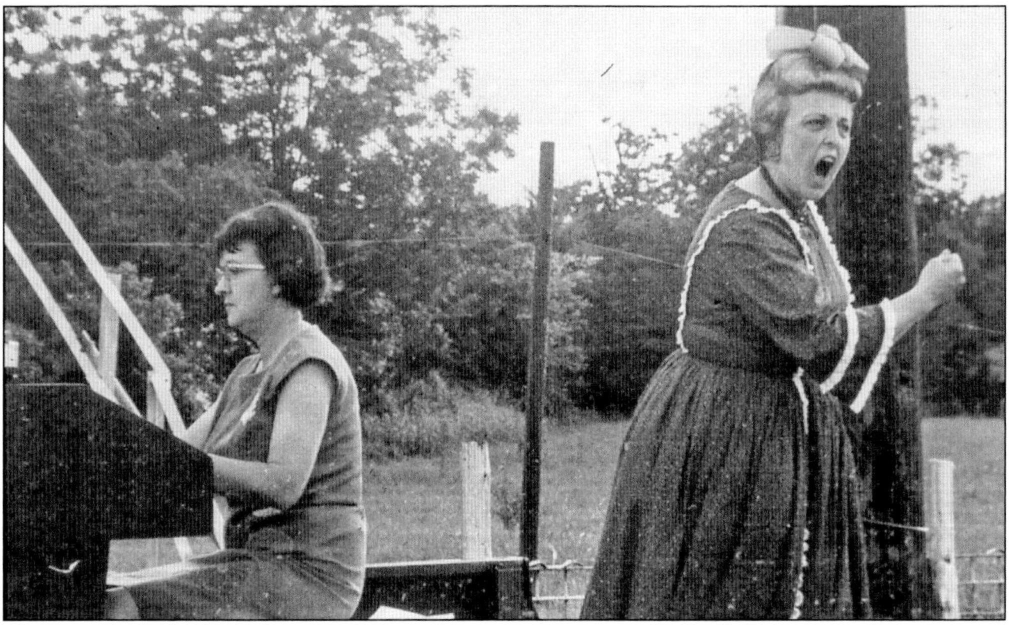

Frances Bradberry played the piano as Dorette Barr led the audience in singing "God Bless America" during bicentennial festivities in 1976. (Author's collection.)

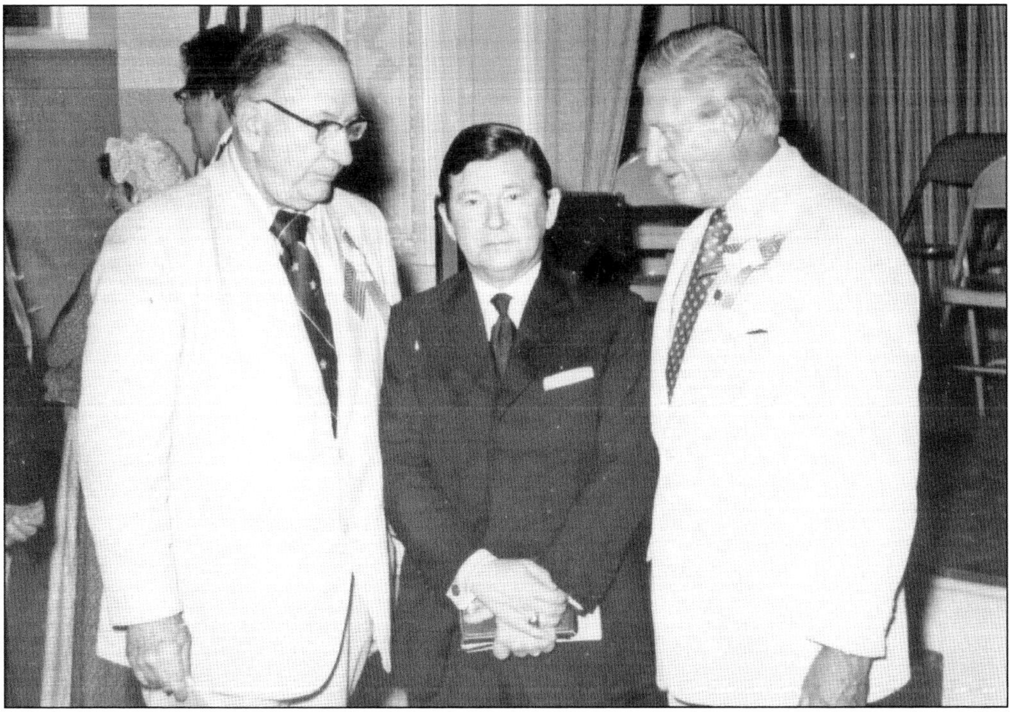

In July 1976, three well-known San Augustinians returned home for the Fourth of July bicentennial celebration. Ambassador to Australia Edward Clark, U.S. senator from Texas John Tower, and federal judge Joe J. Fisher were all participants in the patriotic program. (Courtesy of *San Augustine Tribune*.)

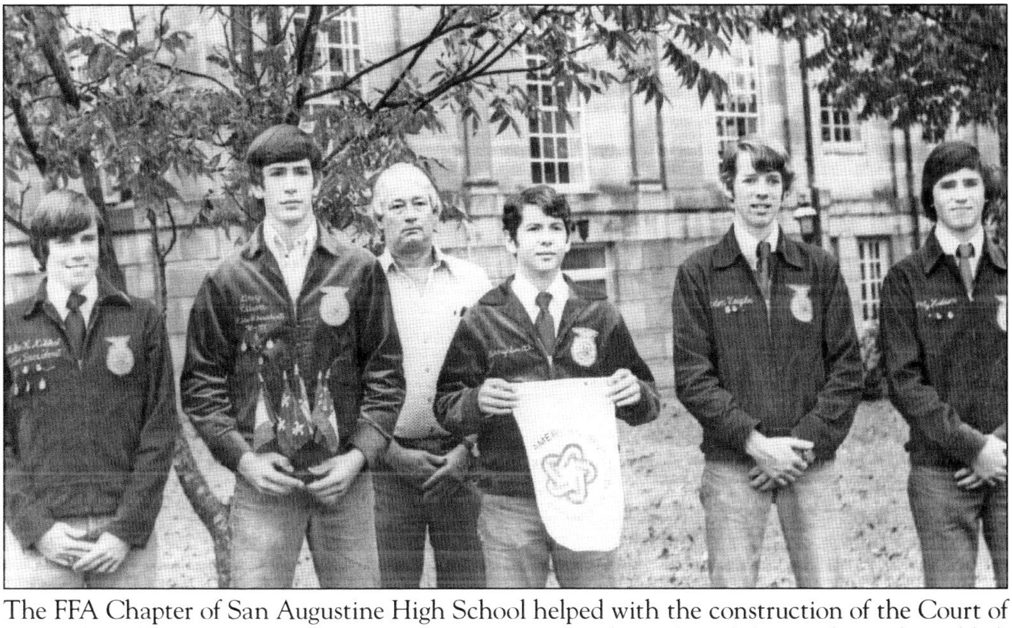

The FFA Chapter of San Augustine High School helped with the construction of the Court of Eight Flags during the bicentennial celebration. Pictured are, from left to right, Mike Nikkel, Greg Elliott, advisor Jim Watson, Larry Smith, Gordon Vaughn, and Monty Hudson. (Courtesy of *San Augustine Tribune*.)

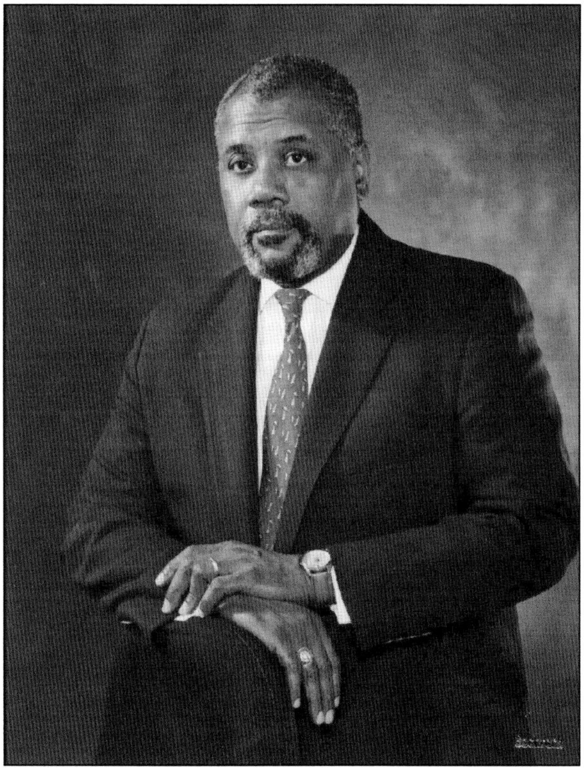

Attorney Fred McClure of San Augustine is the managing partner of the Washington, D.C., office of Sonnenschein, Nath, and Rosenthal and has broad experience with the executive branch of the U.S. government. He has served under Pres. George H. W. Bush and Pres. Ronald Reagan in the field of legislative affairs. While a student at Texas A&M University, he was elected president of the student body. (Courtesy of Mayme McClure.)

In 1976, veteran attorney C. S. Ramsey administered the oath of office to city council members John Matthew Cartwright (left) and Joe Bickley. (Courtesy of *San Augustine Tribune.)*

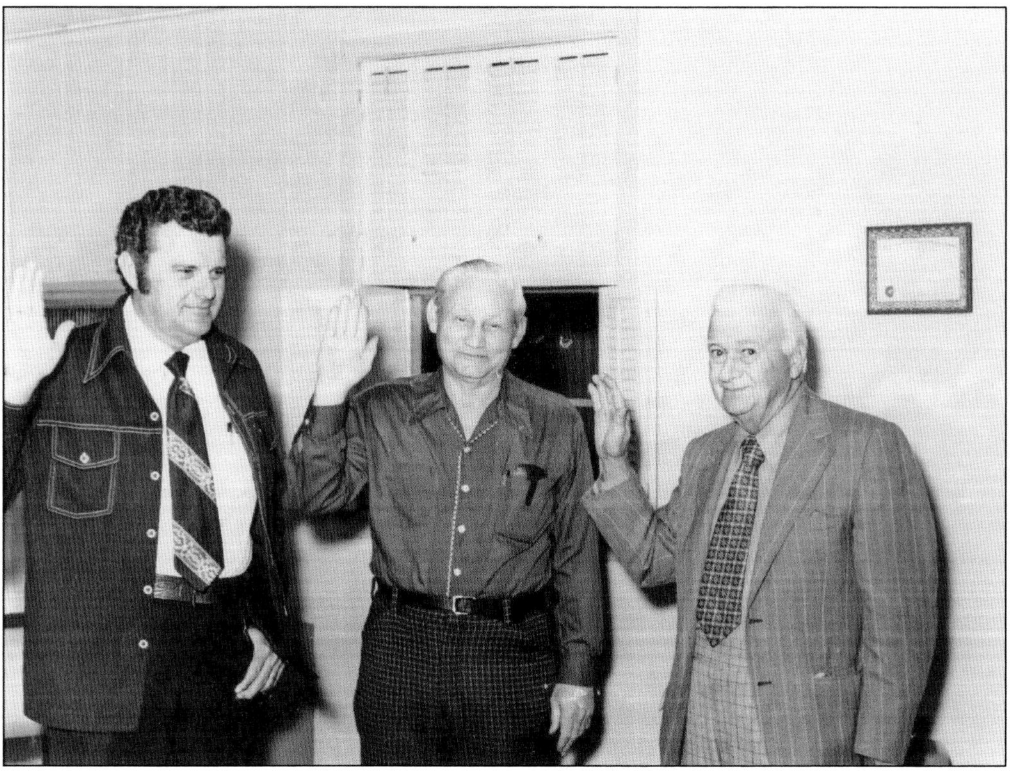

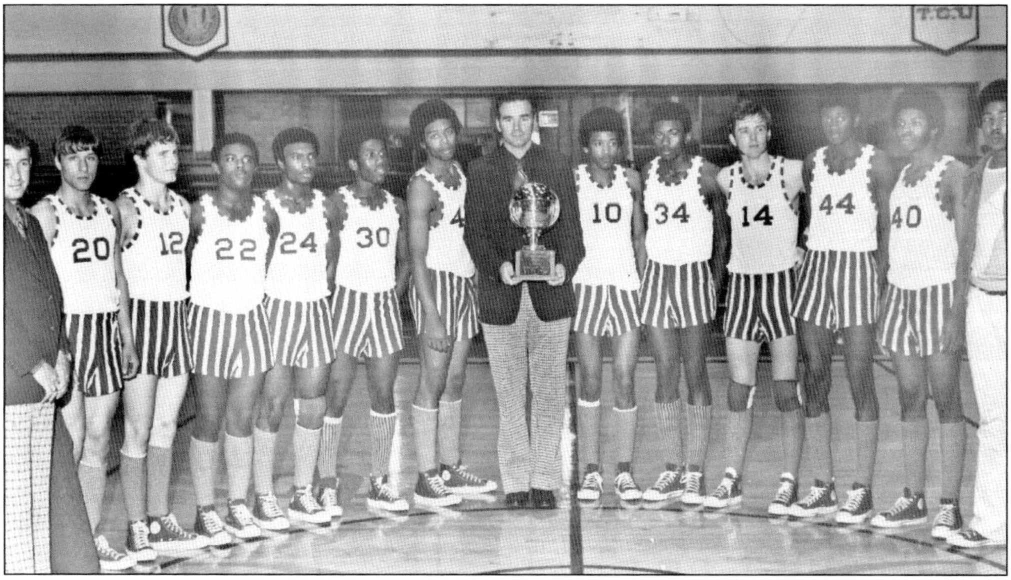

Under the leadership of legendary coach Marion Neill, the Broaddus Bulldogs won the Class A State Basketball Championship in 1976 and 1977, and narrowly missed winning in 1975 and 1978. Neill retired in 1987 after 31 years of successfully coaching the Broaddus team. Terry Teagle (44) went on to become the all-time Southwest Conference scoring leader while playing for Baylor University, then went into the NBA as the Houston Rockets' first pick. (Courtesy of Marion and Patti Neill.)

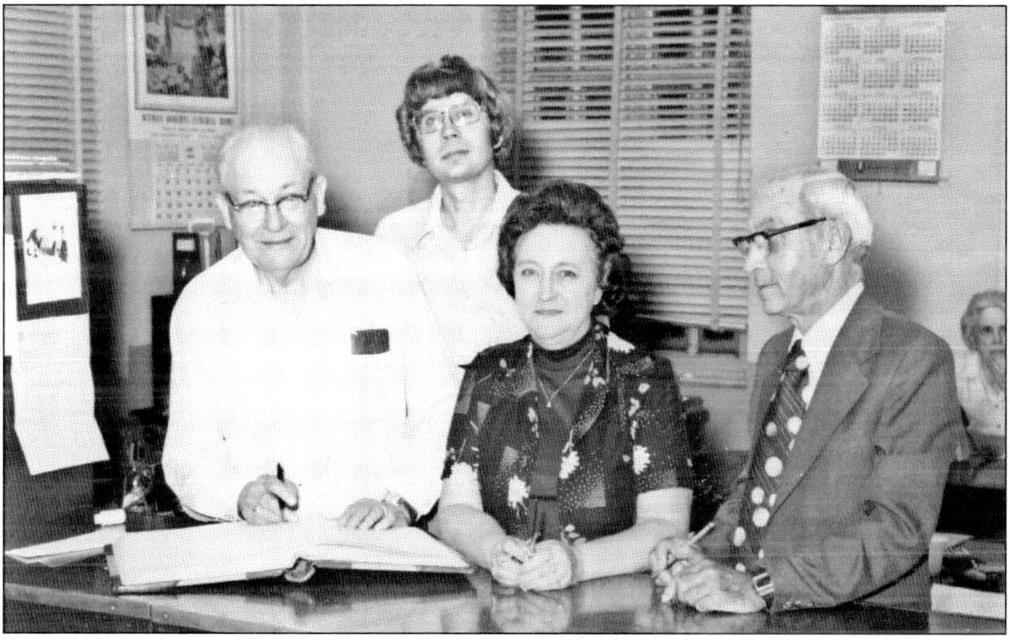

In 1978, *San Augustine Tribune* publisher Arlan Hays wrote, "Cecil Murphy, left, has recorded the returns of over a hundred elections in his day, and just couldn't stay away Saturday night when the returns started coming in. He had been County Clerk 38 years when he retired last year . . . With him are his nephew, Interim County Clerk Larry Woods, Geraldine Smith, the newly nominated County Clerk, and County Judge Wyatt C. Teel." (Courtesy of *San Augustine Tribune*.)

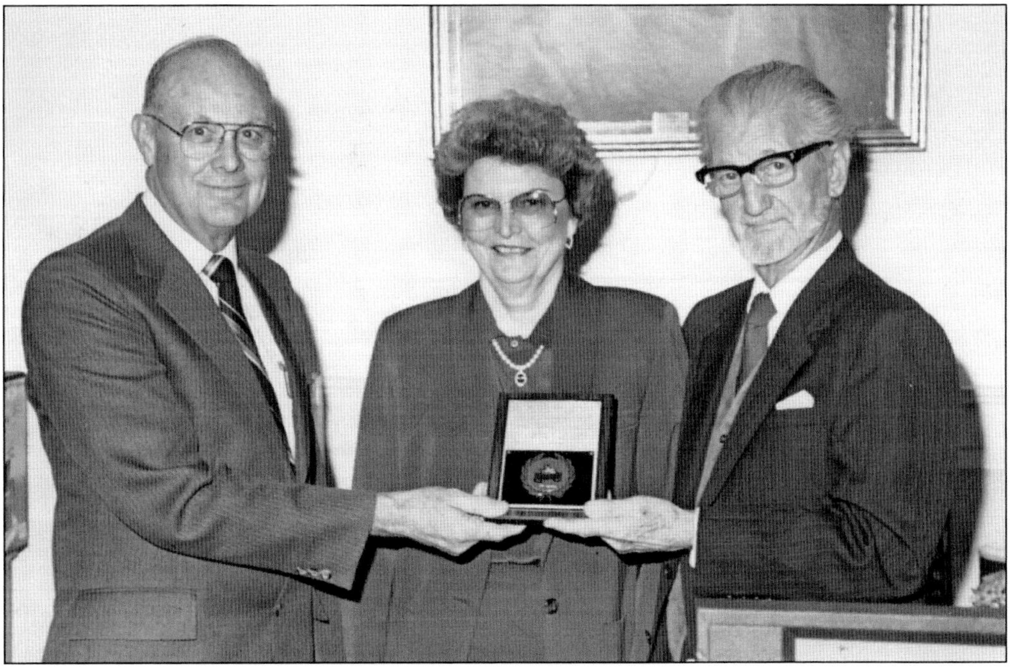

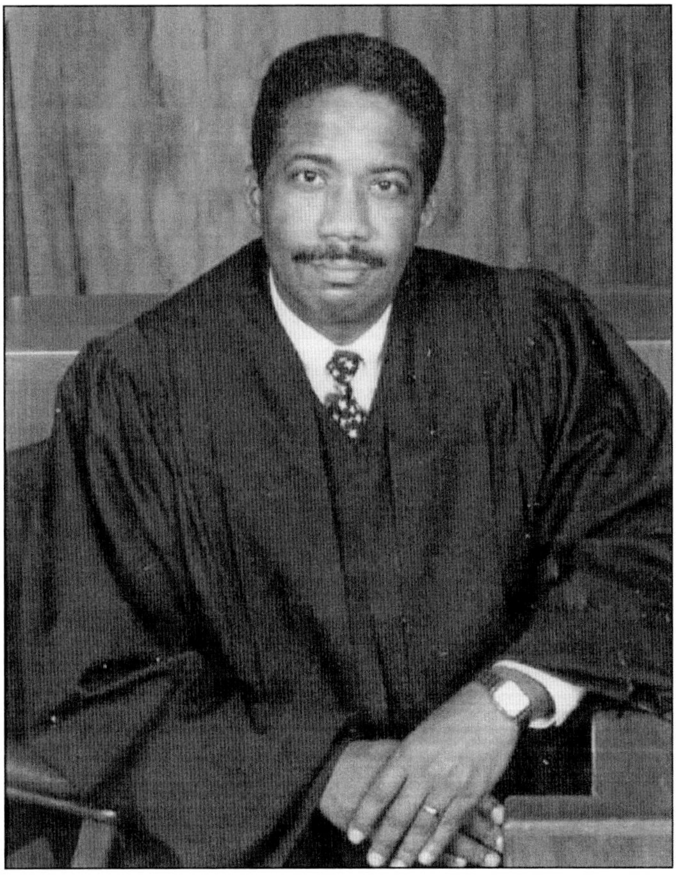

In 1988, San Augustine Drug, a landmark business in the county, was destroyed by fire. Owners Therman and Virginia Bridges immediately built again at the same decades-old location. The Bridges are shown receiving a chamber of commerce "Faith in the Community" award from chamber director Arlan Hays. (Courtesy of *San Augustine Tribune.*)

San Augustine native son federal judge Kenneth Hoyt was nominated in 1987 by Pres. Ronald Reagan and confirmed by the U.S. Senate in 1988 as judge for the U.S. District Court, Southern District of Texas. (Courtesy of *San Augustine Tribune.)*

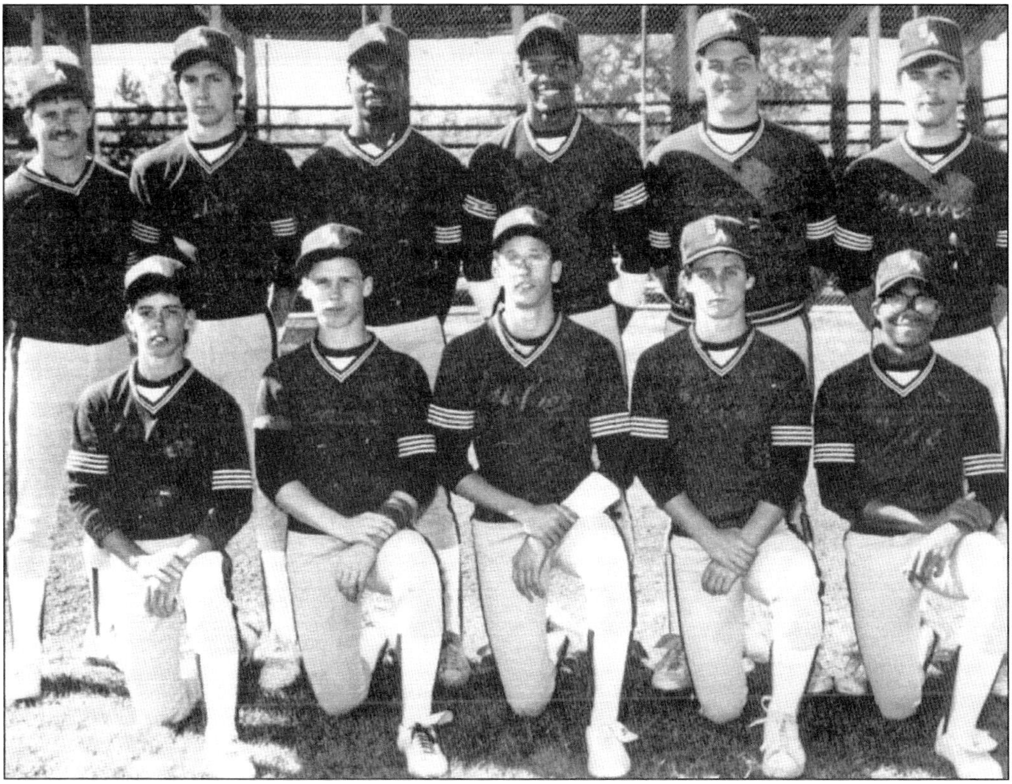

In 1988, the SAHS baseball team won the state championship with pitcher Steve Hughes chosen as MVP for the entire play-off tournament. (Courtesy of SAISD superintendent Walter Key.)

The following year, the 1989 SAHS baseball team played in the state championship game, losing 2-1. Sen. Bill Haley (left) presents the runner-up trophy to team members Abbott Clack, Tony Edwards, Michael Canton, and Forrest Oglesbee. (Courtesy of *San Augustine Tribune*.)

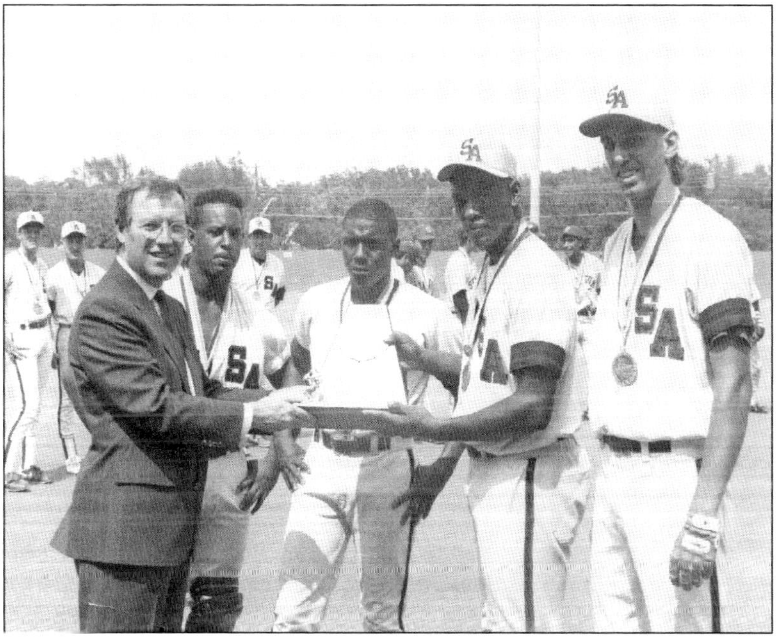

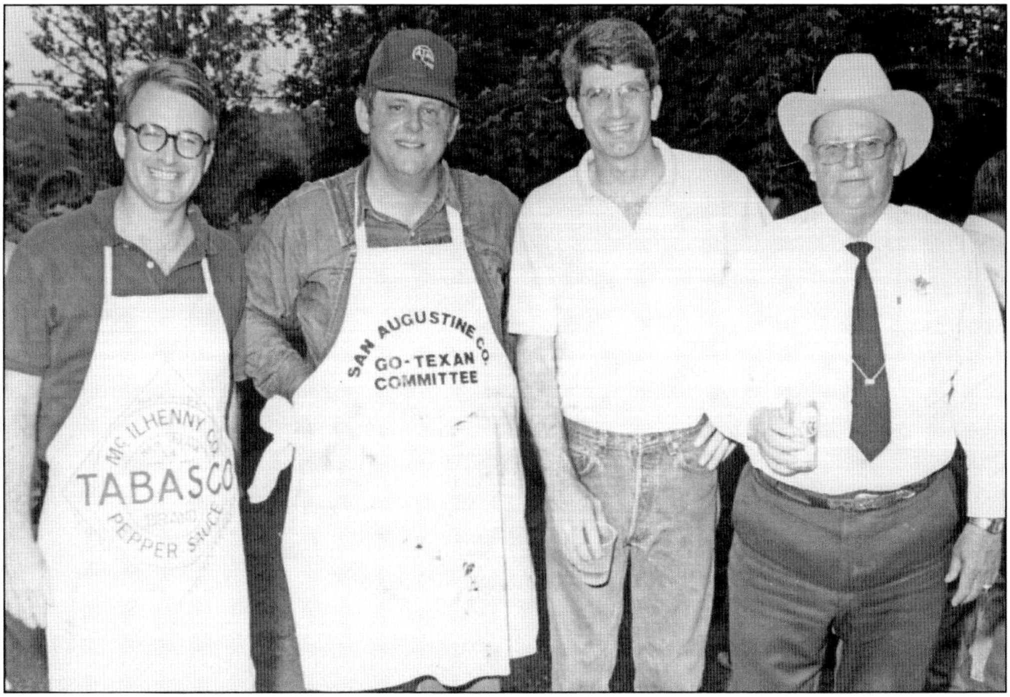

An election celebration barbecue was held at the Mitchell Farm inside the restored Santa Fe Depot in 1988. Shown are, from left to right, district judge John Mitchell, county judge Jack Nichols, district attorney-elect Charles Mitchell, and Sheriff N. L. Tindall. (Courtesy of *San Augustine Tribune.*)

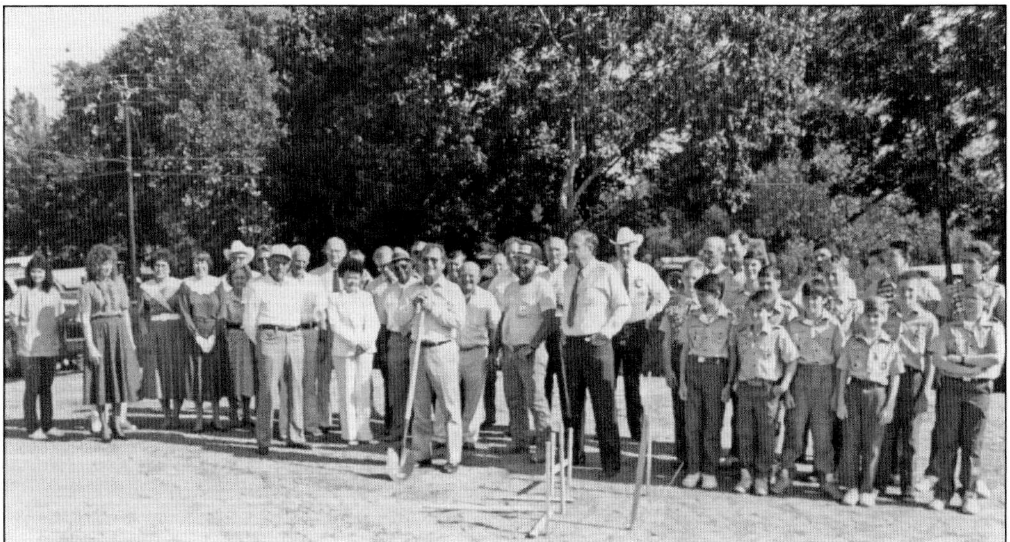

In 1989, the Boy Scout troop and a crowd of interested citizens watched as Mayor Curt Goetz broke ground for the new civic and tourism center, a project initiated and spearheaded by the Scouts. (Courtesy of *San Augustine Tribune.*)

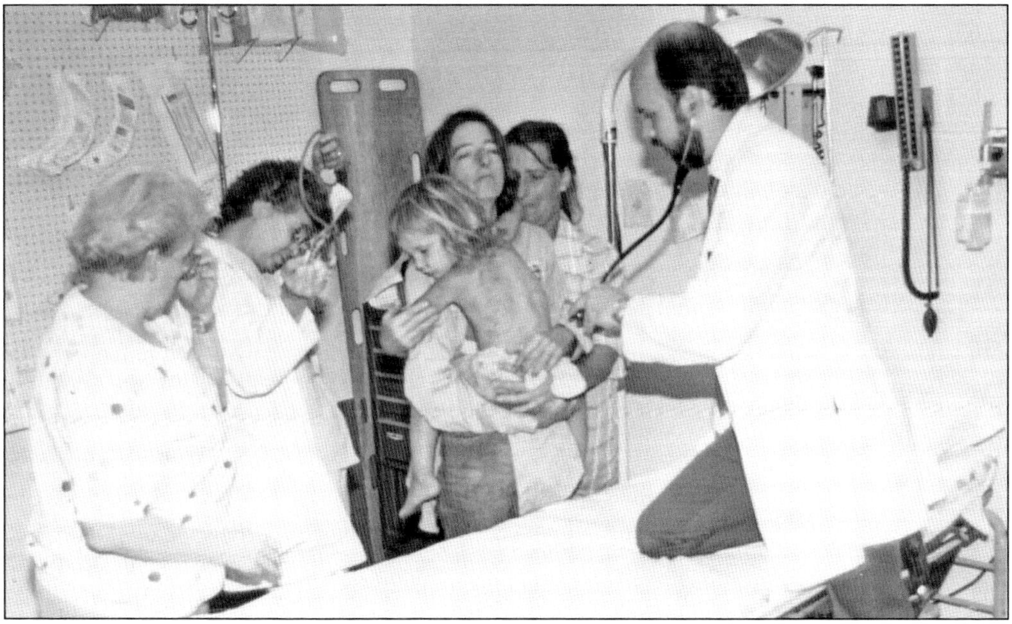

Dr. John Oglesbee at the San Augustine Memorial Hospital Emergency Room examines little Jamie Lynn Bryan after she was found on a Sunday at noon in May 1989. Her mother and grandmother, Patricia Bryan and Willie Mae Medley, hold Jamie while director of nurses Carrie Bryant and nurse Arbell Howard assist. Although the little girl was suffering from exposure, she fully recovered. (Courtesy of *San Augustine Tribune*.)

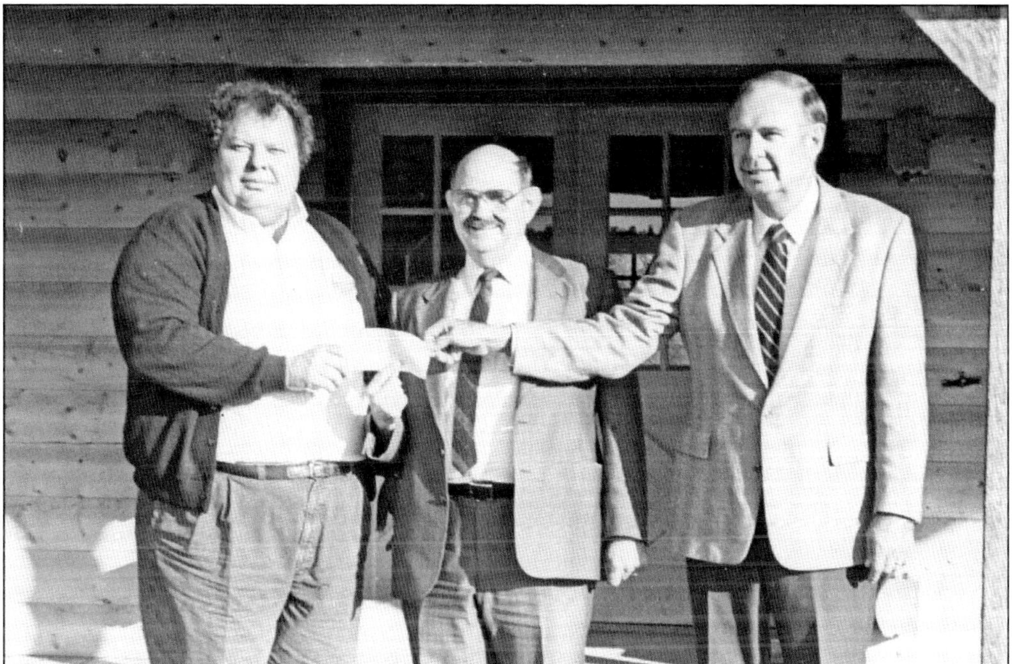

Flanked by assistant scoutmaster Dan Fussell (left) and scoutmaster John Oglesbee, regional manager Ken Wood presents a donation from Southwestern Bell to the Scout troop's Civic and Tourism Center project. (Courtesy of *San Augustine Tribune*.)

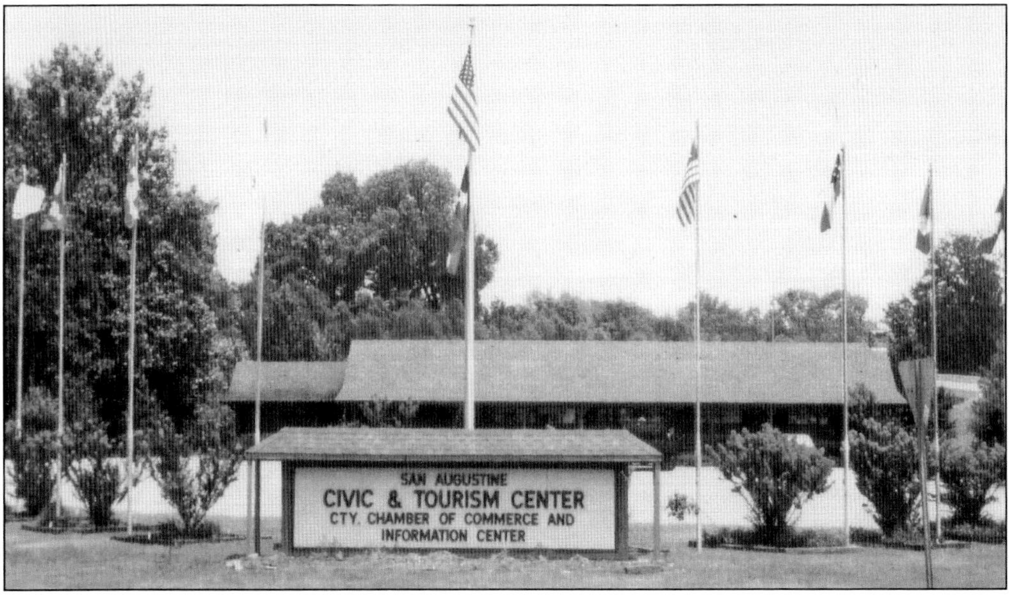

With a spirit of cooperation between the Scouts, city and county officials, Texas Department of Transportation, San Augustine County Chamber of Commerce, individual citizens, banks, businesses, and civic organizations, the completion of the "Cabin on the Bayou" was made possible in 1990. Once again, the historic Ayish Bayou became the chosen location for a San Augustine County landmark. The Boy Scout room is the extension on the left side of the building. (Photograph by the author.)

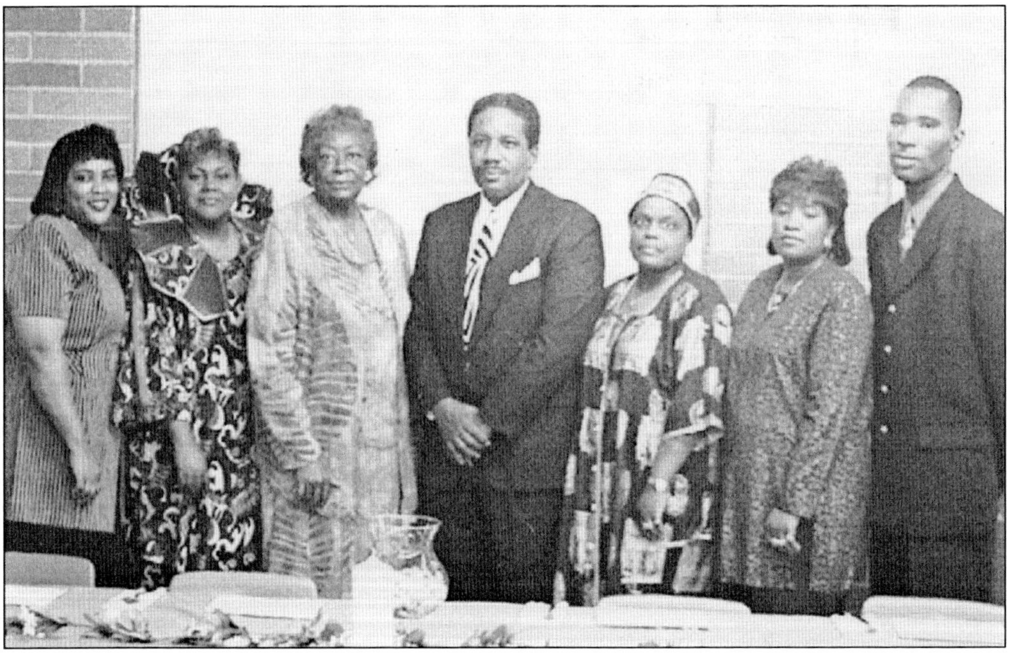

Local citizens welcomed Judge Kenneth Hoyt to the San Augustine County Juneteenth Event in the late 1990s. Pictured from left to right are Gloria Garrett, Mearline Davis, Mayor Gertrude Lane, Judge Hoyt, councilwoman Evelyn Watts, Carolyn Wilson, and Robert Brown. (Courtesy of *San Augustine Tribune*.)

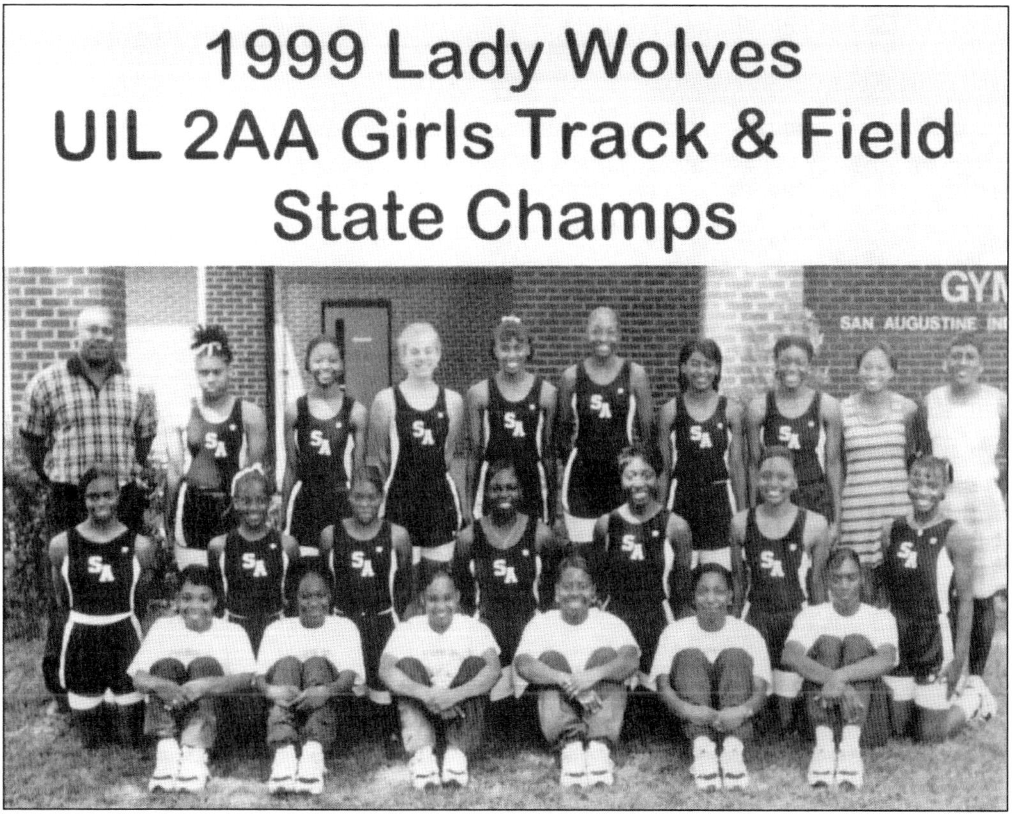

San Augustine High School Lady Wolves Girls Track and Field were state champs in 1999. Coaches Barry Ford (left) and Fleashia Jones Ford (right) are shown with the girls. (Courtesy of SAISD superintendent Walter Key.)

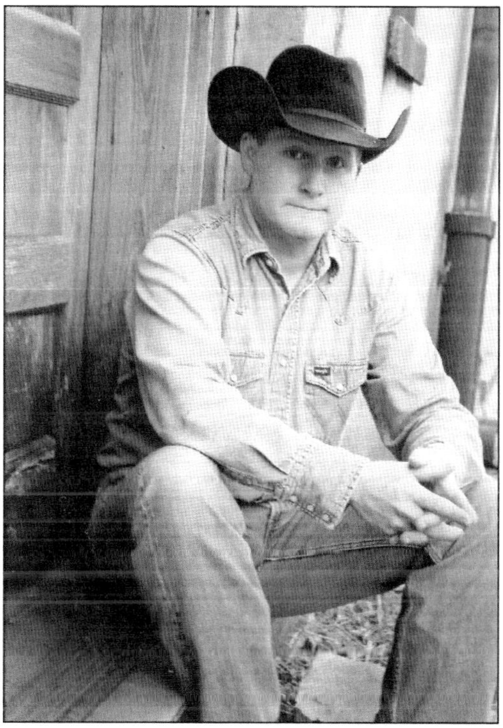

Shane Mathews of San Augustine County is a talented singer, songwriter, and self-taught musician and is a nationally televised Texas Country Reporter talent search winner. In 2007, Shane was named Ambassador of the Texas Country Music Hall of Fame Showcase in Carthage, Texas. (Courtesy of Bette Hodges, Neillrae Music.)

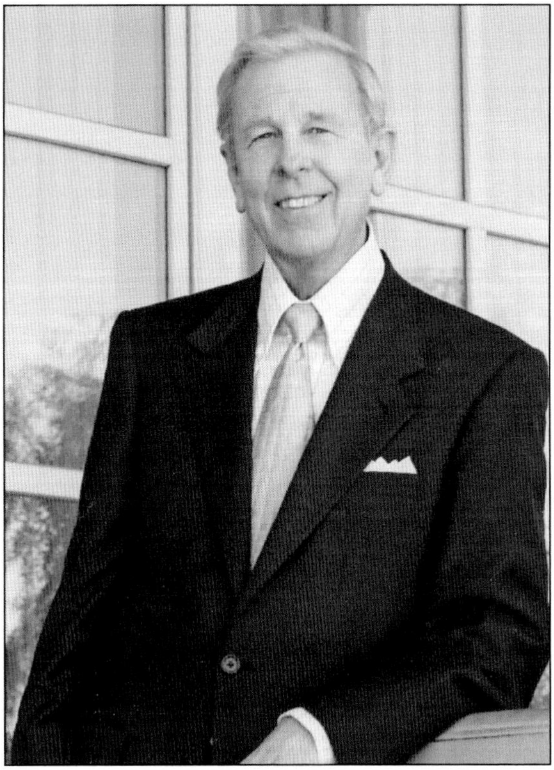

Attorney Gilbert I. (Buddy) Low is a partner in the law firm of Orgain, Bell, and Tucker L.L.P. and a founding director of the Beaumont Foundation of America. A 1950 graduate of San Augustine High School, Low and BFA began giving four-year college scholarships to three local graduating seniors a few years ago in honor of three of his former teachers, Dorette Barr, Harlowe Johnson, and Anna Kathryn Holbrook. In 2010, Teaching Excellence Awards were added to the scholarship program. (Courtesy of Orgain, Bell, and Tucker.)

In the late spring each year, rodeo fans flock to the San Augustine County Youth Arena for the Professional Rodeo Cowboys Association (PRCA) Rodeo. Pictured is county agent Jerry Nickerson preparing for the promotional posters and advertising for this popular event. (Photograph by the author.)

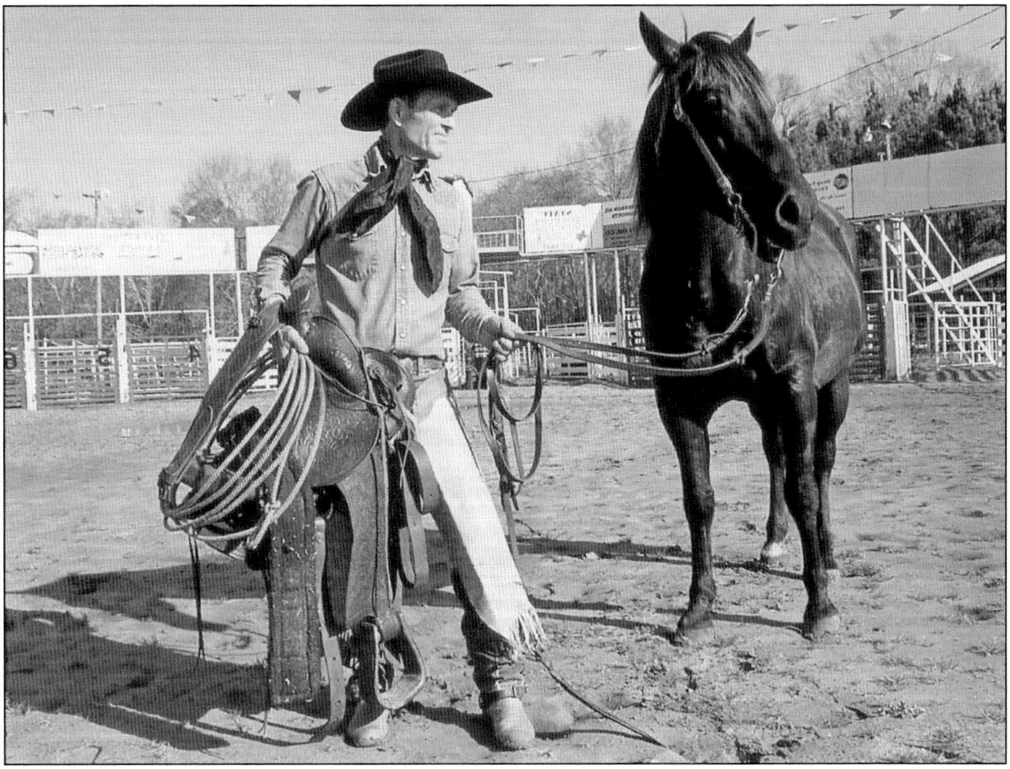

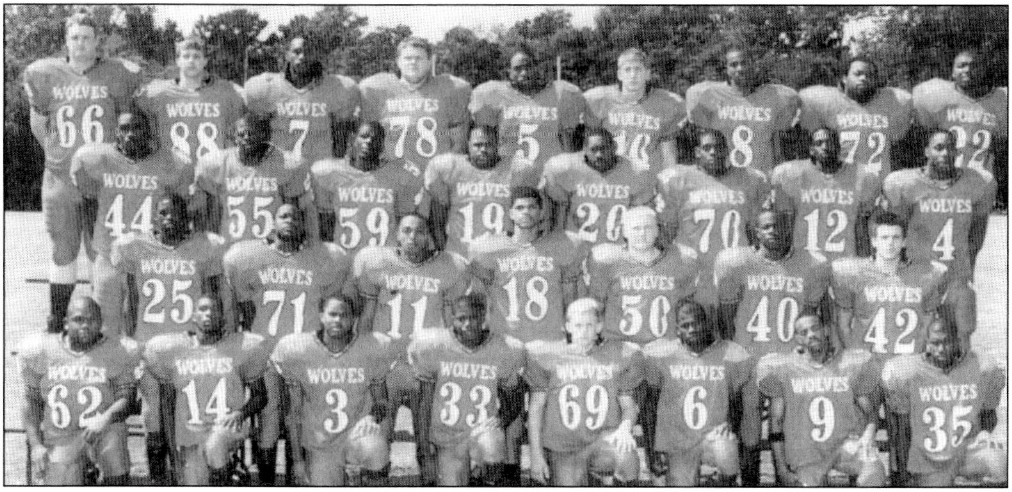

In 2003, the San Augustine High School Wolves varsity football team, under the leadership of head coach Lynn Graves, won the state championship. Team member Dominique Edison went on to play for Stephen F. Austin State University and now is with the Tennessee Titans professional team. (Courtesy of SAISD superintendent Walter Key.)

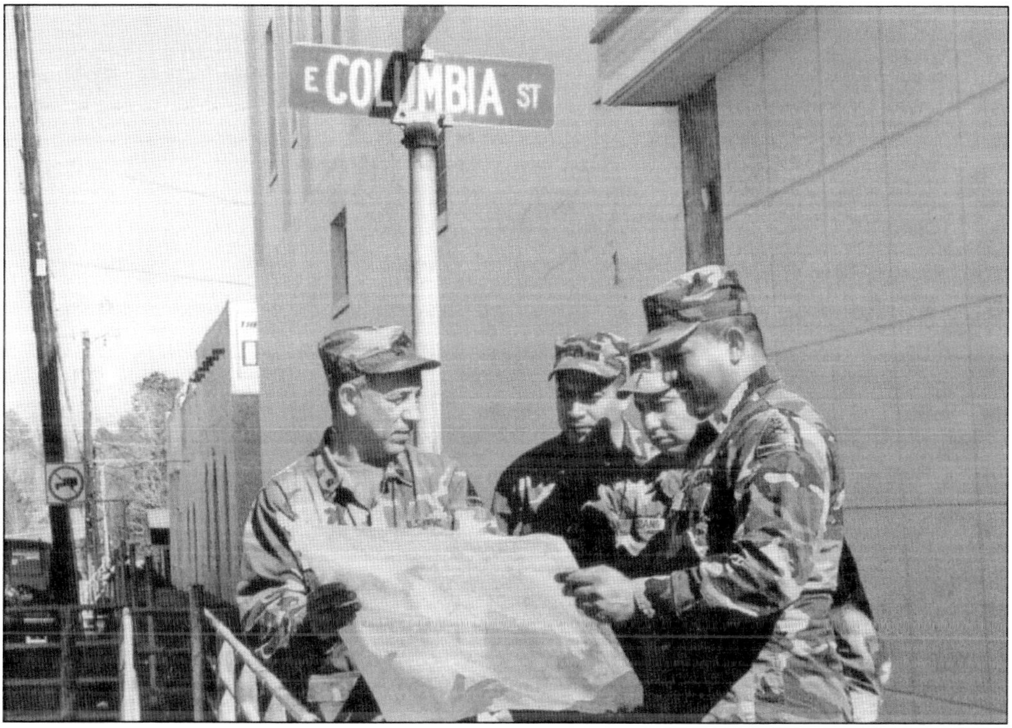

In their usual hospitable way, the folks of San Augustine County turned out en masse to help with recovery efforts after the Columbia shuttle disaster on February 1, 2003. Debris from the shuttle was scattered over a broad path covering Nacogdoches, San Augustine, and Sabine Counties. Recovery workers from law enforcement, military, and governmental agencies made San Augustine's Civic and Tourism Center their headquarters in the San Augustine County vicinity. These National Guardsmen are pictured on the corner of Columbia Street in downtown San Augustine examining an aerial map showing debris locations. (Photograph by the author.)